Decentralizing the
Civil Service

Public Policy and Management

Series Editor: Professor R.A.W. Rhodes, Department of Politics, University of Newcastle.

The effectiveness of public policies is a matter of public concern and the efficiency with which policies are put into practice is a continuing problem for governments of all political persuasions. This series contributes to these debates by publishing informed, in-depth and contemporary analyses of public administration, public policy and public management.

The intention is to go beyond the usual textbook approach to the analysis of public policy and management and to encourage authors to move debate about their issue forward. In this sense, each book describes current thinking and research and explores future policy directions. Accessibility is a key feature and, as a result, the series will appeal to academics and their students as well as to the informed practitioner.

Current titles include:

Decentralizing the Civil Service

From Unitary State to Differentiated Polity in the United Kingdom

R.A.W. Rhodes, P. Carmichael,
J. McMillan and A. Massey

Open University Press
Buckingham · Philadelphia

Open University Press
Celtic Court
22 Ballmoor
Buckingham
MK18 1XW

email: enquiries@openup.co.uk
world wide web: www.openup.co.uk

and
325 Chestnut Street
Philadelphia, PA 19106, USA

First Published 2003

A catalogue record of this book is available from the British Library

ISBN   0 335 21234 4 (pb)   0 335 21235 2 (hb)

Library of Congress Cataloging-in-Publication Data
Decentralizing the civil service: from unitary state to differentiated polity in the
United Kingdom / R.A.W. Rhodes – [*et al.*].
      p. cm.
   Includes bibliographical references and index.
   ISBN 0-335-21235-2 – ISBN 0-335-21234 -4 (pbk.)
   1. Civil service – Great Britain.   2. Great Britain – Politics and
government – 1945–   I. Rhodes, R.A.W.

JN425.D356 2003
351.41–dc21   2002074968

Typeset in 10/11.5pt GraphBembo by Graphicraft Limited, Hong Kong
Printed in Great Britain by Biddles Limited, www.biddles.co.uk

Contents

List of figures and tables

Preface and acknowledgements

Writing this book has proved to be a challenging experience during a period of momentous upheaval in the nature of British governance and the civil service. When we embarked on our research in 1997, devolution had yet to occur. Five years later, it is a reality. While the political arguments continue over the wisdom and longer-term impact of the devolution process, those charged with administering the state, both at the central government and devolved administration level, have quietly continued to fulfil their duties. As such, the British civil service has been the subject of exhaustive inquiry over many years, but a gap persists in the literature about the variations that exist across the UK. Over thirty years have elapsed since Gladden's seminal work in 1967 on the theme of intra-UK variation. Hence, a fresh examination is timely and forms the essential rationale for this book.

The core aim of the book is to update and interpret the map of the civil services of the UK beyond Whitehall. It explores two controversial propositions. First, it asks whether Britain is moving from the unitary, strong executive of the Westminster model to a differentiated polity characterized by institutional fragmentation. Second, it considers whether an unintended consequence of recent changes is a 'hollowing out of the state'. Simply, is the British executive losing functions downwards to devolved governments and special-purpose bodies and outwards to regional offices and agencies with a resulting loss of central capacity? In seeking to secure agreements for policy formulation and implementation, senior Whitehall officials will now need to cross the domestic borders as emissaries, not as proconsuls. Devolution and the redefinition of the role of the British civil service represents the most substantial addition to the process of the hollow-ing out of the state since Britain signed the Treaty of Rome (1972). The civil service is changing, but we do not yet know into what it is changing. The uncertainty is compounded by two decades of public sector management reforms and 'new' Labour's constitutional reform programme, most not-ably devolution to Scotland, Wales and Northern Ireland, as well as its more hesitant steps towards administrative deconcentration in England through the existing government offices for the regions.

Each of the authors lectures and conducts research in the field of public administration and territorial government. The material contained in the book is based on our individual and combined research efforts. Inevit-ably, a project of this size requires a division of labour. Rod Rhodes acted as the coordinator for the research, securing the financial support of the Economic and Social Research Council without which the research would have been impossible for us to undertake. He provided much of the theoret-ical framework for analysis within which our empirical work is located and by which it could be assessed and interpreted. Janice McMillan undertook the analysis of Scotland and helped compile policy case study evidence from Wales. She also organized the collation of the statistical data, liaising closely with officials within the Cabinet Office in London. Andrew Massey undertook analysis of Wales and the government offices for the regions in England. Paul Carmichael was responsible for analysing the Northern Ireland Civil Service, as well as helping to compile policy case study evidence from Wales. He has also been the coordinator for this book. Although the following chapters are provided by each of us based on our respective tasks in the research, we have been careful to act collectively in reviewing our respective contributions and to ensure consistency between chapters. In short, each chapter is a collective effort, as is the book as a whole.

The rationale for and structure of the book are outlined in Chapter 1, as is an overview of the established Westminster model. In Chapter 2, we consider the new governance in the UK, focusing on the merits of the differentiated polity model. In Chapters 3 to 6, we provide a country-by-country analysis of the civil service arrangements in each of the four com-ponent parts of the UK. In addition, we provide an analysis of policy and administrative differentiation in the UK using case study evidence of two key policy areas – economic development and community care – and how these vary in the three smaller countries of the UK. Our conclusions are outlined in Chapter 7.

A large number of individuals and organizations have assisted us in the course of the research for this book. We have interviewed scores of civil servants across the UK, the vast majority of whom have spoken candidly and expansively about their experiences, their views of the changes that have occurred during recent times and on the prospects for the future. As our research shows, the days of civil service anonymity may well be under serious challenge. However, in the interests of preserving the willingness of officials to continue to engage so positively with academic researchers, we have undertaken to observe Chatham House rules on the confidentiality of our interviews. We extend our profound gratitude to all our interviewees.

Additionally, we would like to thank various other individuals and organizations without whose assistance this book would never have materialized. First, thanks go to the Economic and Social Research Council for their award of a grant to fund our work. Second, several other individuals were associated with our research project at different stages of its evolution, including Dr B.M. O'Toole, Dr Christopher Lanigan, Dr Dylan Griffiths and, latterly, Mr Doug Miller who assisted with the compilation and processing of statistical material. Third, our work benefited considerably from collaboration with Mr Derek Coggle, Personnel Statistics Division, Central Support Services, Cabinet Office. Fourth, Rod Rhodes would like to thank Mark Bevir (University of California) and David Marsh (University of Birmingham) for their helpful comments on Chapters 2 and 7.

Rod Rhodes, Paul Carmichael,
Janice McMillan and Andrew Massey

1

Introduction

Since the late 1970s, British government and public administration have been through an extended period of transition. Waves of public sector management reform have challenged and replaced many long-established operating principles. More recently, the impact of constitutional changes, notably devolution, has highlighted and accentuated the real and long-standing differences that exist in the political and administrative systems of both the UK as a whole and its component parts, bringing a transformation of the territorial settlement within the UK. In a real sense, the UK has witnessed a shift – from the government of a unitary state to governance by and through networks.

   This book is concerned with developing a more fruitful avenue for facilitating an understanding of this transformation than the 'Westminster model' that has predominated in many accounts of British government. It does so through a case study of the differentiated polity thesis. That is, it examines one of the pivotal institutions in the process of change, namely the British civil service and the interaction between civil servants and the political systems and subsystems of the UK. We focus on its three smaller constituent countries to raise important issues about the nature of British government and public administration and its future direction. The British civil service has been the subject of exhaustive inquiry over many years. However, remarkably, almost all of the existing studies tend to focus on the senior civil service in London and fail to discuss the organization of the civil service outside Whitehall (Hennessy 1992), or are outdated (Gladden 1967; Hogwood and Keating 1982), or both.

2 Decentralizing the civil service

General texts on the civil service abound (Greenwood and Wilson 1989; Drewry and Butcher 1991; Dowding 1995; Pyper 1995; Theakston 1995; Barberis 1996; Richards 1997; Horton and Farnham 1999) and all argue that significant changes have occurred and continue to occur in the spatial structure and responsibilities of departments, agencies, non-departmental public bodies and civil servants in the UK. Indeed, it is widely accepted that the British civil service has been changing and continues to do so. We remain uncertain, however, about what it is changing into. The uncertainty has two causes. First, there have been decades of public sector management reforms, including the creation of executive agencies, privatization, marketizing public services, managerial decentralization, regulation and the devolution of responsibility for personnel recruitment and pay bargaining to individual departments. Also, central government reformed the governmental regional offices and regional development agencies in England. These developments have created a more territorially differentiated and institutionally federated civil service than previously existed (Pyper 1995). 'New' Labour's constitutional reform programme, most notably devolution to Scotland, Wales and Northern Ireland, accentuated these trends. However, most existing work seldom proceeds to explore in any great detail the differential impact of these changes across the UK. The focus remains the English civil service but there is a clear lacuna in the literature on variations across the UK. Until recently, such oversight may have been attributable to the fact that the devolved parts of the UK Civil Service represented only a small proportion of the total civil service. However, there are clear signs that the unitary institution of the civil service always possessed a much greater degree of internal variety in practice, both in the English regions as well as between England, Wales and Scotland given territorial ministries whose powers are not congruent. And, of course, the existence of a constitutionally separate Northern Ireland Civil Service (NICS) is further evidence of diversity across the UK. Moreover, the need to fill this gap is underscored by devolution, which entrenches the already significant differentiation apparent in the UK.

Over thirty years have elapsed since Gladden's pioneering study (Gladden 1967) and a fresh and rigorous examination is overdue. Our core aim is to update and interpret the map of the civil services of the UK beyond Whitehall. Specifically, we wanted:

- to describe the civil service outside Whitehall, for example, numbers of employees and functions;
- to analyse the factors propelling change in the civil service outside Whitehall;
- to describe how those who work in the civil service outside Whitehall perceive both their work and the civil service; and
- to explore the tensions between territorial and functional politics.

In so doing, however, the book is also intended to be more than a detailed description of spatial variation across the civil service in the UK. The book also explores two related and controversial propositions. First, we assess whether Britain is moving from the unitary, strong executive of the Westminster model to a differentiated polity characterized by institutional fragmentation. Second, we ask whether an unintended consequence of recent changes is a 'hollowing out of the state'. Simply, is the British executive losing functions downwards to devolved governments and special-purpose bodies and outwards to regional offices and agencies with a resulting loss of central capacity (see Chapter 2), and upwards to the European Union.

The civil service is an excellent vehicle for exploring broader themes in the territorial governance of the UK. The current Labour government and many senior interests in the civil service remain strongly attached to maintaining a unified civil service in the UK, even though elements in the devolved administrations of Scotland and Wales favour separate civil services, along the lines of that of Northern Ireland.

The definitional problem in existing research

There is an immediate definitional problem to confront. Most international comparisons of the internal governmental arrangements of states are broad categorizations, typically contrasting unitary systems with federations. Such generic distinctions have manifest shortcomings. The UK is ordinarily said to be a unitary state with a political system that adheres to the tenets of the Westminster model. In truth, the reality is more complex. We need to unpack these terms, examining each in turn.

Unitary state

The nation state is the conventionally accepted form of territorial organization that originated in western Europe. The term 'unitary state' is a black hole in the political science literature; a taken-for-granted notion for which it is rare to find a definition (an honourable exception is Rose (1982: 51–2)). It is all too often treated as a residual category, used to compare unitary with federal states to highlight the characteristics of the latter (Elazar 1997). In this book, we use it to refer to the *politically sovereign, centralized governments of unified nation states*. It is an institutional and constitutional notion; political sovereignty refers to international recognition that a government rules a specified territory. It is centralized because the decision to decentralize can be revoked by the central authority.

There are various types of unitary state. The UK is an example of the Anglo-Saxon state that draws a clear boundary between state and civil society. There is no legal basis to the state. As Rose (1982) noted, 'the idea of the state as a thing in itself, an institution independent of and superior to members of society . . . is alien to British political thinking' (p.47). In the UK, the Crown represents the sum of formal political authority. Combining parliamentary sovereignty and a strong executive makes the British unitary state one of the most centralized in western Europe. Britain can also be seen as a union state. Scotland, Wales and Northern Ireland have distinctive administrative arrangements because the English centre chose an operating code which was flexible and accommodating, stressing indirect control of the periphery and representation of the periphery in the centre (Bulpitt 1983). Constitutional reform in the late 1990s reinforced functional decentralization by devolving political authority to the constituent territories of the UK.

No unitary state is wholly homogeneous. No unitary state is completely centralized. Decentralization is a common strategy for coping with diversity. There are types and degrees of decentralization: deconcentration (prefectoral and functional), delegation, and devolution to both regional and local governments (Rhodes 1992).

Decentralization refers to the distribution of power to lower levels in a territorial hierarchy, whether the hierarchy is one of governments within a state or offices within a large-scale organization (Smith 1985: 1). Or more briefly, it refers to the areal division of powers (Maass 1959). So defined, the term encompasses both political and bureaucratic decentralization, federal and unitary states, and decentralization between levels of government and within units of government.

Deconcentration, sometimes referred to as field administration, involves 'the redistribution of administrative responsibilities . . . within the central government' (Rondinelli and Cheema 1983: 18). A broad distinction can be drawn between prefectoral and functional systems. In the prefectoral system, a representative of the centre – the prefect – located in the regions supervises both local governments and other field officers of the centre. He is the superior officer in the field, embodying 'the authority of all ministers as well as the government generally and is the main channel of communication between technical field officials and the capital' (Smith 1967: 45). The classical examples are the French prefect and the collectors or district commissioners in India. In the functional system, field officers belong to distinct functional hierarchies. The administration of the several policy areas is separate. There is no general, regional coordinator. Coordination occurs at the centre. This system of multifarious functional territories is typified by England (see Hogwood and Keating 1982).

Delegation refers to 'the delegation of decision-making and management authority for specific functions to organisations that are not under the direct control of central government ministries' (Rondinelli and Cheema 1983: 20). Such organizations are referred to as parastatal organizations, non-departmental public bodies or quangos (quasi-autonomous non-governmental organizations). They include public corporations and regional development agencies. This category is also used to cover the transfer of functions to the private sector or voluntary bodies through marketization, privatization or contracting out, cumbersome neologisms which refer to the various ways of delivering 'public' services using markets or quasi-markets. Decentralization understood as managerial delegation and market-ization has fuelled major reforms of the public sector throughout the world in the 1980s and 1990s (Kickert 1997).

Devolution refers to the exercise of political authority, by lay, mainly elected, institutions within areas defined by community characteristics (Smith 1985: 11). Thus, 'local units are autonomous, independent and clearly per-ceived as separate levels of government over which central authorities exer-cise little or no *direct* control' (Rondinelli and Cheema 1983: 22). Historically, the *locus classicus* of devolution is said to be British local government, but the most significant trend in the decentralization of political authority is the growth of regional government in Europe (Jones and Keating 1995). Most recently, the UK has devolved power with the creation of a Scottish Parlia-ment, Welsh Assembly and Northern Ireland Assembly.

Centralization is an easy target for advocates of decentralization. The arguments for and against are clear even if there is no foreseeable end to the debate. So, centralization promotes territorial justice and equality. Central authorities uphold service standards, rationalize resource allocation and coordinate local development. There is a need for national plans, especially when resources are scarce, and only the centre can ensure territorial equality by the central provision of funds and supervising the uniform implementa-tion of national policies. Centralization is encouraged by financial weakness, national elites, including the bureaucracy, eager to protect their interests, and by political instability.

On the other hand, decentralization is often said to be the counter-weight to central power. Liberal-democratic theory assumes decentraliza-tion promotes democratic participation, especially local self-government. Nationally, decentralization is said to promote political education, training in political leadership and political stability. In local government, it pro-motes the values of equality, accountability and responsiveness (Sharpe 1970; Smith 1985: 20). It is also said to have many managerial or adminis-trative advantages. First, it is seen as a way of surmounting the adminis-trative incompetence of the centre, that is, the limits of national planning by getting closer to problems, cutting through red tape and meeting local needs. Second, it improved central 'penetration' of rural areas, spreading knowledge of, and mobilizing support for, the plan and bypassing obstruc-tive local elites. Third, it encouraged the involvement of various religious, ethnic and tribal groups, promoting national unity. Fourth, it increased the speed and flexibility of decision-making, encouraging experimentation and reducing central control and direction. Fifth, it increased the efficiency of the centre by freeing top management from routine tasks and reducing the diseconomies of scale caused by congestion at the centre. Sixth, it increased the administrative capacity of the localities and regions and improved the coordination or service delivery. Finally, it institutionalized participation, provided opportunities for many interests to obtain a 'stake' in the system, trained citizens for democracy and politicians for government, and promoted political maturity and democratic stability (paraphrased from Rondinelli and Cheema 1983: 14–16 and Smith 1985: 186–8).

To raise the topic of centralization is to raise an emotive issue. Centralization is 'bad'; decentralization is 'good'. There is a clear implication that a federal state is a more decentralized form of government than a unitary state. Any such conclusion should be resisted. A federal state can devolve limited powers to its constituent governments. The theory and practice of federalism can diverge markedly and, as the case of Denmark shows, a unitary state can devolve considerable powers to local and regional governments. The unitary state cannot remain a taken-for-granted notion. The degree of centralization, and its varied political and administrative consequences, must become matters of empirical inquiry. That is our task in looking at the civil services of the UK. So, following Rokkan and Urwin (1982: 11), we distinguish between the unitary state and the union state. The unitary state is 'built up around one unambiguous political centre which enjoys economic dominance and pursues a more or less undeviating policy of administrative standardisation. All areas of the state are treated alike, and all institutions are directly under the control of the centre'. In the union state, 'integration is less than perfect . . . [and while] administrative standardisation prevails over most of the territory . . . in some areas pre-union rights and institutional infrastructure . . . preserve some degree of regional autonomy and serve as agencies of elite recruitment'.

Confusion persists both at home and abroad because the terms 'UK', 'Great Britain', 'Britain', 'England' and 'the British Isles' are erroneously interchanged (see Davies 2000). The UK is a multinational political entity whose geographical extent has emerged over centuries. At present it comprises Great Britain (England, Wales and Scotland) and Northern Ireland. Reflecting its composite nature, many rights and institutions that predate the Union persist in each of the UK's four component parts, as do varying degrees of policy and administrative autonomy. In the chapter that follows, we chart the imperfections.

The Westminster model

For decades, the Westminster model has exercised a pervasive influence over how practitioners and academics alike understand British government. The Westminster model refers to the language, map, questions and historical story used to capture the essential features of the British system that, through sheer longevity, form the conventional or mainstream story.[1] The model's characteristics include:

> strong cabinet government based on majority rule; the importance attached to constitutional conventions; a two-party system based on

single member constituencies; the assumption that minorities can find expression in one of the major parties; the concept of Her Majesty's loyal opposition; and the doctrine of parliamentary supremacy, which takes precedence over popular sovereignty except during elections.

(Verney 1991: 637)

There are many similar definitions. For example, Gamble (1990: 407) adumbrates a unitary state characterized by: parliamentary sovereignty; strong cabinet government; accountability through elections; majority party control of the executive (that is, prime minister, cabinet and the civil service); elaborate conventions for the conduct of parliamentary business; institutionalized opposition, and the rules of debate.[2] Obviously, every author varies both the list of characteristics and their relative importance. The model has been criticized and modified and there are several variants but there is a clear baseline to any discussion of the Westminster model and there are marked family resemblances between the several varieties. The most prominent family characteristics are the focus on rules and institutions; the use of legal-historical methods, a Whig historiography, and a personalized view of power.

The Westminster narrative focuses on institutions – that is, the rules, procedures and formal organizations of government – that are the historical heart of political science. As Leftwich (1984: 16) points out, the discipline traditionally had two foci: the study of the institutions of government and the study of political thought (see also Rhodes 1997a: ch. 4). Greenleaf (1983: 7–9) argues that constitutional law, constitutional history and the study of institutions form the 'traditional' approach. Indisputably these topics are central to the Westminster narrative where they are reflected in a prevalent language of machine metaphors and phrases such as 'the machinery of government'.

This narrative also contains a shared set of methodological assumptions. These assumptions involve using the inductive tools of the lawyer and the historian to explain the constraints on both political behaviour and democratic effectiveness. It firmly rejects the deductive approach of the economist. Indeed, as Gamble (1990: 409) highlights, it often embodies an idealist philosophy, seeing 'institutions as the expression of human purpose' and focusing, therefore, on the interaction between ideas and institutions. For example, Johnson's (1975: 276–7) rationale for the study of political institutions argues:

political institutions express particular choices about how political relationships ought to be shaped; they are in the nature of continuing injunctions to members of a society that they should try to conduct themselves in specific ways when engaged in the pursuit of political ends. This is to define political institutions as necessarily containing a normative element.

Here the Westminster narrative typically goes with a Whig historiography that comes perilously close to telling the story of a single, unilinear, progressive idea, reason or spirit underlying the evolution of the British political system. It emphasizes gradualism and the capacity of British institutions to evolve and cope with crises; it provides 'capacity for independent action, leadership and decision' while ensuring that 'British political institutions would remain flexible and responsive'. This narrative, with its implicit Whig historiography, was esteemed by political scientists who 'were largely sympathetic' (Gamble 1990: 411), being 'convinced that change needed to be evolutionary'; and willing to celebrate 'the practical wisdom embodied in England's constitutional arrangements' (Gamble 1990: 409).

The Whig tradition also makes some important, if implicit, assumptions about power. As Smith (1999) argues, it focuses on behaviour, motivations and institutional position. Power is an object that belongs to the prime minister, cabinet or civil service. So, 'power relationships are a zero-sum game where there is a winner and a loser' and power is 'ascribed to an institution or person and fixed to that person regardless of the issue or the context'. Personality is a key part of any explanation of an actor's power.

The UK – a union state and differentiated polity

Just as we question the notion of Britain as a unitary state, we also probe the inadequacies of the Westminster model. Since the 1970s, the Westminster model has faced sustained challenge. Increasingly, it was found lacking, unable to interpret and explain recent developments. Rhodes (1997a) argues that the 'differentiated polity model' is better able to deal with recent trends.

In essence the differentiated polity model disputes that the institutions of the centre can direct all levels of government in the UK. Building on the intergovernmental relations approach and the power-dependence model (Rhodes 1988), it emphasizes the resources of the supposedly subordinate tiers of government that can be deployed to frustrate central control and direction. The prime minister and cabinet, supposedly accountable to the electorate through parliament, do not decide policies; rather, policies 'emerge' from the deliberations of discrete, organized, closed networks of policy actors, although ministers and their departments are important players. Policy networks or policy communities involve actors exchanging resources according to certain understood 'rules of the game' and are too complex to be understood by the notion of central control so central to the Westminster model.

In political science, models indicate what is worthy of study. Thus, whereas the Westminster model focused attention on the prime minister, cabinet, Westminster and Whitehall, the differentiated polity model forces political scientists to look further afield. In our case, we look at the activities of the civil service beyond one part of central London, arguing that this facet of UK government may have something useful to tell us about how government responds to problems in different parts of the country and how (and how successfully) government policies to reform the civil service and public administration are implemented in practice (for a fuller discussion see Chapter 2).

The changes occasioned by devolution are potentially seismic. However, the civil service in the UK was never monolithic. As befits the union state tradition, the existence of territorial ministries in Scotland, Wales and Northern Ireland attests to the considerable administrative diversity that has always been a characteristic of the British polity. Even the most cursory examination of the system of civil administration in the UK reveals that one must refer to 'civil services' – the UK or Home Civil Service, the Northern Ireland Civil Service and, until 1999, the Colonial and Overseas Civil Services. We have limited our analysis to the 'domestic' services. Thus, the UK was already differentiated long before the introduction of devolution. Devolution and other recent reforms reinforce the long-existing pattern of functional differentiation with decentralized political authority. These trends contribute to the hollowing out of the British centre, further eroding the capacity of the British centre to implement its policies effectively and creating the potential for a *dis*United Kingdom.

Statistical background to government beyond Whitehall

While the British civil service experienced many public management reforms after 1979, the incidence of these reforms varied across the UK. The overall decline in the total number of civil servants is well documented, the national total falling by over one-third to about 450,000, before rising again to around 500,000 (see Drewry 2000). To examine these changes more closely, we draw on three main sources of information: official statistics, primary sources (for example, official publications) and elite interviews. Below, we summarize the main findings. The main source for the data was the annual *Civil Service Statistics* publication. There were problems in standardizing the data across time. For example, the units employed in *Civil Service Statistics* changed from thousands until 1982 to full-time equivalents from 1983. There were also specific sources and problems for each constituent territory of the UK. Thus, for the Northern Ireland Civil Service, separate statistics from those for the UK Civil Service have always been compiled. They were reported separately in the *Northern Ireland Digest of Statistics* and, since 1985, in the publications of the NICS's own Equal Opportunities Unit.

For the Home Civil Service, the period for which the most reliable information could be collected was 1975 to 1996, with more detailed information from 1997 to 2000 (see Tables 1.1 and 1.2).

Table 1.1 Non-industrial civil service staff by economic planning region/location (as a percentage of the annual totals)

Location	1975	1976	1977	1978	1979	1980	1981	1982	1983	1984	1985
Northern Region Departments	6.07	6.11	6.21	6.28	6.47	6.36	6.56	6.49	6.44	6.32	6.21
Yorkshire and Humberside	5.15	5.19	5.27	5.40	5.46	5.49	5.60	5.82	5.88	5.97	6.10
East Midlands	3.58	3.63	3.72	3.79	3.75	3.76	3.83	3.88	3.86	3.90	3.93
East Anglia	1.91	1.93	1.90	1.99	2.33	2.26	2.27	2.29	2.33	2.39	2.51
South East	42.83	42.95	42.18	41.43	40.74	40.55	40.01	39.71	39.33	39.07	38.75
South West	8.93	8.93	9.00	9.12	9.15	9.39	9.29	9.21	9.24	9.34	9.34
West Midlands	4.78	4.89	5.13	5.11	5.19	5.23	5.27	5.42	5.48	5.59	5.65
North West	9.36	9.55	9.78	10.00	10.11	9.94	10.01	10.08	10.26	10.12	10.05
Wales	4.93	5.22	5.42	5.56	5.57	5.54	5.57	5.57	5.66	5.62	5.64
Scotland	8.88	9.00	9.02	9.10	9.22	9.26	9.36	9.44	9.46	9.61	9.73
Northern Ireland	0.77	0.76	0.75	0.65	0.65	0.62	0.63	0.62	0.62	0.61	0.61
Elsewhere or not specified	2.83	1.84	1.61	1.57	1.36	1.59	1.60	1.46	1.45	1.46	1.48
Total staff ('000)	**534.0**	**564.6**	**569.7**	**567.0**	**566.0**	**548.4**	**542.6**	**532.9**	**520.3**	**508.9**	**503.3**
Inner London						16.41	15.90	15.54	15.19	15.12	14.99
Outer London						8.44	8.39	8.43	8.53	4.18	4.19
Intermediate										4.24	4.01
Rest of South East									15.61	15.53	15.57

Location	1986	1987	1988	1989	1990	1991	1992	1993	1994	1995	1996
Northern Region Departments	6.15	6.16	6.27	6.28	6.29	6.37	6.42	6.48	6.56	6.80	6.39
Yorkshire and Humberside	6.03	6.14	6.37	6.21	6.37	6.30	6.48	6.81	6.66	6.60	6.74
East Midlands	3.91	3.99	4.01	4.02	3.83	3.81	3.91	4.05	4.04	4.20	4.25
East Anglia	2.62	2.65	2.75	2.72	2.71	2.76	2.91	2.88	2.91	2.91	3.33
South East	38.79	38.49	38.38	38.18	37.78	37.32	37.17	35.95	36.09	35.87	35.17
South West	9.47	9.36	8.98	9.08	9.14	9.17	9.14	9.17	9.47	9.64	9.48
West Midlands	5.71	5.88	6.01	6.00	6.03	6.05	6.15	6.27	6.21	5.70	6.23
North West	9.85	9.99	10.24	10.34	10.25	10.47	10.63	10.93	11.08	11.59	11.53
Wales	5.53	5.41	5.37	5.46	5.65	5.57	5.47	5.35	5.22	5.12	5.08
Scotland	9.71	9.84	9.55	9.51	9.60	9.55	9.29	9.48	9.40	9.20	9.33
Northern Ireland	0.62	0.60	0.61	0.62	0.63	0.65	0.65	0.68	0.64	0.66	0.69
Elsewhere or not specified	1.61	1.50	1.48	1.56	1.72	1.98	1.79	1.93	1.72	1.71	1.77
Total staff ('000)	**497.9**	**506.7**	**506.6**	**499.8**	**495.2**	**490.0**	**504.2**	**502.8**	**487.4**	**474.9**	**458.4**
Inner London	15.02	14.86	14.75	14.84	14.68	14.37	14.23	13.97	13.71	13.57	
Outer London	4.08	3.97	3.90	3.86	3.83	3.72	3.74	3.77	3.80	3.83	
Intermediate	4.02	4.06	4.04	3.88	3.79	3.64	3.99	3.70	3.75	3.97	
Rest of South East	15.67	15.59	15.69	15.60	15.47	15.59	15.20	14.51	14.83	14.50	

Table 1.2 Non-industrial civil service staff by principal department (as a percentage of the annual totals)

Department	1975	1976	1977	1978	1979	1980	1981	1982	1983	1984	1985
Agriculture etc	2.62	2.55	2.49	2.40	2.30	2.30	2.25	2.18	2.17	2.14	2.10
Cabinet Office	0.67	0.69	0.65	0.60	0.64	0.66	0.64			0.33	0.33
Civil Service Department											
Courts Service											
Custom and Excise	5.07	5.19	5.16	5.04	5.11	4.99	4.96	4.95	4.92	4.94	5.07
Defence	24.38	23.19	22.28	21.55	21.36	21.69	21.13	20.70	20.33	20.52	20.16
Defence (Royal Ordnance Factories)											
Education and Science	0.73	0.71	0.68	0.65	0.65	0.47	0.46	0.47	0.47	0.47	0.48
Employment Group	6.61	7.74	8.77	8.98	9.10	9.00	9.25	10.66	10.82	11.01	10.53
Energy	0.22	0.25	0.23	0.23	0.23	0.24	0.22	0.21	0.21	0.21	0.21
Environment	8.11	8.18	7.95	7.81	7.58	7.58	7.28	6.93	6.79	6.92	6.92
Health and Social Security	16.20	16.17	16.53	17.04	17.21	17.34	18.05	18.13	18.14	17.68	18.54
Social Security											
HMSO	0.60	0.58	0.58	0.56	0.57	0.57	0.55	0.51	0.44	0.43	0.40
Home Office	4.98	5.08	5.04	5.15	5.25	5.45	5.80	5.84	6.06	6.32	6.67
Inland Revenue	13.74	14.00	14.48	14.97	15.02	14.38	14.04	13.76	14.13	13.85	13.74
Land Registry	0.84	0.87	0.86	0.90	0.95	1.06	1.03	1.05	1.11	1.30	1.35
Lord Chancellor's Department			1.74	1.78	1.80	1.80	1.84	1.86	1.96	1.99	2.01
Management and Personnel Office											
National Savings	2.51	2.39	2.18	1.94	1.87	1.86	1.82	1.75	1.60	1.56	1.54
National Statistics											
Ordnance Survey	0.77	0.73	0.68	0.63	0.58	0.58	0.59	0.56	0.53	0.52	0.55
Office of Population Census and Statistics	0.52	0.48	0.44	0.46	0.44	0.46	0.48	0.49	0.42	0.41	0.41
Scottish Office	1.72	1.75	1.72	1.69	1.78	1.79	1.82	1.80	1.80	1.82	1.79
Scottish Prison Service (SHHD)											
Social Security											
Trade, Industry and Prices and Consumers	3.20	3.10	3.02	2.91	2.90	2.86	2.84	2.76	2.70	2.44	2.40
Transport											
Treasury	0.21	0.19	0.19	0.19	0.19	0.18	0.18	0.54	0.55	0.52	0.50
Welsh Office	0.24	0.27	0.28	0.26	0.42	0.44	0.41	0.39	0.40	0.40	0.43
Other departments	4.21	4.11	4.04	4.00	4.05	4.28	4.29	4.24	4.21	4.22	3.86
All departments ('000)	**534.1**	**564.8**	**569.9**	**567.0**	**566.0**	**548.6**	**542.8**	**532.8**	**520.3**	**508.9**	**503.3**

Department	1986	1987	1988	1989	1990	1991	1992	1993	1994	1995	1996
Agriculture etc	2.11	1.96	1.92	1.92	1.91	1.98	1.86	1.92	2.02	2.17	2.13
Cabinet Office	0.33	0.32	0.31	0.32	0.30	0.31	0.29	0.46	0.45	0.51	0.63
Civil Service Department											
Courts Service											
Custom and Excise	5.05	5.00	5.20	5.29	5.42	5.52	5.24	5.00	5.15	5.08	5.06
Defence	18.88	18.49	17.54	17.75	18.15	18.43	17.98	17.48	16.98	16.81	16.83
Defence (Royal Ordnance Factories)											
Education and Science	0.48	0.47	0.50	0.49	0.52	0.54	0.53	0.50	0.49	0.53	8.90
Employment Group	10.84	11.56	11.36	10.90	10.50	9.98	11.32	11.40	11.13	10.43	
Energy	0.21	0.20	0.19	0.21	0.21	0.19	0.18				
Environment	7.10	6.92	6.80	6.70	6.90	6.48	5.98	5.13	4.14	1.34	1.88
Health and Social Security	18.59	18.91	19.75	18.42	17.41	17.04	16.45	17.81	18.82	19.73	21.00
Social Security											
HMSO	0.40	0.40	0.39	0.40	0.41	0.44	0.42	0.40			
Home Office	6.81	6.82	7.13	7.54	8.00	8.35	9.28	9.62	9.74	10.12	10.73
Inland Revenue	14.11	13.50	13.15	13.41	13.34	13.41	13.66	13.23	12.80	12.44	12.32
Land Registry	1.41	1.44	1.62	2.11	2.17	2.05	1.89	1.95	1.77	1.79	1.78
Lord Chancellor's Department	2.04	2.01	2.11	2.18	2.11	2.29	2.30	2.37	2.38	2.44	2.45
Management and Personnel Office											
National Savings	1.54	1.49	1.44	1.45	1.42	1.37	1.24	1.21	1.17	1.15	1.02
National Statistics											
Ordnance Survey	0.56	0.56	0.52	0.51	0.49	0.49	0.46	0.45	0.43	0.42	0.43
Office of Population Census and Statistics	0.42	0.41	0.39	0.41	0.43	0.43	0.42	0.38	0.38	0.37	
Scottish Office	1.82	1.81	1.81	1.88	1.95	1.97	1.94	2.06	2.05	1.97	1.99
Scottish Prison Service (SHHD)											
Social Security											
Trade, Industry and Prices and Consumers	2.44	2.41	2.41	2.47	2.33	2.32	2.22	2.31	2.21	2.14	2.15
Transport											
Treasury	0.51	0.50	0.51	0.52	0.51	0.50	0.48	0.33	0.28	0.24	0.21
Welsh Office	0.43	0.42	0.40	0.42	0.44	0.45	0.46	0.46	0.46	0.45	0.45
Other departments	3.90	4.41	4.55	4.70	5.10	5.46	5.39	5.65	7.15	7.25	6.98
All departments ('000)	497.9	506.7	506.6	499.8	495.2	490.0	504.2	502.8	487.4	474.9	458.4

There are several problems with the centrally collected data that limit the usefulness of the statistics. First, in official statistics there are various entries that are registered as 0–50 (or N/A). Precise figures are therefore impossible to calculate, even for the smaller departments of state. Second, there are gaps in the official statistics summary tables of staff in all areas by department. Third, there are individual instances of large variations in staff numbers that cannot be explained through known history of the departments. Probably the greatest problem with the centrally collected statistics, however, derives from the recording mechanism because certain departments have not made annual returns. Even today the method used to gather data puts heavy onus on individual departments. They interpret what information is sought and the form in which it should be provided. Given the criticism often levelled at British government that it is overly bureaucratic and preoccupied with detail, it is perhaps surprising that until recently civil service statistics were neither fully systematized nor fully reported. Indeed, to this day departmental returns have no uniform, universal reporting mechanism. Two main sources are employed: Mandate, a central computer-based recording system, and staff record files that are used to compile manually departmental returns.

For Northern Ireland, the reporting arrangements were even more lax than those for the Home Civil Service. In this case the main statistics were provided by the Department of Finance and Personnel, the *Digest of Statistics*, the Department of Economic Development and the Civil Service Commission. The time series of total number of staff employed in Northern Ireland departments uses different sets of departments over time and only has data for selected years. As far as any civil service statistics are complete, Northern Ireland is probably in the worst situation for a consistent time series. Given the background of the Northern Ireland polity, it should be no surprise that civil service statistics include elements that are not collected elsewhere, for example, religious affiliation. For Northern Ireland, then, the reporting provides greater detail but within a more limited time series.

In spite of these limits, the statistics still tell an interesting story. Tables 1.1 and 1.2 show that, against the backcloth of overall national decline, there has been a major and continuing shift of civil servants from London and the South East. By contrast, as a proportion of the overall total, almost all regions recorded an increase though, proportionately, the greatest increases occurred in East Anglia and, to a lesser extent, Yorkshire/Humberside, Wales and the West Midlands. Unlike the 1960s and 1970s, there has been no corresponding increase for the English peripheral regions. Civil service numbers have remained fairly constant in Scotland, Wales and Northern Ireland. In functional terms, the major shifts have been the sharp declines recorded in the Agriculture, Defence and Environment Departments and the increases posted in Employment, Home Office and Social Security Departments.

For Scotland, Wales and Northern Ireland, the statistics also tell an interesting story. In Scotland, there was a decline in total civil service numbers from 47,400 to 42,600 in the period 1975–96 (Scottish Office 9200 to 4700). However, despite these decreases, Scottish civil servants account for a greater proportion of UK civil service staff, increasing by 0.45 per cent (and 0.27 per cent for the Scottish Office).

In Wales the story is slightly more complex. An overall decline in civil service numbers in Wales (26,300 in 1975 to 23,300 in 1996) has run alongside a rise in the numbers working in the Welsh Office (from 1300 to 2100 in the period 1975–96). Yet both these sets of figures represent an increase in staff working in Wales as a percentage of the total UK Civil Service. Percentages have risen for all Wales by 0.15 per cent to 5.08 per cent in 1996 (and by 0.21 per cent to 0.45 per cent in 1996 for staff employed in the Welsh Office).

Northern Ireland differs from Scotland and Wales in that there has been a rise in both total number of civil service staff and staff employed in the Northern Ireland Office 1975–96. Indeed, Northern Ireland had the largest increase in total numbers of any of the territorial offices, with staff doubling from 1500 in 1975 to 3600 in 1996.

More recently, with devolution, Scotland and Wales required more civil service staff and embarked on recruitment campaigns with set targets. The methods by which the devolved administrations intend to meet these targets have, as one may expect, differed. Scotland has made more extensive use of the transfer and secondment system whereas Wales has externally advertised posts (Parry 2001). Importantly for future civil service staffing levels and the strategies used in recruitment, Parry (2001) has noted a subtle shift in attitudes from 'joining the civil service' to 'joining the devolved administration'.

The case studies: economic development and community care

To better illustrate the extent of the differentiated polity, each chapter on Scotland, Wales and Northern Ireland includes evidence from case studies of the extent of variation in the application of policy across the UK. The cases focus on two key aspects of public policy, namely economic development and community care. For each policy area, we outline the distinctive development of policy in Scotland, Wales and Northern Ireland. Then we examine the institutions in each country responsible for the oversight and delivery of policy before assessing the effects of any differences.

Economic development – mapping the policy area

Economic development policy, by its nature, varies across the UK because it aims to promote the economic well-being of those parts of the country that have either lagged behind the general pace of the economy or have experienced pronounced dislocation as a consequence of global economic restructuring. By evaluating this policy area, it is possible to see how the policy is both framed and implemented in the component parts of the UK and to see whether the differences are explained solely by institutional and political variation.

Any examination of economic development as a policy area confronts an immediate problem: government decisions on macroeconomic policy, especially public expenditure, can render irrelevant any initiatives geared specifically to economic development. Generally, a good working definition is that economic development should 'raise the quality of life of . . . people through increasing economic opportunities for all, on a socially and environmentally sustainable basis' (Scottish Executive 2000b: viii). It therefore concerns international integration, regional development, social integration and sustainability. The main drivers to economic development are a supportive macroeconomic environment, supportive national physical, human and electronic infrastructures; competitiveness of enterprises and economic policies to secure favourable social, regional and environmental outcomes. Two of these drivers of economic development are outwith the direct realm of responsibilities of the devolved administrations. First, macroeconomic policy is the responsibility of the UK government, which in turn is influenced by EU policy. Second, the competitiveness of enterprises cannot be determined by public policy, a key factor given that it is widely accepted that private enterprise should be the primary driver of economic growth. So, the influence of the devolved administrations on economic outcomes will be limited. Further it is argued that there is now considerable consensus that private enterprise should be the primary driver of economic growth. The influence of the devolved administrations on outcomes may be limited despite the fact that the definition itself does not vary greatly from that held centrally, for example as set out in plans for regional development agencies outlined in *Our Competitive Future: Building the Knowledge Driven Economy* (DTI 1998) and *Regional Development Agencies: Regional Strategies* (DETR 1999).

The problems of defining and understanding economic development are recognized by government. One factor that makes economic development elusive is the fact that 'the knowledge and understanding of what drives economic development is continually evolving both within the UK and internationally' (Scottish Executive 2000b: 84). Indeed, the definitions of, and policies for, economic development have changed considerably over time, look set to remain fluid for the foreseeable future, and, therefore, make any evaluation of policy success and failure particularly difficult. A further complication arises, however. Simply, the literature (both academic and official) uses such terms as 'economic development', 'planning and development', 'industrial development', 'regional development', 'regional policy' and so on, interchangeably. The problem is more than one of semantics since, even if precise definitions could be offered for each of these terms, there remains a substantial overlap between them. Such terminological confusion makes for difficulties in securing meaningful and legitimate comparisons. Hence, to ensure a thorough exploration of the literature, we adopt a fairly inclusive analysis in which any and all of the above terms are accepted. Finally, matters are complicated further by the manner in which institutional structures and nomenclature vary across the UK. For ease of exposition, we consider the position in Scotland, Wales and Northern Ireland respectively by chapter.

Community care – mapping the policy area

To provide a contrast with economic development policy and its implementation across the UK, we provide a case study of variations across the UK in community care. Community care differs from economic development in that the main aims and objectives are more clearly expressed and the outcomes easier to identify, although debate surrounds interpretation of those outcomes. In contrast to economic development policy, community care policy should in theory be applied uniformly given that the incidence of need is not primarily a function of geography. In the differentiated polity, however, we contend that there will be territorial variations. Moreover, like many policy areas, community care illustrates the non-executant nature of the British central state. That is, there are no implementation functions vested with government departments. It is other public bodies and providers that deliver services. Civil service involvement is confined to policy initiation rather than implementation.

What is community care? The term does not lend itself to straightforward definitions. It

> apparently unites politicians, planners, social services professionals and a wide range of pressure groups . . . It has been a prominent policy goal of governments of both political parties since the Second World War . . . But for such an important concept, it has proved to be remarkably elusive and has been subject to surprisingly little critical attention over its long life.
>
> (Walker 1982: 1)

For decades, while the mantra of 'community' was repeated, attempts to define it were studiously avoided. Implicitly, the terms 'not hospital' and 'closing asylums' represented a belief shared by many professionals, politicians and members of the public alike.

During the 1970s, NHS reorganization 'attempted to overcome the divide between health services in the community and hospital-based services, only to create another gulf in community care between health and social services' (Allsop 1984: 110). Additionally, there was an 'emphasis on normalisation' with a philosophy of 'integration rather than isolation' (p.108).

Wolfenden (1978) highlighted the 'mixed economy' of welfare. It 'widened the discussion about community care so that more recent policy debates have been concerned with the respective roles of the statutory agencies, the commercial or private sector, the voluntary sector and the informal sector that is through family, friends and neighbours caring for the dependent in the community' (Allsop 1984: 109). In the 1980s, the Conservative government's *Care in Action* (DHSS 1981a) stressed that the voluntary and informal sectors were the 'primary sources of community care if not community treatment, and statutory and private sources are seen as supplementing and supporting this provision' (p.109). The House of Commons Social Services Select Committee captured the flavour of the terminological confusion when it observed that 'the phrase "community care" means little by itself', having 'come to have such general reference as to be virtually meaningless' (House of Commons Social Services Select Committee (1985), cited in Salter 1994: 120).

For consistency, we employ the definition offered by the 1987–92 Conservative government in its legislation. That is, the concept of community care involves

> providing the services and support which people who are affected by problems of ageing, mental illness, mental handicap or physical or sensory disability need to be able to live as independently as possible in their own homes or in 'homely' settings in the community . . . which enables such people to achieve their full potential.
>
> (DHSS 1989: 3)

The stated objective is

> to enable people to live as normal a life as possible, with the right amount of care and support to achieve maximum possible independence, while giving people a greater individual say in how they live their lives and the services they need to help them to do so.
>
> (DHSS 1989)

The policy of community care with which we are familiar today is rooted in a series of developments that can be charted back to the postwar creation of the welfare state. Barnes *et al.* (1998) observed that, from the 1960s, the changing nature of government policy on community care was driven by a combination of resource, ideological, professional and social considerations. Financially, the budget for residential care had spiralled sharply. Simply, in an era of retrenchment, more cost-effective solutions were needed. Politically, both Left and Right advanced the case for reform. For the New Right, the old methods such as long-stay hospitals and residential homes smacked of the 'collectivist' solutions of the social democratic welfare state, solutions that were deemed inconsistent with their individualist philosophy. In keeping with the new thinking, family provision and self-reliance nested more comfortably with the language of the family and personal responsibility. Also, it saved a great deal of money, an ines-capable albeit welcome fact for politicians anxious to control govern-ment budgets. For the Left, an emphasis on equal rights and status, with notions of living within the community being a right, had encouraged the belief that services must recognize the individuality of clients. Professionals, too, had become sceptical about the psychological impact of institutional care.

During the 1980s, community care 'gained momentum' (Prior 1993: 119). A consultative document, *Care in the Community* (DHSS 1981b), signalled community care was the best alternative for most people in insti-tutionalized care settings. The Griffiths Report (Griffiths 1988) on NHS management that led to the introduction of general management in health services as part of the drive for economy, efficiency and effectiveness gave added impetus. The Health and Social Services Adjudication Act 1983 established 'a modest increase in the amount of money made available for joint finance, a relaxation of the rules on use of joint finance to allow support to be provided over a longer period of time, and a change in the law to allow joint finance to be used on education for disabled people and housing' (Ham 1992: 89). For community care, this Act formally tied the NHS and local authorities in joint finance as the main actors in imple-mentation. These moves, however, had the impact of clearing hospitals but of moving people into residential accommodation; in other words the move to the community (either own homes or other establishments) had not been achieved. Further reform was necessary. When both the House of Commons Social Services Select Committee (1985) and the Audit Commission (1986) expressed concern about community care services, gov-ernment action seemed inevitable. The government commissioned Sir Roy Griffiths to consider community care arrangements and to make recom-mendations. His report (published in 1988) on community care was pivotal in prompting a shift in public policy.

Despite its disappointment and dismay (especially over the proposed enhanced role for local authorities), the government published its White Paper *Caring for People* (DHSS 1989), accepted Griffiths' main recommen-dations and proposed that all changes be implemented by April 1991. It proposed that: (a) local authorities were to have the lead role in securing community care services; (b) the needs of individuals were to be deter-mined by a multidisciplinary assessment, coordinated by social workers acting as care managers; and, (c) funds for purchasing the care element of residential and nursing home care would be transferred from the benefits system to local authorities.

Caring for People was a prelude to legislation – the NHS and Commun-ity Care Act 1990. The Act was a watershed that established community care as a distinct policy area, the culmination of a series of reports and inquiries set up to explore reasons for the slow and uneven implementa-tion of community care policy. Despite being declared government policy since the early 1970s, services remained dependent on institutional and hospital-based resources. For Means and Smith (1998), the Act involved a top-down movement in which central government brought to bear financial pressures and offered national guidance on good practice and legislation (p.12). Under the Act, local authority social services departments (social work departments in Scotland; Northern Ireland was outside the scope of the Act) were designated as the lead agencies for developing community care. Each local authority received a ringfenced addition to its government grant, an estimate based on the cost of delivering a standard level of community care to its residents (Lunt *et al.* 1996: 372). The Act delayed full introduction of the changes, with community care plans not becoming a statutory requirement until April 1992 and a new funding regime delayed until April 1993 (Means and Smith 1998: 58). For Barnes *et al.* (1998), there was a shift in focus in favour of consumer over producer interests.

Social services departments are responsible for producing community care plans consistent with the plans of the health authorities and other relevant agencies. These plans must be submitted to the Social Services Inspectorate of the Department of Health. To assist them in their planning, central government has issued a mass of guidance on how best to implement legislation and on how local authorities might improve the quality of the services they deliver or commission. Much of the advice is from the Social Services Directorate of the Department of Health. In addition, the Audit Commission published 'some of the most influential reviews of local authority performance in the provision of community care services' (Means and Smith 1998: 14). Together, 'since July 1996, the Social Services Inspectorate and the Audit Commission have been carrying out a rolling programme of joint reviews of 20 social services authorities per year' (p.14).

Hunter and Wistow (1987) suggest two reasons for studying community care. First, community care has had cross-party support for decades. Thus, it permits a longitudinal examination of the extent to which the Department of Health and Social Security (DHSS) (subsequently, the Department of Health (DH)) in England has functioned as the 'lead' department in the development of policy. Also, it allows an assessment of the extent to which territorial departments replicated or deviated from this lead. Second, as a longstanding policy area in its own right, community care is an important aspect of social policy in the UK. Hunter and Wistow (1987: 3) contended that the 'assumption of a unitary state in which Westminster/Whitehall gives the policy lead is shown to be grossly misleading in the case of community care policy. Considerable variations exist not only in policy means but also in policy ends'. Analysis of community care exposes the extent of differentiation that exists within the supposedly unitary structure of the UK. Frequently, the 'existence of quite distinct and separate arrangements for the administration of health and social care within the constituent parts of the UK has received no more than a fleeting acknowledgement' (p.3). The DH is usually regarded as the 'lead' department for health and personal social service matters. The conventional wisdom is that the three territorial departments had a predominantly reactive role, taking their cue from Whitehall 'rather than developing initiatives of their own. The ascription of policy leadership to the DHSS [now, the DH] is, however, only a particular example of the leadership role more generally associated with the functional departments in Whitehall' (p.4). In the highly centralized constitutional and political framework within which the territorial departments are obliged to function, the imperatives of policy homogeneity prevail (Kellas and Madgwick 1982; Keating and Midwinter 1983; Kellas 1984). In as much as diversity exists, it is about means rather than ends.

However, a conventional critique exists in which policy varies as well as implementation. Hunter and Wistow (1987) queried just how much the DHSS/DH operated as the lead department and 'how far such diversity as exists is confined to variations in the means through which common policies are pursued, rather than reflecting more fundamental divergences in the policy stances adopted by different departments' (p.5). They contended that the 'twin notions of policy uniformity and the lead department are neither straightforward nor self-evident' (p.5). Among the many complicating factors is the role of the UK's three territorial offices. The territorial offices are, according to Kellas and Madgwick (1982: 10) 'more corporate in their organisation and style than the giant functional departments based in London' which is held to ensure greater coherence and consistency in policy at the respective centres (Edinburgh, Cardiff and Belfast) than in England. However, before devolution, apart from the cabinet, there were no formal links at an administrative level and no regularized meetings of health ministers from the four countries. There were, however,

> strong informal links between the permanent secretaries, and the NHS chief executives, who meet some 3–4 times per year to discuss policy developments. Moreover, at assistant secretary level, there is lots of to-ing and fro-ing. We give each other advice and look at how things affect us. Given devolution, there is now a concordat across departments going ahead to formalize these informal mechanisms.
>
> (interview)

Centripetal and centrifugal forces are at work. Under devolution, in each new administration, the politicians want to be seen to be doing (and achieving) things. Already, while such issues as developing new standards and techniques may be resolved on a national (UK-wide) basis, other structural and process issues may see divergent approaches. To explore how the civil service has impacted on the policy-making and implementation aspects of community care policy, we again consider the evidence from each of the UK's three smaller countries.

The structure of the book

The aim of this book is to challenge long-held assumptions about the UK being a unitary state whose governmental system is based on the Westminster model. The remainder of the book develops these arguments. Chapter 2 outlines in detail the differentiated polity model. Chapters 3 through 6 examine each of the four countries of the UK (Northern Ireland, Scotland, Wales and England). Each chapter is self-contained, but we use a standardized format. Each charts the history, major characteristics and trends in the territorial civil service, concentrating on the period 1970 to 2000. We cover the impact of public sector reforms and the transition to devolved administrations. Chapter 6 examines England and the steady development of the regional tier of administration since the 1960s, concentrating on the government offices for the regions and regional development agencies. Chapters 3, 4, and 5 consider Northern Ireland, Scotland and Wales, respectively. These chapters also contain the case studies of economic development and community care. Finally, Chapter 7 draws together the findings of the empirical chapters and analyses the material comparatively. We also assess the extent of differentiation and reply to critics of the differentiated polity thesis.

Notes

1 Tivey (1988) provides a useful guide to the mainstream literature and its many variations, thereby removing the need for a lengthy list here.
2 See also, among many others, Parker (1979), Weller (1985: 16) and Wilson (1994: 190–3).

2

The differentiated polity

In the 1980s and the 1990s, British government underwent many changes. One obvious role for the academic is providing an anthology of such changes; explaining what changed and why. Thus, Britain has shifted from the government (of a unitary state) to governance (by and through networks). But our description and explanation can fall on uncomprehending ears. We may say what words mean and produce only misunderstanding. So, Peter Riddell, political editor of *The Times*, said:

> The language in which political scientists operate is divorced from that of practitioners and commentators. Every time I see the word 'governance' I have to think again what it means and how it is not the same as government. Terms such as 'core executive', 'differentiated polity' and 'hollowed out executive' have become almost a private patois of political science, excluding outsiders, rather like the jargon of management reform in the civil service. The current generation of political scientists should look back a century to the elegance and clarity – though not the views – of Dicey and Bryce, and even perhaps the wit of a Bagehot.

This chapter defends the 'private patois of political science', revisiting the notions of the differentiated polity, governance, networks, the core executive and hollowing out. We provide a guide to one way of understanding British government, to what we are trying to understand and how we understand it.

The shorthand name for the conventional story of how British government works – and academics and practitioners alike share the story – is the Westminster model. This model focuses on such features as cabinet government and the role of the prime minister, majority party rule, parliamentary supremacy and a neutral, permanent civil service. It would be foolish to deny that these are important characteristics of British government, but the Westminster model paints an incomplete picture. For example, the growth of the welfare state made many professions powerful: they could change and at times openly resist the policies of the elected government. If a powerful executive could pass new policies, it could not always make sure those policies would be put into practice as intended. So, if the Westminster model is characterized by a strong executive and a tradition of 'leaders know best', an interesting puzzle is why do so many of their policies fail. The much-vaunted, seemingly all-powerful Mrs Thatcher, 'handbagged' the professions of the welfare state. Yet, as we write, the newspapers are filled with stories about arrogant consultants in the NHS and the problems of holding them to account. What is missing from the Westminster model is an account of 'the sour laws of unintended consequences' (Hennessy 1992: 453).

To compound the problems of the Westminster model, much has changed in the half-century from Attlee to Blair. The Empire is no more. The European Union exercises an influence few anticipated when Britain joined in 1972. Respect for authority and falling trust in government go with the decline of class and the growing importance of race, gender, religion and nationality as cleavages in British society. Globalization is the cliché of the present day, with nation states seemingly powerless to resist. The Westminster model acts as a symbol of continuity in this sea of change, a tribute to the eternal verities of British government and its capacity to adapt. It is a myth, but in so saying we do not seek to trivialize the Westminster model. Myths express truths and help us to impose some order on a complex, anarchic world. The Westminster model encapsulates shared values about British government, including Britain's qualities of heroism and independence. But the brute fact of life is that Britain can act alone only rarely. In an interdependent world, diplomacy, agreement and compromise are unavoidable and many of the economic and political decisions that impact on Britain are taken in forums where we are but one voice among many.

Of course, academic colleagues are not blind to the changes. Many identify the weaknesses of the Westminster model and seek to assess whether it remains useful. But they do so within this map of British government. The language they use is the language of the Westminster model and they often call for a return to the everlasting verities of cabinet government and parliamentary sovereignty. Again as we write, there are debates about Blair's presidentialism, about the death of cabinet government, and about whether No. 10 has become a prime minister's department in all but name. These debates assume the issues and problems confronting the British executive concern institutional positions and their current incumbents. Again we do not dispute that these trends are important. We do dispute that they can be adequately explored using the language of the Westminster model.

The 1980s and 1990s have seen a second language widely used to talk about British government, commonly referred to as either managerialism or the New Public Management (NPM). Managerialism encompasses disparate reforms (see, for example, Wright 1994). They include: privatization or selling the assets of the former nationalized industries; regulating both public utilities and the internal workings of the bureaucracy; the political control of the civil service by ministers; and decentralization which initially referred to decentralization within government departments but latterly has also covered devolution to Scotland, Wales and Northern Ireland. But marketization and corporate management are of greatest relevance to explaining the rise of governance. Marketization refers to the use of market mechanisms in the delivery of public services to strengthen competition and increase choice (for example, contracting out). Corporate management refers to introducing private sector management methods into the public sector (for example, setting objectives and measuring performance, value for money, and Investors in People).

More recently the emphasis has shifted to responsiveness and closeness to the customer. British government has undertaken reforms in both these areas and many commentators employ such phrases as the managerial state, the state under stress and the audit explosion to capture the changes in the Westminster model. A pervasive storyline of British government is the clash between the Westminster model and the emerging managerial state. Thus, the search for greater economy, efficiency and effectiveness has led to 'agencification' and separating policy from management. Ministers delegated responsibility to agency chief executives but remained accountable to parliament for policy. For many commentators this trend weakened ministerial responsibility to parliament. But the concerns of NPM are often too narrow, focusing on, for example, the internal management of central departments rather than on managing the links between departments, the rest of the public sector, the voluntary and private sectors. The reforms have been evaluated but rarely, and when they are evaluated the emphasis falls on narrow financial and efficiency indicators, not their effectiveness. Reforms are often reformed before we can assess what impact they have had. The supporters of managerialism claim much but prove little. The outcomes of managerialism may include greater efficiency and less accountability, but analysis cannot be confined to these normal concerns of the Westminster model.

The Westminster model and managerialism provide narratives of British government that influence, indirectly, how practitioners and citizens view the system. This chapter offers a different narrative. The object is to edify, that is to offer metaphors which clarify social life, to find new ways of speaking and to open new avenues of exploration. Does the new story change existing stories? Does it account for more of the 'facts'? Is the new story persuasive? Does it open new lines of inquiry? We seek a new map of British government. To do so, we employ the language of governance, networks, core executive and hollowing out. We use these concepts to show that central government is hampered by the sour laws of unintended consequences and that there is considerable territorial policy variation both in policy initiation and implementation.

Governance and networks

Finer (1970: 3–4) defined government as 'the activity or process of governing' or 'governance' (as in the *Oxford English Dictionary*); 'a condition of ordered rule'; 'those people charged with the duty of governing' or 'governors'; and 'the manner, method or system by which a particular society is governed'. Present-day use does not treat governance as a synonym for government. Rather, governance signifies a change in the meaning of government, referring to a *new* process of governing; or a *changed* condition of ordered rule; or the *new* method by which society is governed. How has the Westminster model changed? What is new in British government?

To answer this question we must start with the notion of policy networks. The term refers to those sets of organizations clustered around a major government function or department. These groups commonly include the professions, trade unions and big business. Central departments need the cooperation of these groups to deliver services. They need their cooperation because British government rarely delivers services itself. It uses other bodies. Also, there are too many groups to consult, so government must aggregate interests. It needs the 'legitimated' spokespeople for that policy area. The groups need the money and legislative authority which only government can provide (for a fuller account see Rhodes 1988, 1999a; Marsh and Rhodes 1992).

Policy networks are a long-standing feature of British government. They have developed a consensus about what they are doing which serves the aims of all involved. They have evolved routine ways of deciding. They are a form of private government of public services, scathingly referred to by the New Right as producer groups using government for their own sectional interests.

The government of Margaret Thatcher sought to reduce the power of policy networks by using markets to deliver public services, bypassing existing networks and curtailing the 'privileges' of professions, commonly by subjecting them to rigorous financial and management controls. But these corporate management and marketization reforms had unintended consequences. They fragmented the systems for delivering public services and so created pressures for organizations to cooperate with one another to deliver services. In other words, and paradoxically, marketization multiplied the networks it was supposed to replace. Commonly, welfare state services are now delivered by packages of organizations. So what is new is the multiplication of networks in British government.

Fragmentation not only created new networks but it also increased the membership of existing networks, incorporating both the private and voluntary sectors. Also, the government swapped direct for indirect controls and central departments are no longer either necessarily or invariably the fulcrum of a network. The government can set the limits to network actions. It still funds the services. But it has also increased its dependence on multifarious networks, and devolution to Scotland, Wales and Northern Ireland simply adds layers and varieties of bureaucracy to what was already there, with implications for the traditional unity of the civil service. In many ways, devolution illustrates how the civil service acts as both a mechanism for integrating the differentiated polity and for expressing difference between the parts. That is, it speaks *for* the centre in the constituent nations and regions and *to* the centre for those nations and regions.

In short, governance refers to the changing role of the state after the varied public sector reforms of the 1980s and 1990s. In the UK context, where there is no state tradition comparable to the continental tradition of *rechtsstaat*, the literature on governance explores how the informal authority of networks supplements and supplants the formal authority of government. It explores the limits to the state and seeks to develop a more diverse view of state authority and its exercise.

If networks are the defining characteristic of governance, how do they differ from more widely understood notions such as markets and hierarchies (or bureaucracies)? Table 2.1 shows the distinctive features of networks compared with markets and hierarchies as mechanisms for allocating and coordinating resources and public services.

Again, the aim is not to bore the reader with endless definitions but to provide, at a glance, characterization to show that networks are a distinctive coordinating mechanism and, therefore, separate from markets

Table 2.1 Characteristics of markets, hierarchies and networks

	Markets	*Hierarchies*	*Networks*
Basis of relationships	Contract and property rights	Employment relationship	Resource exchange
Degree of dependence	Independent	Dependent	Interdependent
Medium of exchange	Prices	Authority	Trust
Means of conflict resolution and coordination	Haggling and the courts	Rules and commands	Diplomacy
Culture	Competition	Subordination	Reciprocity

and hierarchies. Of these characteristics, trust is central because it is the basis of network coordination in the same way that commands and price competition are the principal mechanisms for bureaucracies and markets, respectively. It is 'the most important attribute of network operations' (Frances *et al.* 1991: 15). Shared values and norms are the glue which holds the complex set of relationships together; trust is essential for cooperative behaviour and, therefore, the existence of the network. As a working axiom, networks are high on trust and contracts are low on trust. With the spread of networks there has been a recurrent tension between contracts on the one hand, with their stress on competition to get the best price, and networks on the other, with their stress on cooperative behaviour.

So, governance refers to governing with and through networks or, to employ shorthand, it refers to *steering networks*. We use governance in three ways. First, it describes public sector change; it refers to the fragmentation caused by the reforms of the 1980s and 1990s. Second, we use it to interpret British government. To talk of the governance of Britain is to say the Westminster model is no longer acceptable and we have to tell a different story of the shift from government (by the strong executive) to governance (through networks). Third, we use governance to prescribe the next round of reforms; for example, management by negotiation and other measures designed to improve coordination between government departments and other agencies. But whether we use the term to describe, interpret or prescribe, it still refers to the changing form of the British state in general and the ways in which the informal authority of networks supplements and supplants the formal authority of the state in particular (for a more detailed discussion see Rhodes 1997a, 2000a).

Core executive

There is a conventional debate about the British executive that focuses on the relative power of prime minister and cabinet. Many have pointed to its limited nature but it continues to this day as commentators rail against Tony Blair's presidentialism. This analysis assumes the best way to look at the executive is to examine principal positions and their incumbents. Instead of such a positional approach, the executive can be defined in functional terms. So instead of asking which position is important, we can ask which functions define the innermost part or heart of British government. The core functions of the British executive are to pull together and integrate central government policies and to act as final arbiters of conflicts between different elements of the government machine. These functions can be carried out by institutions other than prime minister and cabinet; for example, the Treasury and the Cabinet Office. By defining the core executive in functional terms, the key question becomes, who does what? (Rhodes and Dunleavy 1995).

There is a second strand to the argument favouring a focus on the core executive rather than prime minister and cabinet. The positional approach also assumes that power lies with specific positions and the people who occupy those positions. But power is contingent and relational, that is it depends on the relative power of other actors and, as Harold Macmillan succinctly put it, 'events, dear boy, events'. So, ministers depend on the prime minister for support in getting funds from the Treasury. In turn, the prime minister depends on his ministers to deliver the party's electoral promises. Both ministers and prime minister depend on the health of the American economy for a stable pound and a growing economy to ensure the needed financial resources are available. This power-dependence approach focuses on the distribution of such resources as money and authority in the core executive and explores the shifting patterns of dependence between the several actors (see Rhodes 1999a: ch. 5; Smith 1999).

So, the term 'core executive' directs our attention to two key questions: who does what, and who has what resources? If the answer for several policy areas and several conflicts is that the prime minister coordinates policy, resolves conflicts and controls the main resources, we will indeed have prime ministerial government.

The search for better coordination lies at the heart of Labour's reforms. As Kavanagh and Seldon (2000) point out, under 'new' Labour we have seen prime ministerial centralization in the guises of institutional innovation and more resources for No. 10 and the Cabinet Office, and strong political and policy direction as No. 10 seeks a tight grip on the government machine. The pendulum swings yet again as the centre promotes coordination and strategic oversight to combat Whitehall's departmentalism and the unintended consequences of managerialism. As Norton (2000: 116–17) argues, 'Ministers are like medieval barons in that they preside over their own, sometimes vast, policy territory'. Crucially, 'the ministers fight – or form alliances – with other barons in order to get what they want' and they resent interference in their territory by other barons and will fight to defend it'. So, the core executive is segmented into overlapping games in which all players have some resources with which to play the game and no one actor is pre-eminent in all games.

In sum, power dependence characterizes the links both between barons and between the barons and prime minister. Looking at the heart of the machine as if it were a core executive characterized by power dependence and game-playing reveals the limits to the Westminster model view that Britain has a strong executive.

The argument about the strength of the British executive is overstated. It is clear that there were always many constraints. But with the trend from government to governance the constraints become ever more insistent. The storyline of the 1980s and 1990s is one of fragmentation confounding centralization as a segmented executive seeks to improve horizontal coordination among departments and agencies and vertical coordination between departments and their networks of organizations. The unintended consequence of this search for central control is a hollowing out of the core executive. It is a present-day illustration of Enoch Powell's comment that, in politics, 'the test of success or failure is so unsure that one is tempted to wonder whether there is such a thing as true political success at all: failure, or frustration, or reversal, seems so much to be the essence of any political career' (cited in Hennessy 1996).

Hollowing out

Hollowing out of the state means simply that the growth of governance reduced the ability of the core executive to act effectively, making it less reliant on a command-operating code and more reliant on diplomacy. In what ways has the capacity of the British core executive been eroded? The state has been hollowed out from above (for example by international interdependence), from below (by marketization and networks), and sideways (by agencies). Internally, the British core executive was already characterized by baronies, policy networks and intermittent and selective coordination. It has been further hollowed out internally by the unintended consequences of marketization that fragmented service delivery, multiplied networks and diversified the membership of those networks (see Rhodes 1994; Weller et al. 1997). It will not be long before devolution to Scotland, Wales and Northern Ireland imposes further constraints. Indeed, there may be a demonstration effect that gives added momentum to the demand for regional devolution in England.

Externally, the state is also being hollowed out by membership of the EU and other international commitments. Menon and Wright (1998) conclude that there is 'no doubt' the UK has 'forged an efficient policy making and coordinating machine' because the government speaks and acts with one voice. It has also been successful in its 'basic strategy of opening up and liberalising the EU's economy'. However, its 'unjustified reputation' for being at the margins of Europe is justified for EU constitution-building and 'an effective and coherent policy making machine becomes ineffective when it is bypassed' for the history-making decisions.

Few would consider the problems of steering an ever more complex, devolved government machine and being bypassed for constitutional, history-making decisions as evidence of the core executive's ability to act effectively. It is important to distinguish between intervention and control. Indisputably the British centre intervenes often, but its interventions do not have the intended effects and so cannot be considered control.

'New' Labour recognizes the problem. In its drive for 'better government', the Labour government merged the Office for Public Service (OPS) into the Cabinet Office, giving the revamped Cabinet Office a new focus as the civil service's 'corporate headquarters', included in which is a Centre for

Management and Policy Studies (incorporating the Civil Service College). The government strongly promoted public private partnerships (PPPs), asset disposals, a revamped Private Finance Initiative (PFI), Fundamental Spending Review, and modifications and relaunch of the Citizen's Charter in 1998. Proposals in the government's White Paper *Modernising Government*, 'consolidate and develop changing ideas about the relationship between the citizen, as consumer of public services, and the state as a service provider or, in many contexts, a facilitator of service provision through contractual and quasi-contractual partnerships with the private and voluntary sectors' (Drewry 2000: 170).

Improved central coordination lies at the heart of its policy agenda. Prime Minister Tony Blair (1996) stated the aims succinctly: 'joined-up problems need joined-up solutions' and this theme runs through the *Modernising Government* White Paper with its frequent references to 'joined-up' government and 'holistic governance' (Cm 4310 1999; see also Cabinet Office 2000a and 2000b). Both phrases are synonyms for steering networks, and the White Paper is a response to the government's belief that 'too little effort has gone into making sure that policies are devised and delivered in a consistent and effective way across institutional boundaries'. It describes the challenge as 'to get different parts of government to work together' by, for example, 'designing policy around shared goals', 'involving others in policy making' and 'integrating the European Union and international dimension in our policy making'.

Joining up takes various forms. For example, there are area-based programmes or 'action zones' (26 in health, 25 in education) linking central and local government, health authorities, the private sector and voluntary organizations; and group-focused programmes such as the Better Government for Older People pilot (Cm 4310 1999: 18, 26–7, 29). The Labour government stresses developing networks to promote cooperation and these networks are supposed to be based on trust. Blair describes such trust as 'the recognition of a mutual purpose for which we work together and in which we all benefit' (Blair 1996: 292). Quality public services are best achieved through cooperative relations based on trust, and the Labour government's reform proposals base the delivery of public services on such networks (see Rhodes 2000c).

However, the practice of British government remains familiar. Ministers, the barons at the heart of British government, continue to defend their fiefdoms; it was ever thus. Equally, action zones show the limits to vertical coordination. There is an epidemic of zones, to the point where the solution (to fragmentation) becomes part of the problem (by adding to the bodies to be coordinated). For example, John Denham (1999), then a junior minister in the Department of Health, conceded that 'zones can sometimes make government look more, rather than less complicated to the citizen' and there is the danger of 'initiative overload' because the zones do not join up.

Zones show the government adopting an instrumental approach to network management that assumes the centre can devise and impose ways to foster integration in and between networks and realize central government's objectives. The reforms have a centralizing thrust. They seek to coordinate departments and local authorities by imposing a new style of management on other agencies. So, they 'do not want to run local services from the centre' but '[the] Government is not afraid to take action where standards slip'; an obvious instance of a command operating code (Cm 4310 1999: 35, 37, 45, 53, 55). The centre owns zones and local agendas are recognized in as far as they help the centre. Such a code, no matter how well disguised, runs the ever present risk of recalcitrance from key actors and a loss of flexibility in dealing with localized problems. Gentle pressure relentlessly applied is still a command operating code in a velvet glove. When you sit at the top of a pyramid and you cannot see the bottom, control deficits are an ever present unintended consequence.

'Diplomacy' or management by negotiation, is the hands-off alternative to hands-on management. Such skills lie at the heart of steering networks. Network structures are characterized by a decentralized negotiating style that trades off control for agreement. This style of hands-off management involves setting the framework in which networks work but keeping an arm's length relationship. For example, a central department can provide the policy framework and policy guidance, prod the network into action by systematic review and scrutiny of its work, use patronage to put 'one of its own' in principal positions, mobilize resources and skills across sectors, regulate the network and its members; and provide advice and assistance (Cm 2811 1995). Such steering is imperfect. Just as there are limits to central command, so there are limits to independent action by networks. Above all, such management by negotiation means agreeing with the objectives of others, not just persuading them that you were right all along or resorting to sanctions when they disagree.

In sum, the task confronting British government is to manage packages; packages of services, of organizations and of governments. This is not the picture of British government painted by the Westminster model. Its account of Britain as a unitary state emphasizes political integration, centralized authority, a command operating code implemented through bureaucracy and the power of the centre to revoke decentralized powers. The differentiated polity narrative highlights political devolution, fragmentation and interdependence, and functional decentralization. Centralization coexists with fragmentation and interdependence, where policy intentions drown under their unintended consequences. The contradictions between authority and interdependence, bureaucracy and networks, and political and functional politics, underpin the sour laws' unintended consequences. And while complete political integration and administrative standardization have never been achieved within the UK, devolution makes their attainment a still more distant prospect. Put simply, government and policy in Britain have become messy. Indeed, British territorial governance is rapidly becoming a case of many exceptions and few rules.

The consequences of this approach for studying the civil services are obvious. It raises several distinct questions:

- Are there territorially specific policy networks?
- Are territorial ministries the core executive for their country?
- Do the territorial networks and executives initiate territorially specific policies?
- Do the territorial networks and executives modify UK-wide policies when they implement them?
- Do the territorial civil services speak *for* the centre in the constituent nations and regions of the UK?
- Do the territorial civil services speak *to* the centre for the constituent nations and regions of the UK?
- To what extent do the territorial civil services have distinctive histories and ways of working?
- What are the consequences of these traditions and practices for policy initiation and implementation?

All of these questions are but specific parts of a much larger question about the extent of integration and differentiation of the governance of the UK. To the extent that we find distinctive civil services with their own ways of working and servicing territorially specific networks, we can conclude that the UK is a differentiated polity. The greater the territorial variation in policy initiation and implementation, the lower the degree of integration in UK policy-making and, again, the stronger the case of the differentiated polity.

Of course, research is never that straightforward. If the case for Britain as a centrally coordinated unitary state is often overstated, we must not fall into the trap of overstating the centrifugal forces. Civil service distinctiveness may be evidence of differentiation, but these differences may help the civil service to play an integrating role. To be an effective voice for a territory at the centre, it may also have to speak for the centre in the territory. The civil service could play an important integrating role. We are exploring the oscillating balance between integration and differentiation and the role of the civil service in striking that balance – a balance that devolution may change irrevocably.

So, to our questions about differentiation, we can also add questions about integration:

- Do regional and territorial civil services act to bridge the policy and political differences between centre and periphery?
- Will devolution require territorial loyalty of its civil servants and so undermine their bridging role?

34   Decentralizing the civil service

And so to the grand question which subsumes all others: does territorial politics in general and devolution in particular hollow out the British state? We begin our answers by looking at the most deconcentrated system of public administration and differentiated part of British governance, Northern Ireland.

3

Northern Ireland

Introduction

There is one part of the UK in which the notion of a national unitary civil
service is undermined completely. In Northern Ireland, the operations of
the Home Civil Service are accompanied by those of the Northern Ireland
Civil Service (NICS). Usually, NICS is accorded footnote status save from
some worthy exceptions (for example, Birrell 1978; Bell 1987; Connolly
and Erridge 1990; Loughlin 1992; and, in comparison to Scotland and Wales,
Levy 1995; McConnell 2000). The rationale is understandable. It is tempt-
ing, when considering the civil service in Northern Ireland, to employ the
clichés with which so much analysis of the province is replete – 'governing
without consensus', 'a place apart', and so on. Northern Ireland is detached,
geographically and, for the most part, politically, from the British 'mainland'. As one former senior civil servant recalled, 'this is a damned funny
country. There's one crowd singing "Wrap the Green Flag Round Me" and
another crowd sings "Rule Britannia" and there's a lot of bloody civil servants up there in Stormont drawing twenty pounds a week and laughing
at the lot of us' (comment made in 1939 to Patrick Shea, cited in Shea 1981:
205). Anderson (1983) styled Northern Ireland as a 'frontier region' – 'an
area adjacent to an international boundary, whose population is affected in
various ways by the proximity of the boundary' (p.2). The peculiarities
of governing Northern Ireland might make for tenuous comparison with
the rest of the UK. That said, Northern Ireland is neither a colony nor a
dominion but an integral part of the UK, and the practical functioning of

its various administrative arrangements is relevant. For all its difference, it is governed according to many of the criteria pivotal to the uniquely British way of doing things, a process consolidated by the progressive integration of many aspects of its government with those of the UK. Perhaps a better description would be 'parity with particularity'.

If Northern Ireland represents an enigma in understanding the system(s) of British government and administration, it remains a tantalizingly attractive one. For fifty years, no matter how controversially at times, the 'local agents' managed the province (Harvey Cox 1987: 82). Moreover, through all the horrors of the euphemistically termed 'troubles', public administration continued as an essentially provincial concern, notwithstanding the disputed role of civil servants from the Republic of Ireland after the Anglo-Irish Agreement of 1985. Northern Ireland offers a fascinating picture of civil administration under both devolved and London-directed government. Thus, Bell (1987) contended that it could cast light on problems common throughout the UK. First, there are 'those faced by any minister (including the territorial ministers) in controlling and giving direction to multi-functional ministries'. Second, the centre–periphery relationship in government needs to be considered in terms of 'central and territorial ministries; between functional ministries and territorial departments; and between the resource control and personnel functions of both territorial and functional ministries and the operational "line" departments and divisions' (p.191). To Bell's list must be added the impact of recent devolution, into which, having already experienced devolved government, Northern Ireland offers valuable insights.

This chapter provides an overview of the nature of the civil service in Northern Ireland. Briefly, it outlines NICS's origins under the Stormont era before focusing on the position since 1972 (when Direct Rule was introduced) in four substantive subsections: the transition from devolved government to Direct Rule; structures; policy issues; and public management reform. Then, it presents case studies of economic development and community care policy. Finally, the chapter assesses the impact of devolution.

Devolution, 1921–72

Northern Ireland's existence stemmed from the inability of successive British governments to reconcile the irreconcilable. The aspirations for Home Rule (devolution) of mainly Catholic Irish Nationalists (sentiments that, after 1916, shifted decisively towards full independence) clashed with those of the mainly Protestant Ulster Unionists (concentrated in the north-eastern province of Ulster) who strenuously objected to any 'dilution' of Ireland's union with Great Britain. In the febrile atmosphere of Irish politics, the ineluctable logic of these mutually exclusive positions degenerated into violence, leading to a partition-based 'solution'. The Government of Ireland Act 1920 effectively paved the way for most of Ireland to secede in 1922 to form an overwhelmingly Catholic Irish Free State (later the Republic of Ireland). Six counties remained within the UK as Northern Ireland, solidly Unionist but with a substantial Nationalist minority. The uneasy balance of opinion within Northern Ireland has ensured that it has always operated as a mini-political system nested within a larger entity, the UK.

The terms of the Irish settlement marked a novel development in British constitutional practice, introducing a system *sui generis* in the UK. Uniquely, Northern Ireland was provided with a devolved parliament and government (usually known as Stormont, the location of the devolved institutions from 1932) modelled on Westminster lines (Loughlin 1992). Devolution required a delineation of legislative and policy competences. The Government of Ireland Act 1920 identified three categories. 'Excepted' or 'reserved' remained the responsibility of the UK government, classed as 'Imperial' matters to be administered by UK ministers and the Home Civil Service. Matters 'transferred' were administered by NICS that was formed by transferred staff who previously worked in British government departments in Dublin. NICS was 'an independent and autonomous body rather than a regional organisation' (Birrell and Murie 1980: 153), being a unique example of a regional civil service within the UK completely separate from the UK civil service (Birrell 1978: 305). Nonetheless, despite its separate status, structure and *modus operandi*, NICS paralleled the Home Civil Service (CAB 1964, 1966). NICS has always had its own head, civil service commission (to deal with recruitment and promotion) and internal grading system.

Three distinct phases can be discerned in examining government in Northern Ireland: devolution (1921–72); Direct Rule (1972–99) and devolution-*plus* (1999 to the present). Space constraints limit our consideration to the second and third periods. Readers interested in pursuing inquiries on the creation and early years of NICS might consult Lawrence (1956, 1965), Birrell and Murie (1980) and Follis (1995).

Direct Rule, 1972–99

The transition from devolved government to Direct Rule

In 1968, Home Secretary James Callaghan asked 'will they [the NICS] be loyal or will it be another Rhodesia?' On that matter, if few others, his fears were groundless though his remarks betrayed a fundamental ignorance of Ulster among many in Westminster, Whitehall and beyond. The fundamentally *British* Unionist culture (as distinct from a narrower Ulster variant) of senior NICS personnel explains much, not least the wearing of sponges after Wilson's infamous 'spongers' television broadcast in 1974, as a token of their resentment at the insinuation that Northern Ireland had an effectively parasitical dependence on the Treasury. The challenge to Westminster became intolerable as Northern Ireland descended deeper into civil and political disorder after 1969. By 1972, faced with mounting instability, the Conservative government in London prorogued Stormont and imposed Direct Rule. A senior official in Stormont and later head of NICS, Sir Ken Bloomfield, remarked that 'all that was left was the ritual of an orderly and responsible take over' (1994: 165). According to one former Northern Ireland minister, Lord Windlesham, 'despite its traumatic impact the change to direct rule was accomplished without any interruption in the day to day business of government. For this transition the NICS deserves the highest praise' (p.263). Similarly, a former permanent secretary, John Oliver (1978), confirmed, 'administrative life was going on all the time; we were not just concentrating on emergencies, not by a long chalk' (p.96). A former permanent secretary and ombudsman, Maurice Hayes (1995), was 'struck by the ease with which the civil service has adapted to direct rule' (p.163).

The term 'Direct Rule' is misleading. Outwardly, it implies that, in revoking devolution, Northern Ireland would be governed along the same lines as Great Britain. The history of devolution and local governmental traditions explain its use. No reference has ever been made to Direct Rule operating in Scotland, Wales or England. Unlike Great Britain, UK-based Northern Ireland ministers under Direct Rule had a 'non-elective relationship with the recipients of policy' (Bloomfield and Lankford 1996: 146; see also Loughlin 1992). Unlike ordinary parliamentary bills, legislation specific to Northern Ireland was passed in the form of orders in council (a long-established parliamentary device) to which no amendments can be tabled. Ministers never represented a Northern Ireland Westminster constituency since Labour and the Liberal Democrats do not field candidates in elections in the province, and the Conservatives' forays onto the local scene have been marked by ignominious defeat. A democratic deficit became the foundation of political representation in a liberal democracy; the vote had little direct influence on the policy content of government in the province for almost thirty years. With its parochial political party system, the absence of the main UK parties allowed local politicians the luxury of opposition offering 'all the advantages of political activity with none of the disadvantages of responsibility' (Prior, cited in Bogdanor 1999: 99). In addition to the effective disenfranchisement from the British political mainstream, Northern Ireland returns only 18 out of 659 MPs at Westminster. Thus, unless there is a hung parliament (1974, 1977–79) or the government's majority vanishes (1995–97), the Irish contingent is marginal to the main proceedings.

In a province whose fiscal capacity has always been weak, the reliance on the Exchequer transfer (or subvention) of £3.5 billion (or 35 per cent of annual public expenditure) to sustain the 'parity principle', compounds the deficiencies in democracy (Borooah 1997). Intergovernmental fiscal transfers are not unusual in industrialized societies to assist areas of relative deprivation. However, their magnitude in Northern Ireland raises questions since the relationship between taxpayer and government is tenuous.

Another factor exacerbating dissatisfaction with Direct Rule concerned concurrent changes in *sub-regional* governance. In 1970, the Macrory Report (Macrory 1970) recommended transferring many erstwhile local government services (notably education, libraries, housing, personal social services) to central (Stormont) government departments and ministerially appointed boards and quangos. This was done to improve service delivery and to overcome structural weaknesses in the old system of local government. In practice, it heightened the democratic deficit in the policy process, as the continued existence of an elected provincial government was a *sine qua non* to Macrory. However, Stormont's demise brought a dramatic loss of local accountability, occasioning what was dubbed the 'Macrory Gap'.

Structures

The most important change to emerge from Direct Rule was the establishment of a new UK government department: the Northern Ireland Office (NIO). The NIO was (and remains) based in London and Belfast. The political head is the secretary of state for Northern Ireland, a minister with UK cabinet status. Up to four juniors completed the ministerial team (now down to two since devolution). The London office was created from the existing Home Office divisions responsible for Northern Ireland (Windlesham 1973: 196). The Belfast office was the 'lineal descendant of the old Stormont Cabinet Office' (Bell 1987: 212). Indeed, the former Stormont ministries continued more or less as before, staffed by the same civil servants (see Table 3.1). Interestingly, in 'an unusual variant of the Westminster model' (Bloomfield, in interview), British junior ministers were sometimes responsible for two Northern Ireland departments. Under all legislation for Northern Ireland government since 1921, the legal entity is the department not the minister. That is, the department is the 'corporation sole' and Northern Ireland departments (NIDs) have a legal existence separate from their heads of department. Thus, the position of senior NICS civil servants is anomalous (Hayes 1997). Under the Northern Ireland Act 1974, no head of department could be appointed in the 'interim period' of Direct Rule. The department itself performs the functions of a political head of department. The term 'minister' is a courtesy title – incumbents have no formal constitutional powers. 'High policy' matters such as policing, security, criminal justice, plus constitutional and political developments like the Anglo-Irish Agreement (1985) and interparty talks processes in the 1990s fell within the NIO's bailiwick. The NIO was a UK department of state but not a ministry as it is only part of the secretary of state's brief. Even the NIO and the NIDs combined are not a ministry since they 'do

Table 3.1 Departmental structure of Northern Ireland government since 1921

Year	Prime minister / Secretary of state	Finance		Commerce			Agriculture	Home Affairs		Labour				Education	
1921	Prime minister	Finance		Commerce			Agriculture	Home Affairs		Labour				Education	
1940	Prime minister	Finance		Commerce			Agriculture	Home Affairs	Public Security	Labour				Education	
1944	Prime minister	Finance		Commerce			Agriculture	Home Affairs	Health and Local Government	Labour				Education	
1964	Prime minister	Finance		Commerce			Agriculture	Home Affairs	Health and Social Services		Development			Education	
1969	Prime minister	Finance		Commerce			Agriculture	Home Affairs	Health and Social Services		Development			Education	Community Relations
1972	Secretary of state; central secretariat; NIO	Finance		Commerce			Agriculture	Home Affairs	Health and Social Services		Development			Education	
1974	Secretary of state; NIO central secretariat	Finance		Commerce			Agriculture	Home Affairs	Health and Social Services	Manpower Services	Environment	Housing, Local Government and Planning		Education	
1976	Secretary of state; NIO central secretariat	Finance	Civil Service	Commerce			Agriculture		Health and Social Services	Manpower Services	Environment			Education	
1982	Secretary of state; NIO central secretariat	Finance and Personnel		Economic Development			Agriculture		Health and Social Services		Environment			Education	
1999	Secretary of state; NIO central secretariat/Office of First and Deputy First Minister	Finance and Personnel		Enterprise, Trade and Investment	Regional Development	Social Development	Agriculture and Rural Development		Health, Social Services and Public Safety		Environment		Culture, Arts and Leisure	Education	Higher and Further Education, Training and Employment, since renamed Department of Employment and Learning (DEL)

not jointly comprise in law a unified organisation' (Bell 1987: 193). The NIO staff establishment has fluctuated over time but in 2002 numbers around 1200 staff. Most NIO staff are seconded from NICS although they remained classified as NICS personnel, usually returning to NICS departments after completing their secondment. The secretary of state's wide responsibilities led one former incumbent to see himself as a mini-prime minister (Connolly 1990: 88). Bloomfield (1997) stressed that the Stormont departments 'which currently operate under the "direction and control" of the Secretary of State for Northern Ireland are as much a part of central government as the NIO itself is of the Northern Ireland operations of United Kingdom wide-departments' (p.1). Therefore, 'in the strict sense, [the NIO] is one of the series of Whitehall departments, enjoying in this case relatively broad territorial rather than narrow functional responsibilities' (p.2).

Direct Rule has been integrationist in many respects, bringing approximation to administrative styles in Great Britain. Although a substantial degree of territorial specificity remains, undeniably, Northern Ireland's machinery of government and administrative structures have become steadily entangled with those of Whitehall. Such developments were inevitable given the ministerial team's origins. However, it also reflected an implicit acknowledgement that Direct Rule was not going to be quickly abandoned. Hence, in 1976, the post of head of NICS was also made the 2nd permanent undersecretary (PUS) of the NIO, occupying the position of cabinet secretary/head of NICS that was abolished when Stormont was prorogued. The change was partly symbolic, partly functional. Irrespective of the rationale, however, the effect was to bring the two bureaucratic pyramids (of the NICS and the NIO) together at their apex. The head of NICS was (and remains) based in Belfast, heading an organization 30,000 strong but with no direct executive responsibilities (these rest with the permanent secretaries of each department). However, the position did permit him to attend the weekly meetings of the Whitehall permanent secretaries. There has been a relatively limited amount of staff exchange between the NIO and NIDs. Complete integration of NICS into the Home Civil Service has never been seriously proposed. Rather, NICS has always been viewed as an organization in waiting ready to serve a new devolved government. A further complication stems from the Macrory Report (Macrory 1970). Since Macrory's recommendations led to the absorption into central government of many erstwhile local government functions and corresponding expansion in NICS, NICS cannot be compared directly with the Home Civil Service since its functional responsibilities are not the same.

There are several other points worthy of note about the structure of NIDs. The experience of power-sharing in 1973–74, as well as the new devolved arrangements since 1999, illustrate how 'functions can be brigaded together in different ways according to the emphasis one wishes to give to this or that' (Bloomfield 1994: 183). The exigencies of political arithmetic mean 'the final outcome was a fairly shameless piece of pork-barrelling in a sort of Parkinsonian calculus' (Hayes 1995: 165). Moreover, Wilson (1989) noted that the mistrust felt by nationalists towards the civil service was tempered by their experience of government during the ill-fated 1974 Sunningdale Agreement. There 'can be no doubt that their experience in government was an instructive one for the SDLP . . . The SDLP were . . . to learn that the civil servants were not the mere lackeys of the Orange Order' (Wilson 1989: 178). For example, Brian Faulkner (1978) remarked of John Hume and Paddy Devlin that 'both agreed that on the basis of their first week in office and that day's meeting they were willing to admit that the Northern Ireland civil service had been much maligned' (p.240) (see also Devlin 1993).

Policy issues

The policy process in Northern Ireland can be understood most easily as government by policy network (Rhodes 1988). Territorial policy communities have the following characteristics: stability of relationships; continuity of a highly restricted membership; vertical interdependence based on shared delivery responsibilities, insulation from other networks, the public and even from parliament; and highly integrated (Connolly 1990). The Northern Ireland territorial policy community was broadly, though not fully, congruent with its Scottish and Welsh counterparts, for while 'the differences between the territorial ministries are now less marked, the NIO remains the most autonomous: a legacy of devolution and insulation from Westminster and Whitehall' (Rhodes 1988: 152). Administrative interests predominated. Since Direct Rule, ministers often ran up to two departments as well as fulfilling their Westminster obligations, and often they were not consulted or were consulted only superficially. Senior NICS officials became closely involved with (overtly) political affairs. Their profile in the media was more prominent. They acquired a series of 'glad-handing' roles, all of which brought a loss of anonymity. Thus, in lieu of an agreed form of stable democratic devolved government, NICS developed its own extensive and direct relationship with numerous groups and agencies, which were many and various, reflecting dissatisfaction with sterile local electoral politics. Local notables, though lacking electoral mandates, still exert influence over aspects of public policy, especially in activities funded by partnership arrangements. Through partnership arrangements, which sponsor local community groups, voluntary associations and others, a kind of local corporatism has emerged.

The NIO attempted 'to provide an overall coherence to policy in Northern Ireland' (Loughlin 1992: 70). However, whatever policies were formulated in London, they were not blithely imitated in Northern Ireland. Much depended on the policy in question. For national UK politicians, a posting to Northern Ireland was regarded as internal exile, with a series of

cabinet 'dissidents' (or wets, as they were known in the Thatcher governments) being banished to the troubled outpost. Conflicting interpretations
exist over the extent to which, once dispatched, such ministers could prac-
tise a 'wetter' range of policy options. 'As James Prior once said (in not
entirely benign terms): "In Northern Ireland we're all Keynesians" ' (O'Leary
et al. 1988: 109).

Successive British governments adopted a series of measures designed
to smooth the functioning of the system. Financially, in accordance with
the 'parity principle' (the UK has uniform national taxation and, in theory,
uniform benefit and service levels that meet need), the Treasury's Needs
Assessment (1979) indicated that the province's high public expenditure
was justified by its low gross domestic product and higher needs. Thus,
from the early 1970s, a fairly lax fiscal regime prevailed in the province
in comparison with that in Great Britain. Borooah (1997: 4) recorded how
a period of 'catch up' occurred (given the fact that much of Northern
Ireland's infrastructure, especially housing, lagged seriously behind that
within Great Britain). Public expenditure rose rapidly under the 1974–79
Labour government, before it 'reached a plateau' during the 1980s and 1990s.

Loughlin's (1992: 70) interpretation of how policy is applied in Northern Ireland regards it as 'a continuum going from a high degree of convergence to a high degree of divergence'. During both the devolved Stormont
and Direct Rule periods, there has been a recurrent tension between the
twin imperatives of *parity* and *particularity*. During the Stormont era, for
example, Greer (1994) illustrated the role of local policy networks in
agriculture policy. Indeed, he characterized the whole Stormont period as
possessing a conflict between the imperatives of parity and particularity,
though concluded that considerations of parity eventually prevailed. Under
Direct Rule, there was an inevitable degree of tension between the NIDs and
their Whitehall counterparts (where these existed – note the exceptions of
the Department of Economic Development (DED) and, partially, the Department of the Environment (DoENI) and the Department of Education
(DENI)). In all three territorial ministries (Scotland, Wales and Northern
Ireland), departments often looked to the corresponding functional English
or British ministers to determine priorities. In respect of community care
policy, for instance, one senior official from the DHSS(NI) insisted that
'we maintain an entirely separate system, funded separately, and with separate accountability mechanisms [but] we would consider the Department of
Health as the lead department' (private interview). By contrast, Collins
(1995: 666) noted how, in respect of agriculture, 'within the constraints of
financial dependence, DANI [the Department of Agriculture] has sought to
maintain a position of maximum adaptability'. The resulting trust that
emerged ensured that 'the tendency towards indiscriminate intervention
waned and the NIO role became much more one of fitting Northern Ireland's social and economic matters into the wider ministerial and official
matrix of Whitehall' (Bloomfield 1997: 3–4).

Connolly and Loughlin (1990) suggested that Northern Ireland's policy experience was best understood within an 'adoption or adaptation' continuum. Gaffikin and Morrissey (1990b: 140) observed, however, that 'adoption' does not necessarily entail the application of uniform policies across the UK because of external influences, principally those associated with Britain's membership of the EU. EU policies, notably the structural funds, in Northern Ireland 'may induce differences with other regions which are not beneficiaries of EC aid'. Thus,

> the absence of complete uniformity within Britain itself and the importance of ex-UK influences [mean that] an adoption/adaptation framework is not wholly applicable. Perhaps a better concept would be adaptation within a standard framework of theories, policies and structures. While this would be appropriate for understanding national and regional policy divergences within the whole of the UK, it would be particularly useful for Northern Ireland, given its distinctive features. Moreover, we have already argued that developments in Northern Ireland should be considered in terms of their continuity/discontinuity with policies prior to 1972. *The continuity of approach, especially within the field of economic development, was remarkable for most of the period of Direct Rule.*
>
> (Gaffikin and Morrissey 1990b: 144, emphasis in original)

In the 1970s, the Policy Coordinating Committee (PCC) of departmental permanent secretaries (chaired by the head of NICS) was established to enable greater policy coordination. While sometimes regarded as analogous to a cabinet of civil servants, the PCC was not presented as such (Connolly and Erridge 1990). All legislative proposals were considered by the PCC, which had a 'key role in advising [the secretary of state] on whether legislation in Northern Ireland should follow or vary from that proposed or effected in Britain' (pp.27–8). In 1997, the Civil Service Management Board (CSMB) replaced the PCC, though its composition was in essence the same. Undoubtedly, the emergence of the PCC/CSMB was 'consistent with a move towards a "technocracizing of politics" – a means whereby ordinary issues are voided of moral and ideological imperatives and are thereby seen as technical and procedural problems rather than issues of principle' (Ditch and Morrissey 1979: 111).

> [The] emphasis on administration as opposed to representation has increased the scope for civil service influence over policy. Given the small size of Northern Ireland, the result has been a tight and intimate policy network dominated by administrative interests. The inability of local political parties to influence policy has not, however, abolished the need of the government to stay in contact with the governed. As a result, the civil service has increasingly developed its own extensive and direct relationship with numerous groups and agencies.
>
> (Morrow 1996: 148–9)

Since NICS follows UK precepts on appointment and promotion by merit, the pattern of religious and gender representation in the service remained constant over a prolonged period. Catholics and women continue to be under-represented at the higher levels (grade 5 and above), although the position is being addressed partly by Northern-Ireland-specific legislation, especially on fair employment. The inquiry of the Fair Employment Agency (later the Fair Employment Commission) in 1983 (FEA 1983), prompted the establishment of the NICS Equal Opportunities Unit. The unit has a

> sophisticated monitoring system of employees, which included religion, gender and disability . . . [It] was later extended to cover recruitment and promotion and identified a range of problems concerned with employment tests and the composition of promotion panels.
>
> (Osborne 1992: 12)

During the 1990s, the UK government supplemented existing fair employment legislation by introducing a new initiative entitled Policy Appraisal and Fair Treatment (PAFT). PAFT demanded that considerations of equality had to be inserted into the policy-making process (Osborne 1996). PAFT was followed by a second initiative, Targeting Social Need (TSN), that sought to narrow the disparity between the two communities. PAFT and TSN were amended by the Northern Ireland Act 1998. Section 75 of the Act effectively replaced PAFT, introducing a statutory obligation to uphold an equality agenda covering multiple categories (gender, race, religion, age, disability and sexual orientation). TSN was revised to give it more tightly focused criteria. Together, the new TSN and section 75 of the Act have placed Northern Ireland in the vanguard for promoting equality in the UK.

Northern Ireland's atypicality is underscored in other ways. For example, since 1972, the leading trade union for Northern Ireland civil servants has been the Northern Ireland Public Service Alliance (NIPSA) with a penetration rate of 70–75 per cent across the service as a whole, rising 90 per cent in the Social Security Agency. NIPSA is not affiliated to the UK Trades Union Congress (TUC), being a member of the Irish Congress of Trades Unions (ICTU), but it does belong to the UK Council of Civil Service Unions.

Another illustration is the growing role of civil servants from the Republic of Ireland, with whom NICS and NIO have a special relationship. In its attempts to resolve the province's constitutional imbroglio, the British government engaged more directly with its Irish counterparts, culminating in the Anglo-Irish Agreement (AIA) of 1985. Ironically, the negotiations that led to the AIA excluded many NICS officials, including its then head who was incredulous at not having been consulted (Bloomfield, in interview). He accurately predicted that 'the new agreement would fail to deliver Irish nationalism what it expected to get out of it, but would drive Ulster unionism deeper into a laager of dangerous resentment'

(Tannam 1998: 86). The AIA created an Anglo-Irish secretariat based at Maryfield near Belfast and meant

> a presence of Dublin civil servants (however few) close to the heart of the governing process of Northern Ireland. Indisputably, British ministers, advised by British civil servants, remain in charge of decision-making within the province, which is subject to British law, taxation, and international obligations. Nevertheless, the role accorded to the Irish government in the Agreement is considerable, amounting if not to power without responsibility, at least to influence without much responsibility.
>
> (Harvey Cox 1987: 90–1)

Also, an intergovernmental conference brought together civil servants from the NIO and the Irish government's Department of Foreign Affairs. 'The establishment of an Irish dimension in British policy towards Northern Ireland automatically implies a degree of political/administrative cross-border co-operation' (Tannam 1998: 67).

While the AIA enraged Unionist sentiment in Northern Ireland, Tannam (1998: 160) suggested that cross-border cooperation remained minimal, certainly in the early years, observing a 'compartmentalisation of bureaucratic interests' and 'economic conflicts of interest between Irish and Northern Irish civil servants'. Cooperation chiefly concerned areas of 'high politics' such as Anglo-Irish intergovernmental and Northern Irish multiparty political negotiations over the future of Northern Ireland, with little about the 'low politics' of securing EU funding and economic co-operation and development. Anecdotal evidence suggests that friendly and harmonious informal links developed between Belfast and Dublin. While the precise role of Irish officials is often intangible, nonetheless their influence in advancing the aspirations of Northern Irish nationalists is considerable.

Public management reforms

Although, after 1921, custom and practice in NICS was to follow the Home Civil Service, 'under devolved rule, we took the best bits and ignored the others' (Bloomfield, in interview). Later, while the remit of official reports did not extend to NICS, aspects of their findings invariably found application. The Fulton Report's (Fulton Committee 1968) idea for a civil service college was not adopted. A college would not have been viable, but the Public Service Training Council was established (in 1974). In 1975, a separate Department of the Civil Service (NI) was also established. Because the Macrory changes expanded central government, NICS found itself in the vanguard developing 'agencies'. The DoE NI, as parent department, had been keen to devolve powers to self-contained units like its roads and water divisions. The Northern Ireland Housing Executive (NIHE) (since 1970) and the Industrial Development Board (since 1982) were archetypal agencies long before the Next Steps programme. Previous heads of NICS confirmed that the reforms of the Thatcher and Major eras applied to Northern Ireland, 'sooner or later'. Any slowness of pace reflected, in varying degrees, the different context, a measure of resistance, other pressures (especially security) and a lack of political will among successive secretaries of state. NICS did not experience the sharp decline in absolute numbers employed, seen in the Home Civil Service. The large decline in numbers of industrial civil servants was offset by a growth in non-industrials, especially within the Police Authority of Northern Ireland (PANI). PANI growth stemmed from increased use of civilians to enable police officers to replace the Army in 'front line' security duties, as part of the 'Ulsterization' of law and order.

Other reform initiatives were applied to NICS. As part of the Raynor scrutinies, a small project team of Home and NICS civil servants undertook an analysis of financial administration in Northern Ireland (Raynor Scrutiny 1980). The team recommended merger of the Departments of Finance and of the Civil Service (this occurred in 1982, to form the Department of Finance and Personnel, DFP) arguing that the

> fragmented arrangements prevent NICS from maximising the administrative advantages that should accrue from its relatively small size [being . . .] undesirable in that manpower control should be associated with and supported by responsibility for overall expenditure in order to function effectively.
>
> (Raynor 1980, cited in Bell 1987: 220)

Similarly, a version of Michael Heseltine's Management Information Systems for Ministers (MINIS) was adopted in the NIO, known as the Management Information System (MIS), while the six NIDs developed their own similar systems (Bell 1987).

The later Financial Management Initiative (FMI) in Great Britain was coordinated by both the Treasury and the Management and Personnel Office (MPO). In Northern Ireland, the secretary of state launched a separate but parallel exercise. It would be coordinated by the DFP that 'has a unique and significant responsibility for the approval of departmental expenditure, the central management of the public expenditure block and the civil service manpower total' (Knox and McHugh 1990: 258). The DFP's own report said that the central FMI Unit 'has kept in close contact with the Whitehall Financial Management Unit and benefited considerably from advice and information which that Unit has supplied' (DFP 1984: 2).

> Generally speaking, developments in the NICS keep broadly in step with those in the UK Civil Service. Where there are differences these stem mainly from the smaller size of the NICS and the advantage of centralising certain functions such as recruitment which elsewhere in the UK would be delegated to Departments.
>
> (DFP 1984: 7)

Bell (1987: 216) maintained that the 'administrative logic' of Direct Rule and the Public Expenditure Survey (PES) system encouraged the shift in Northern Ireland to 'something approaching the Whitehall style of doing business'.

The most influential reforms came with the Sir Robin Ibbs *Next Steps Report* (Efficiency Unit 1988). Ibbs' terms of reference did not include Northern Ireland. However, the head of NICS argued that, although many public services were politically sensitive in the province and executive bodies already handled many services, nonetheless, the report would be considered. The DFP was alarmed that agencies would weaken financial control and break up a unified and integrated system (Knox and McHugh 1990). Eventually, however, an Agency Liaison Group was formed (consisting of the undersecretaries of the NIDs and NIO) to identify candidates for agency status. Since 1990, over 72 per cent of NICS staff have been transferred into agencies (with a target for NICS of 80 per cent, compared with 90 per cent in Great Britain) (see Table 3.2). Some of its agencies are very small – eleven have fewer than 200 staff.

The New Management Code in the UK has no NICS equivalent but the old NICS Pay and Conditions of Service (the Blue Book) has been retained, to be revised to reflect changes in the Management Code. Hence, NICS acts as a single entity, as if it were just another Home Civil Service department or agency. The detailed rules abide by changes in the UK Management Code and 'we monitor the situation as far as developments in the Home Civil Service are concerned' (interview). Hence, the Pay and Conditions of Service document (produced by the DFP) acts as NICS's own rulebook within the parameters of the UK Management Code. In 1998, the Civil Service Commission (NI) announced the gradual replacement of the Pay and Conditions of Service code by the new Staff Handbook.

The NICS Code of Ethics is the equivalent of the new Civil Service Code for the Home Civil Service. That document summarizes the constitutional framework within which civil servants work and the values they are expected to uphold. The NICS document draws heavily on it though it is tailored to suit local conditions and includes a new and independent line of appeal to the civil service commissioners in Northern Ireland in cases of alleged breaches of the code or issues of conscience. It is supplemented by the more specific provisions in the conduct section of the NICS Staff Handbook and in departmental or agency guidance that is issued periodically. All such documents were intended for use only during the period of Direct Rule and can be amended by the devolved assembly.

Like their British counterparts, Northern Ireland agencies may seek a delegation to determine their pay and conditions by applying to DFP's Central Personnel Unit. Few requests have been made. Delegation has been granted for non-pay conditions of service matters (such as holiday entitlement), but otherwise the policy has been reactive (to requests) rather than proactive. Most departments and agencies continue using the centralized services for recruitment and promotion leaving them free to concentrate

Table 3.2 Northern Ireland Civil Service agencies

Department	Agency	Permanent staff[b,c]	Launched
Agriculture and Rural Development	Rivers Agency	256	Oct. 96
	Forest Service	242	April 98
Enterprise, Trade and Investment	Industrial Research and Technology Unit	147	April 95
Higher and Further Education, Training and Employment (renamed Employment and Learning)	Training and Employment Agency	1,349	April 90
Culture, Arts and Leisure	Public Record Office	59	April 95
	Ordnance Survey	172	April 92
Finance and Personnel	Construction Service	515	April 96
	Land Registry	170	April 96
	Rate Collection Agency	214	April 91
	Government Purchasing Agency	93	April 96
	Valuation and Lands Agency	252	April 93
	NI Statistics and Research Agency	223	April 96
	Business Development Service	248	April 96
Environment	Environment and Heritage Service	338	April 96
	Driver and Vehicle Testing Agency	283	April 92
	Driver and Vehicle Licensing Agency	262	Aug. 93
	Planning Service	405	April 96
Health, Social Services and Public Safety	NI Health and Social Services Estates Agency	121	Oct. 95
Social Development	Social Security Agency	4,439	July 91
	Child Support Agency	1,132	April 93
Regional Development	Water Service	2,127	April 96
	Roads Service	2,076	April 96
Northern Ireland Office[a]	Compensation Agency	119	April 92
	Forensic Science Agency	115	Sept. 95
	Prison Service	351	April 95
All government departments	Non-agency staff	10,136	
Total		**25,843**	

[a] NIO agencies are not the responsibility of the devolved administration
[b] As at 1 January 2000
[c] 64.3 per cent of NICS staff are employed in agencies. This figure is determined by dividing 18,249 (15,706 agency staff plus 2543 uniformed prison staff who do not appear in the table) by 28,385 (25,842 total number of civil service staff plus the 2543 uniformed prison staff who do not appear in the table)
Source: Northern Ireland government

on their 'core' activity. One problem concerns the NIO. As a Whitehall department, it enjoys full delegation for its Home Civil Service staff but not for the majority of its staff who are seconded from NICS. As it must harmonize these two groups, the NIO asked for delegation to be able to treat its NICS staff in the same way as its Home Civil Service employees. Such problems are inevitable.

Trade unions' fears and reformers' hopes that breaking up a unified service might produce downward pressure on pay proved groundless. If anything, the more focused bargaining that occurs in individual agencies and departments makes for higher pay claims and settlements. Although there is no statutory rule on pay parity between NICS and the Home Civil Service, the expectation is for continued bunching around the norm. Another problem concerns NICS agencies with 'cousins' in Great Britain or where a NICS agency does work for a British agency, such as the Child Support Agency (CSA) and Social Security Agency (SSA). Separate Whitley Councils remain in place for the industrial civil service for each agency and there is evidence that individual agencies are prone to pursue their own line. Since their introduction, agencies have been subject to further investigations. Although the Frazer (Cabinet Office 1991) and Trosa (Cabinet Office 1994) Reports were primarily directed at the Home Civil Service, their provisions were transferred to the NICS. Agencification varies across NIDs. Senior officials accept the need for management reforms, but were unenthusiastic about agencies. For one permanent secretary:

> I was not a great fan of the so-called revolution. At the time, we believed that what we already had before agencification was sensible. Next Steps was a very bureaucratic exercise. Why turn the branches into agencies when they already had autonomy, corporate plans and targets. However, the Government wanted us to go through the exercise even though all it did was increase expense, especially in the very small agencies. Whitehall needed reform, I'm sure of that and I'm sure it brought considerable benefits. God it needed it. But crude application of a formula based on Great Britain's needs to Northern Ireland seemed bizarre. In my experience, Whitehall initiatives have been applied here more and more – government by photocopy, or fax, or email. This is the consequence of the absence of local political influences. Westminster ministers had no reason to query this. During the second part of the 1980s and first half of the 1990s, they had a growing tendency to say 'what they do there, we do here'. The reforms showed a lack of flexibility to suit local circumstances. However, on policy, such as those in the DoENI, there remains considerable divergence, for example, privatisation and CCT. This was for good political reasons though you have to ask what advice civil servants gave that led to certain policy recommendations/outcomes.
>
> (Gerry Loughran, in interview. He subsequently became head of NICS in August 2000)

Since 1997, a new Recruitment Service (part of DFP) has assumed responsibility for recruitment of civil servants, taking over from the Civil Service Commission (Northern Ireland). At senior levels (above grade 5), a new senior civil service (SCS) was established in 1996, comprising departmental permanent secretaries. It determines the methods of filling SCS vacancies (either by internal competition, open competition or Regulation 3 appointments) for all departments and agencies.

Devolution-*plus*, 1999 to the present

A taste of life under a devolved administration returned on 2 December 1999. In accordance with the provisions of the Belfast Agreement (1998), a new Northern Ireland Assembly moved to appoint ten members from among its numbers who, with the first and deputy first ministers (already nominated), formed the Northern Ireland Executive. Apart from a hiatus between February and May 2000 during which the devolved arrangements were suspended, these arrangements remain in place. There have been changes in the departmental configuration of Northern Ireland government. That is, ten departments plus the Office of the First and Deputy First Ministers replaced the six departments established in 1982. The Northern Ireland secretary and NIO retain responsibility for reserved powers in areas such as policing, prisons, security and criminal justice. Other changes included the removal of the Anglo-Irish Agreement and associated secretariat, and the establishment of a North–South Ministerial Council, North–South Implementation Bodies, and other East–West forums (see below). Thus, 'British policy post direct rule can be characterised as an exercise in variable geometry' (Wilford 2000: 578). The new system differs from the old Stormont and merits being styled 'devolution-*plus*' (Carmichael 1999). It is:

> an internal consociation built within overarching confederal and federal institutions; it has imaginative elements of co-sovereignty; it promises a novel model of 'double protection'; and it rests on a bargain derived from diametrically conflicting hopes about its likely long-run outcome, but that may not destabilise it.
>
> (O'Leary 1998: 3)

As an essentially power-sharing arrangement, while a formal grand coalition is not explicitly stipulated in the Belfast Agreement, there is in practice a (permanent) rainbow coalition government drawn in proportion using the d'Hondt method. In essence, to determine the allocation of portfolios (departments) in the Northern Ireland Executive, the Belfast Agreement provided for use of the d'Hondt procedure:

> Using the divisors 1, 2, 3, 4 . . . n, [the procedure] may be seen as a series of rounds. In each round, one portfolio is allocated to highest-scoring party. In the first round, each party's score is the

number of seats it holds in the elected assembly. After the first port-folio is allocated to the winning party, that party's score in the next round is divided by two; the other parties' scores are unaltered, and the party now having the highest score wins a portfolio. When any party wins its second portfolio, its score for the next round is its original seat total divided by three, and so on. The process continues until all portfolios, 10 in the case of Northern Ireland, have been allocated.
>   (information extracted from Professor Brendan O'Leary's letter
>   to *The Times*) from the legislative assembly, itself elected
>   by proportional representation, a modified form of STV
>   (single transferable vote)

Within this executive, the first minister's position is inextricably linked to that of its coequal, the deputy first minister. Ministers 'have full executive authority in their areas of responsibility'. However, 'there are checks on ministerial autonomy . . . [Assembly] members could, on a cross commun-ity basis, effectively sack a Minister'. Moreover, a powerful assembly committee flanks each department. The committees 'act not only as scrut-inising bodies in the manner of Parliamentary select committees, but also will consult with the "target" Department on policy development and legislation: indeed, the Committees can themselves propose legislation in the relevant area(s) of Departmental responsibility' (Wilford 2000: 581–2). Crucially, the reality of devolution-*plus* is underscored by external links, for what is especially innovative is that the internal consociation (within Northern Ireland) and external confederalism (with southern Ireland) are '"mutually interdependent"; one cannot function without the other' (O'Leary 1998: 9). In addition, there is a second confederal relationship, namely the new British–Irish Intergovernmental Council (BIIGC, that subsumes the Anglo-Irish Intergovernmental Council and the Intergovernmental Council) and British–Irish Council (BIC, or Council of the Isles). Indeed, the BIC could 'flourish as a policy formulation forum, if the devolved governments of the UK choose to exploit it as an opportunity for intergovernmental bargaining within the UK, or to build alliances with the Irish Government on European public policy – in which case it will give added impetus to other federalist processes' (O'Leary 1998: 11). O'Leary contended that the Belfast Agreement is 'explicitly federal' because only by breaking its international treaty obligations can Westminster

>   exercise power in any manner in Northern Ireland that is inconsistent
>   with the Agreement . . . In short, maximum feasible autonomy while
>   remaining within the Union is feasible provided there is agreement to
>   that within the Northern Assembly . . . If the Agreement beds down
>   the political development of a federal relationship between the UK
>   and Northern Ireland is assured for the medium term.
>   (O'Leary 1998: 11)

The implications of the Belfast Agreement for public administration are less profound than the political changes but the new territorial dispensation continues to demand flexibility from politicians and civil servants alike. While the NIO and Northern Ireland secretary remain in situ, retaining responsibility for reserved powers in areas such as policing, prisons, security and criminal justice, most of the secretary of state's previous responsibilities have been transferred to the devolved forums. NICS now serves the devolved administration. The head of NICS has ceased to be the 2nd permanent undersecretary (PUS) at the NIO. Although the automatic right to sit on the committee of Whitehall Permanent Secretaries disappeared with devolution, 'I will still be able to attend. The need for inputting a Belfast view is less now since many officials now have some experience of Northern Ireland. On a courtesy basis, I will continue to visit – Richard [Wilson, head of Home Civil Service] values it' (Semple, in interview). The two civil services

> will move apart as we will have different political masters. Joe Pilling [1st PUS at NIO] will remain accountable to the Secretary of State. I have four political masters [the four parties in the executive]. I will deal with the transferred matters though Joe and I will keep in touch.
> (Semple, in interview)

Already, devolution has resulted in the creation of six cross-border (North–South) bodies with chief executives. However, these are useful areas of cooperation but not central functions. All the institutional elements of the Belfast Agreement (the North–South bodies, the British–Irish Council, the British–Irish Intergovernmental Council, the Human Rights Commission, the Civic Forum and the Equality Commission) have now been configured and appointed, and have met at least once. Devolved government brings not only a new era but also a new learning process.

> [We] will start with a blank sheet. I am one of the few senior civil servants who has experience of the last period of devolution . . . Politicians on all sides are resentful of NICS. They are on the outside of the fence looking in. After years of Direct Rule, it will be difficult for many civil servants to adjust to the new circumstances. The traditional anonymity of senior civil servants that is the hallmark of the Westminster/Whitehall model has been substantially eroded during Direct Rule. Under devolution, politicians will want to put their stamp on things and rightly so.
> (Semple, in interview)

Semple's predecessor expressed similar sentiments: 'Devolution will bring much more local scrutiny of NICS than exists at present. Some predict that agencies may not survive since ministers will not like the idea of being the "hole in the mint"' (Fell, in interview). Under devolution, all responsibility for management issues in the NICS is vested with the devolved assembly/executive. 'In theory, all of the [management] reforms could be reversed though it is unlikely that that would happen. That said, some changes are probable'. Under the new '10 + 1' departmental structure, for example, the Training and Employment Agency has been reabsorbed into its parent department. As the devolved arrangements are allowed to bed down, it seems inevitable that the fledgling institutions will want to examine the structures they have inherited, including the role of the NICS.

Local politicians, flushed with the power that is conferred by electoral success, have been eager to put their stamp of authority on a system that they have regarded as being too long remote and unaccountable. Senior civil servants face more intense scrutiny of their actions than at any stage since devolution last operated. Again, anecdotal evidence and selective leaking of information suggest discomfort and resentment among some senior officials, especially about the proactive stance of various assembly committees under devolution. The traditional anonymity of senior civil servants that is the hallmark of the Westminster/Whitehall model was substantially attenuated during Direct Rule. Under devolution, however, there is no automatic reversion to anonymity. The announcement of a review of procedures for appointment and promotion in NICS as part of the Northern Ireland Executive's draft Programme for Government, emphasizes 'modernizing' government and making it more open and accessible to the public. Reflecting developments in UK central government, an implicit distrust of civil servants has occasioned a spate of appointments of 'special advisers', in effect political appointees chosen outside the normal appointments process. In giving policy advice to ministers, there is a problem in delineating their precise role and the potential for conflict with existing civil servants.

Policy case studies

Economic development

Economic development in Northern Ireland differs markedly from that in either Scotland or Wales not least because of the province's previous experience of devolved government. After 1921, economic development policy rested variously with the Ministries of Commerce and Labour before being explicitly recognized in 1982. Thus, from 1982 to 1999, economic development was the responsibility of the Department of Economic Development in Northern Ireland (DED) and its agencies: the Industrial Development Board (IDB); the Local Economic Development Unit (LEDU) – a limited public company; the Northern Ireland Tourist Board (NITB) – a statutory public agency; the Training and Employment Agency (T&EA); and, the Industrial Research and Technology Unit (IRTU). Together, these bodies have a wide-ranging remit which in Whitehall falls to two departments: the Department of Trade and Industry (DTI) and the Department for

Education and Employment (DfEE), and their associated agencies. As one DED official remarked, 'We are really the industry department – the term [economic development] doesn't convey with precision what we seek to do. We cover a lot of ground including regulatory functions. We are industry facing and concerned with wealth creation' (interview). The potential for confusion also afflicts the department's agencies. An official in the Training and Employment Agency, before the agency was reabsorbed in its new parent department in December 2000, noted that there was

> not much contact with the DTI. We are kept informed about policy developments on competitiveness but then so does the DfEE. GB Business people have expressed their liking for the Northern Ireland model. We are an umbrella service – we are the employment service (whereas it is an agency in GB), we are a careers service and we are a disability service. Where should we be in structural terms? Should we be with DED or with DENI [Education]? We are part of the DED network but we have equally close links with DENI. There are also very close links at Chief Executive level to DfEE and increasingly at lower levels too. We are also starting to develop links with the Scots and Welsh. We meet with our Scottish and Welsh counterparts regularly in, for example, the New Deal Committees. Remember that the New Deal was not devolved in GB but was to Northern Ireland.
>
> (interview)

A complicating factor arises from the way that economic development is financed in all three countries. There is no direct equivalent Whitehall department to the DED, so it cannot automatically expect to benefit from any change in the national budget, unlike say, education or health. Consequently, the budgets of the respective economic development divisions grew over the years largely without reference to the UK budget. As in Scotland, they have to be defended within their respective national blocks. Given the pressures on the Northern Ireland block, there is a limit to the pace and extent of growth.

The existence of a 'regional problem' in the UK was especially acute in Northern Ireland where the devolved government enacted a 'range of incentives for new industry [that] was different in form and wider in scope than those provided in Great Britain' (Birrell and Murie 1980: 23). Northern Ireland 'broadly followed the framework established nationally', modified to suit local conditions (Harrison 1990a: 167), though the province's legislation 'offered more generous inducements to industrialists than its British counterpart, the Distribution of Industry Act (1945)' (Arthur 1989: 76). Moreover, 'the provision of grants (rather than loans for the most part, as in the British legislation) and the specific link with employment creation differentiated the policy operating in Northern Ireland in the post-war period' (Harrison 1990a: 153). The Local Economic Development Unit (LEDU) was set up in 1971 as a company limited by guarantee, its board being appointed from among the local business community. The LEDU model had counterparts in Great Britain, namely the Council for Small Industries in Rural Areas and the Small Industries Council for the Rural Areas of Scotland. Additionally, the Northern Ireland Finance Corporation (NIFC) was established in 1972 'to provide loans, guarantees and equity capital to Northern Ireland industrial undertakings threatened with contraction or closure but with good prospects of long-term viability' (Harrison 1990a: 157). In 1973, Enterprise Ulster was established to generate jobs for the long-term unemployed. Its mission states that its purpose is to assist 'the economic development of Northern Ireland by the provision of quality training and the creation of employment projects of lasting value to the community' (Enterprise Ulster annual report 1998).

Generally, Northern Ireland has tended to exhibit the greatest divergence from the UK norm. 'We do "Northern Irelandise" GB programmes as far as possible thereby making it relevant to the situation as it pertains here' (interview). An illustration of the reliance on local actors stems from the fact that the imposition of Direct Rule left intact the pattern of locally specific policy. Gaffikin and Morrissey (1990b: 129) observed that, during the first ten years of Direct Rule, the conception of the economic problems facing Northern Ireland did not change. Only over time was there a partial convergence with the wider UK agenda. One area of policy convergence with Great Britain was the replacement of the NIFC by the Northern Ireland Development Agency (NIDA) in 1976. Not only did this broaden the scope of the province's main government development agency but it 'closely followed the emerging legislative and administrative framework in the rest of the UK' (Harrison 1990a: 157). The models of the UK National Enterprise Board (NEB), Scottish Development Agency (SDA) and Welsh Development Agency (WDA) formed the rationale for NIDA. NIDA itself had a strong investment banking function 'intended to complement the package of regional policy instruments then prevailing in Northern Ireland' (Harrison 1990a: 160). As with the SDA and WDA, NIDA was 'supplementary to the regional policy package rather than a replacement of it' (p.160), although, relative to the SDA and WDA, NIDA's functions were more narrowly constrained. Other measures were adopted, some varying from UK policy. In 1976–77, Regional Employment Premium in Great Britain was abolished (as part of the International-Monetary-Fund-inspired austerity), whereas in Northern Ireland selective financial assistance was upgraded, increasing the maximum rate of selective capital grant from 40 per cent to 50 per cent. Factory rental concessions and interest relief grant were also raised, while grants for research and development were introduced. 'Thus, for a short time at least, there was a clear divergence between policies implemented in Britain and Northern Ireland' (Gaffikin and Morrissey 1990b: 134). A new inner-city initiative, the Belfast Areas of Need (BAN) programme, was introduced, modelled on the Urban Programme's Inner City Partnerships in the UK (Birrell and Wilson 1993).

In 1982, a new Department of Economic Development (DED) assumed responsibility from the old Departments of Commerce and Manpower Services. Additionally, the Industrial Development Board (IDB) was formed by merging the industrial development functions of the old Department of Commerce with those of NIDA into a new unified arm (although excluding LEDU that remained in tact). The IDB operates 'within the framework of industrial development policies for the UK as a whole' (Bell 1987: 224). The IDB has

> its own Board and Executive, a civil service staff strengthened by secondments and short-term contract staff from the private sector, and the intention of acting in an entrepreneurial and businesslike way subject only to the constraints of political and financial accountability.
>
> (Harrison 1990a: 163)

As a government agency, IDB is responsible for promoting industrial development in Northern Ireland. It is a publicly accountable body, an agency of the new Department of Enterprise, Trade and Investment (DETI). Organizationally, the IDB itself was a hybrid. In part, it was modelled on the SDA (without the SDA's local area physical and economic planning emphasis), and on the Republic's IDA (without the range of functions, executive responsibilities and strategic orientation that set the IDA apart as a successful development agency) (Harrison 1990a: 167). However, the IDB model reflected further changes in UK regional policy that played down the emphasis on regions and had instead focused on smaller areas in the large cities – witness the growth of enterprise zones and urban development corporations, and the associated marginalization of local authorities in these areas, especially after the 1981 civil disturbances in major British cities. Usually, however, Northern Ireland is significantly influenced by Great Britain policy developments. Formally, policy is framed by the Department of Enterprise, Trade and Investment (DETI), successor to DED. Before devolution, the position was thus:

> While there is no democratic devolution, there is administrative devolution. The DTI is the right department on trade issues since they have the resources but even then we often do our own thing . . . The regional objective is in harmony with the national objective. But some calibration on a regional basis is needed.
>
> (interview)

For all the convergence with Great Britain, however, the scale of expenditure in Northern Ireland was much higher. Moreover, it is often the *way that things are done* as much as what is done that affects how those things are perceived. One former senior official suggested: 'Had the policy of cutting overdependence on government grants to industry been applied here directly, it would have been seen as Thatcherite. Instead, we did it by meeting with local industry and discussing the problems and how to solve them' (interview). In the end, the policy that was 'agreed' with local industry was still that grants should be cut if more self-reliance was to be achieved. The impression, however, was that it was done differently in Northern Ireland thereby making it more acceptable.

In Northern Ireland, throughout Direct Rule, overall responsibility for policy rested with the Secretary of State for Northern Ireland, assisted by a junior minister, one of whose portfolios was economic development. There was no formal relationship with a Whitehall department but there were informal links that varied with the issue in question. For example, the biggest initiative in recent years was New Deal. 'We are involved in this – but that is exceptional. This is because the structures and responsibilities differ. Our Training and Employment Agency has no equivalent in Great Britain – they have the LECs [local enterprise councils] in Scotland and LEAs [local education authorities] in England/Wales' (interview). There are also some informal links with Wales (the WDA), but especially with Scotland (the Industry Department and Scottish Enterprise), on issues of mutual interest (such as the Scottish–Irish gas and electricity interconnectors, and where 'we compete against the common enemy'. The strongest links are with the Republic of Ireland where there is close cooperation with *Foras Aiseanna Saothoir* (FAS) – the Training and Employment Authority for Ireland 'with whom we are more similar than Scottish Enterprise . . . In an increasingly all-Ireland labour market, we face common problems. We have a very open relationship. There is a joint board that meets as and when required but there is constant contact by phone in the meantime' (interview). Overall, cross-border relations

> are very cordial. For every trip we make to London, we make three to Dublin. I wouldn't compare the experiences of London and Dublin. London visits are often on obscure matters whereas with Dublin it is the bread and butter issues, especially inter-connection, the all-Ireland energy markets, and tourism. On industry competition, we have a more competitive relationship with Scotland and Wales than the Republic. The South's tax regime is more favourable than ours is so our packages are focused on capital investment. It all depends on what companies are looking for. Pharmaceuticals love the tax regime in the Republic whereas we attract those needing upfront capital investment, especially engineering.
>
> (interview)

Under Direct Rule, 'the nature of the minister–department relationship is that they cannot devote enough time to the department' (interview). On everyday matters, while high-level policy comes from the government, the framework locally is set by the DED. 'A lot of national policy makes sense everywhere so there is no need to depart from it' (interview). Even on the London-based initiatives, responsibility for policy and its implementation rested with DED and its various agencies. Perhaps the main distinction with London is the extent to which NICS staff had greater prominence.

> Civil servants do have a considerable degree of responsibility for running services. This has extended to glad-handing, giving speeches and attending public events. There are tensions. It is inconsistent with the classic British model and our culture doesn't prepare us for this. I had no basis on which to draw to prepare for this very uncomfortable situation. It does create problems for civil servants and is not particularly healthy.
>
> (interview)

Similarly, one agency chief executive remarked how

> I am very much first reserve in terms of regularly being asked to stand in for the minister. We are expected to answer parliamentary questions of an operational nature. The procedure is that the chief executive deals with them in a written reply that appears in Hansard. A policy matter requires a ministerial response. Also, agency staff are often interviewed in the media. Indeed, if we get calls from the media and say 'Would you prefer to speak to the minister?', they often say that they want the civil servant instead. We see it as part of our accountability role. There is a decline of anonymity and increasingly large representational role or duty to perform. It is natural that people come to us given that ministers are very busy, especially in Northern Ireland, where they hold more than one portfolio and have to travel to Great Britain regularly. Ministers are notoriously unreliable for missing their public appointments.
>
> (interview)

The relationship between DED and its agencies was clear:

> I like to see it that we are the 'holding' company – the others are the 'subsidiaries'. We have a departmental board that includes me and the chief executives of our subsidiaries and which meets quarterly or more often if needed. Each subsidiary has high autonomy, a three-year corporate plan and operating agenda. Each is different however. The T&EA are civil servants, while the NITB and LEDU are not, for example.
>
> (interview)

Another distinguishing factor is the role of local authorities. While the tenor of central–local government relations deteriorated in Great Britain, as central government vested more powers with quangos and other single-purpose bodies, notably in the area of urban regeneration, local government in Northern Ireland had already been divested of most functions in 1973, albeit for different reasons. Paradoxically, while local authorities in Great Britain during the 1980s and 1990s saw their role sharply attenuated, Northern Ireland's local authorities were allowed to exploit their limited powers in respect of economic development. Indeed, the area has been one of only a handful in which councils had a growing role (see Knox and Carmichael 1998; Carmichael and Knox 1999).

Frequently, Northern Ireland acquired ministers who were adjudged to be 'dissidents' (or 'wets') in the Thatcher governments. A degree of licence seems to have been granted in so far as there was autonomy to practice a 'wetter' range of policy options. Thus, the IDB 'retains a remit which allows a high degree of support and subsidy. Even die-hard free marketeers like Rhodes Boyson, when minister for industry in Northern Ireland, adopted a hands-on policy' (Gaffikin and Morrissey 1990a: 87).

Community care

Developments in Northern Ireland have tended to follow broadly similar principles to those in Great Britain although with distinctive methods of implementation. Largely, recent differences stem from historical patterns established decades beforehand. The early development of health services in Northern Ireland 'was, in some ways, more advanced' in Great Britain (Birrell and Murie 1980: 245). Certainly, after partition, the organization of health services differed significantly from that in Great Britain, with responsibility vested with the Ministry of Home Affairs – there was no equivalent to the (English) Ministry of Health set up in 1919. A mixture of constitutional uncertainty before partition coupled with financial and economic circumstances thereafter ensured that the difference remained. In the interwar period, 'health services in Northern Ireland began to fall further and further behind provision in Britain' with 'no central authority responsible for all health matters . . . There was, moreover, the continued failure to develop policies and provision for the care of certain categories of the mentally disordered' (Evason et al. 1976: 70–1). The development of a comprehensive National Health Service in Northern Ireland gathered pace during the war, with the creation of a Ministry of Health and Local Government in 1944. Until 1972, hospital services in Northern Ireland were provided through a two-tier structure involving a single Hospitals' Authority and local hospital management committees that worked under the general policy direction of the Ministry. The Mental Health Act (NI) 1948,

> taken as a whole, put Northern Ireland ahead of Britain in its provisions and the thinking behind them . . . Northern Ireland acquired a single comprehensive act for mental health. Moreover, a single authority – the Northern Ireland Hospitals Authority – was given responsibility for all mental health services – institutional and community services. In Great Britain, the division of responsibility between

the regional hospital boards and the local health authorities proved a critical obstacle to development of community services and an integrated approach to the needs of the mentally disordered.

(Evason *et al.* 1976: 86–7)

In the late 1960s, developments in Great Britain were again informing those in the province. 'Nothing short of a fully integrated administrative system can provide an adequate framework for comprehensive care today and for an effective response to the problems and challenges of tomorrow' (NIG 1969: para. 24). Thus, the Northern Ireland government agreed to 'integrate hospital and specialist services, general health services and local authority health services into a single administrative structure, and for the new administrative structure to take responsibility for welfare services presently provided by local authorities' (NIG 1972: 2). On reorganization, the personal social services, which were previously the responsibility of the welfare departments of local authorities, were amalgamated with the health service and came under the Ministry (now Department) of Health and Social Services (DHSS) (NI) (Prior 1993). Based on the recommended structure of the management consultants Booz, Allan and Hamilton, the management of personal health and personal social services would rest with four area boards, each serving a minimum population of about 250,000 and each defined by a grouping of district council areas. Thus Northern Ireland adopted a different pattern from that in the rest of the UK. In explaining why, the government remarked that the pattern of local government in Northern Ireland was 'an inadequate base for major social services . . . [Thus,] there is a need for very close links between health services and personal services' (DHSS(NI) 1975: para. 4). While the timing of reorganization paralleled reforms in Great Britain, the changes themselves 'took the logic of unification, co-ordination and rationalisation further by relieving local authorities of their responsibilities for personal services as well as for health services' (Birrell and Murie 1980: 260). These arrangements allowed for better planning and more efficient, cost-effective and comprehensive provision. Contrary to the Seebohm Committee's (HMSO 1968) recommendation and unlike in Great Britain, there was no real debate over the need to retain local control of such services.

In essence, the organizational hierarchy of the post-1973 system had three tiers. The DHSS(NI) was at the top with similar functions to UK Department of Health. Until devolution, the Secretary of State for Northern Ireland had overall responsibility for determining policy and apportioning the budget within the Northern Ireland block. The DHSS(NI) additionally acted as a regional health authority with overall responsibility for all personal social services (including community care activities) and for their coordination with the health services. In the department, the Health and Social Services Committee was the senior management team. It comprised the departmental permanent secretary, NHS chief executive (NI) and the chief inspectors. They met monthly. Then, there was the Health and Social Services Management Executive (HSS-E) acting as the regional tier for health and social services. The HSS-E is the equivalent of the English NHS Executive. It meets monthly and includes the directors of the six directorates (including the Child and Community Care Directorate) and professionals from the various inspectorates. In addition, the HSS-E director meets weekly with the six directors (interview). The HSS-E lays down policy guidelines, determines resource allocations and oversees the execution of policy (Gray and Getty 1999).

The next tier consists of the four health and social services boards covering geographical areas of Northern Ireland – northern, eastern, southern and western. The DHSS(NI) delegated to the boards management responsibility for planning, monitoring, and coordinating services in their respective areas. Each board has four committees: an administrative services committee, a policy and resources committee, a health services committee, and a personal social services committee. The boards have a statutory responsibility to 'promote health and provide care' for their resident population and are the lead agencies charged with implementing community care reforms. In contrast, in Great Britain the lead agencies are the social services departments of the local authorities (be they shire counties, unitary councils or metropolitan districts). Uniquely in the UK, therefore, Northern Ireland has an integrated structure. Following the reforms of the NHS in the early 1990s, the boards have assumed a purchasing role (see below).

The boards are split into units of management – administrative areas that contain varying numbers of hospitals, health centres and other providers of community services. These units – all now NHS trusts – form the lowest tier in the structure (Tonks 1993: 262). There are 19 health service trusts, 7 providing hospital services only, 5 providing community health and social services, and 6 providing a full range of health and social services, plus the ambulance service (Gray and Getty 1999).

Policy in Northern Ireland in essence parallels that in the UK as a whole although officials in the province preferred to speak in broader terms, seeing it as embracing care of the elderly, learning disabled and psychiatric groups. The integrated nature of the system means that the

> definition of the policy is necessarily different since our system combines the benefits of both the national health and local government social services systems, especially in areas like district nursing. That said, the actual definition is very similar to Great Britain's. We tend to regard community care as anyone needing care in the community.
> (interview)

However, even some of those employed in the structure expressed caution: 'Integration is far more evident at senior management level than at the grass roots. The nearer to the patients you get, the greater the divide' (cited in Tonks 1993: 262). Despite these misgivings, a full-scale review of services with mental health problems, initiated in 1980, did not alter the structure (Donnelly *et al.* 1994: 3).

There are differing opinions on whether there is a slavish adherence to UK policy. Generally, it appears that the pace of change is slower in Northern Ireland, with an ability to pick selectively from UK-level developments. As one official maintained, 'you go with what the government of the day does. Our policy here is geared to need. We also have the sectarian issue and try to keep it out of health/social services. It is national policy applied sensibly' (interview). Another official stressed that, on policy discretion:

> we have a bit which we guard quite jealously. The UK Health Secretary is not our boss. We maintain an entirely separate system, funded separately and with separate accountability mechanisms . . . [However, we] would consider DH [the Department of Health] as the lead department. They have the resources to commission research and we don't want to reinvent the wheel. We are pretty selective as to what we take. We alter to suit. They are far better placed to be at the leading edge. They have some very good people.
>
> (interview)

A former permanent secretary at DHSS(NI) echoed these sentiments – the UK DH is the lead department on major policy issues such as the nature and shape of the NHS, the decision to end trusts and commissioning (interview). Periodically,

> we may look to Scotland on clinical issues such as cardiac disease whereas on trust reconfiguration, we've been looking to Wales. Connections with the Isle of Man and Channel Islands are tenuous. Essentially, they consist of service agreements with commissioning individual services under contracts that may include the Isle of Man and Channel Islands as well as authorities in Great Britain. However, currently, there is a legislative block on English health and social services departments purchasing community care from Northern Ireland and vice versa though . . . There are informal means of getting around this . . . More links exist with the Republic of Ireland, including the exchange of patients, though it is still rare. There is some institutional care for children involved, while elderly people have been known to 'filter' across the border via families who have residence in the north.
>
> (interview)

In 1990, for the first time, a policy for Northern Ireland was fully articulated (Prior 1993). *People First* (DHSS(NI) 1990) was introduced as Northern Ireland's version of *Caring for People* (DHSS 1989). *People First* explained that 'Caring for People sets out six central objectives, which apply as much to Northern Ireland as to Great Britain' (p.5). The national policy objectives in *Caring for People* would be pursued in the context of Northern Ireland's unique integrated health and social services, and in the context of the new role which boards will assume in line with *Working for Patients* (DHSS(NI) 1990: 4).

In examining the relationship between health and personal social services, the House of Commons Health Select Committee (1999) gathered evidence from Northern Ireland:

> We strongly endorse the practice we saw in Northern Ireland . . . We consider that it is a pragmatic approach to service provision and has major benefits for users and carers as it allows a seamless service between health and social care to develop. We also consider that there are advantages for the administration of services, for example, it might be argued that unified commissioning is more effective than joint commissioning.
>
> (paragraph 63)

Unlike Great Britain, where local authorities have the main responsibility, Northern Ireland has four health and social services boards (see below) that deal with implementation. The Northern Ireland case illustrates how civil servants there are often thrust into the limelight, unlike their counterparts in Great Britain. One official remarked:

> Our role in Northern Ireland is like Janus. We look at policy nationally and see how it must be interpreted before application in Northern Ireland. We also look at the community here and see how its needs can be satisfied. Political and constitutional points prevent us from being simply like a regional tier of England . . . The civil service here has much greater sense of responsibility. It is uncomfortable to be placed in a position of appearing all-powerful or politicking. There is heightened public exposure. Ministers who don't ask questions actually increase the sense of responsibility. In all major decisions, they make the decision after having had our advice.
>
> (interview)

Civil service management reforms had only limited impact in the DHSS(NI). Apart from the creation of the Child Support and Social Security Agencies, most of the department's work in respect of community care was unaffected. On devolution, one NICS official speculated that:

> there is a strong chance that the new government will end the role of the health boards and centralise responsibility for everything at departmental level. It is likely that there would be more policy advisers. The role of the civil service may increase, as might the number of civil servants, but this is neither certain nor likely. We would have a greater regional planning role but no new operational functions.
>
> (interview)

No firm decisions have yet been announced, although the Review of Public Administration in Northern Ireland may well turn this official's speculation into reality. Similar pressures are at work in Scotland and Wales. Hard-pressed local authority budgets may accelerate the momentum to centralize implementation of community care policy.

Since Direct Rule was introduced, 'the trend towards "similarity in most respects" is clear . . . a trend which reflects the movement towards convergence between Northern Ireland and Britain' (Prior 1993: 162). Certainly, the structures in place differ. However, in policy terms, the evidence suggests that Great Britain and Northern Ireland are converging. The arrangements for administering policy on community care in the province built substantially on the distinctive nature of the previous system under devolved government. In so far as these were changing, Direct Rule accelerated matters. Paradoxically, the potential advantages conferred by integrating health and social services were offset by the loss of local control over local services; lack of the innovation evident in Great Britain (especially Scotland); and a failure to establish workable structures that could allow integration to become a practical reality instead of unfulfilled ambition.

> The convergence of policy between England and Northern Ireland, which has accelerated during the later 1980s, is an example of the far reaching inhibiting effect of the current form of government (Direct Rule) on every aspect of social policy. [This] has left Northern Ireland with no forum for debate and very little room for local initiative.
>
> (Prior 1993: 165)

Thus, while at one level Northern Ireland's integrated structure of health and social services is without parallel in UK terms, the system is riven with contradictions. As one former director of the Northern Ireland Health and Social Services Board observed:

> Much play has been made in the past of the fact that in Northern Ireland, we have integrated primary, secondary and community health and social services. Personally, I believe this form of structure offers advantages over the arrangements pertaining in England and Wales. In the circumstances, therefore, one would reasonably expect policies to be consistent with and even-handed in support of this approach. This, however, is not the case. The 1973 reorganisation was a 'squandered' opportunity.
>
> (interview)

Various reasons for the failure were offered. At departmental level, NICS was 'ten years behind' Great Britain in terms of its approach. In terms of the individual professional groups, social work was regarded as paramedical service with a paucity of qualified staff and so, despite a core central team, the doctors' lobby predominated. Even though steps were taken to build up social work as a profession, a further complication was that different types of accountability are in play. Doctors are under professional codes of ethics and accountability whereas legislation regulates the social work profession. An additional complication under Direct Rule is that ministers from England 'brought their understanding of the English system and also the associated critical analysis. None understood the application of the principles in the given local context. We used to speak of the "English disease" having been imported into Northern Ireland' (interview). However, as another official observed, 'ministers are keen to be consistent and coherent and, to be fair, this is not unexpected in a unitary state' (interview).

People First and the potential for integration in Northern Ireland were, contended one official, undermined by national UK creation of a 'market' in health care and what Evason and Robinson (1996) suggested was a broader process of NHS disengagement from providing long-term and community care. The trusts had a disintegrative effect undermining the structure. The trusts' agenda was to stay in business. There was distrust, rivalry, and a desire to increase 'market share' and enhance status. With 19 trusts, transaction costs inevitably rose. Consequently, broad strategic management gave way to negotiations with and between many trusts, each with its own narrow interest. The trusts have now bedded in and contain directors, 'many of whom are not up to it but who represent, nonetheless, another vested interest' and are a stumbling block to change. The changes have generated 'an inward-looking organisational focus and a preoccupation of securing futures rather than giving primacy to urgent service issues' (interview). While there were odd examples of like-minded people making things happen, organizationally it was not a success. Hence, such integration as has existed since 1973 has done so largely at the civil service and finance levels, not at the level of planning and collaboration between professional groups to benefit clients. A successfully integrated system needs a supportive, planned and managed structure, not one that generates competition, fear of job loss and missed opportunities.

Given the weaknesses that exist, the process of managing in the present structure has been characterized as 'muddling through', with crucial decisions being taken locally on interpretation of national policies (Ham, cited in Smyth, 1996). Rather than admit to muddling through, Smyth (1996) preferred to see the operational methodology as pragmatism. In the new 'marketplace' of health, while a need to manage the individual components of the service continues, the interface between each part should be left to the market. Smyth (1996) rejected this:

> [W]e know our market is not real. If it were, then there would be more product selection, greater concentration of services, winners and losers, and the other paraphernalia of the market place proper. A full blown market is, of course, openly acknowledged as being politically difficult and publicly unacceptable and probably operationally

incapable of meeting the statutory obligations of service to the whole population in a safe, equitable and just manner. As a result, by way of compromise, we are given the so-called 'regulated market'.

For its part, the DHSS

> seems to operate according to the principle – 'Do as I say, not as I do'. That is, while the Health Boards and Trusts are required to consult on a most rigorous time-scale with the public, prior to taking decisions on service change, the Department takes critical decisions without regard not only to the Boards' views but in some cases, to professional opinion.
>
> (Smyth 1996)

With devolution in Northern Ireland, the old DHSS was widened to include responsibility for public safety, becoming the Department of Health, Social Services and Public Safety. The other institutions referred to remain in situ, as do the arrangements for interinstitutional linkages, meetings and lines of accountability, though a fundamental overhaul and rationalization of the system is pending.

Conclusions

Northern Ireland's past and present governmental and policy-making arrangements are different from those of the rest of the UK. Given the absence of mainstream party politics and the vexed constitutional question, this conclusion is to be expected. In exploring the changing nature of Northern Ireland's civil service and its reform, the special provisions for governing the province show that the pure unitary state is a myth. The Westminster model helps to understand only partially the government of the UK. With the Labour government's reforms since 1998, the UK's variegated governmental structure has been further entrenched. Long in gestation, the differentiated polity in the UK is solidifying steadily, most readily in Northern Ireland.

Despite the serious political upheavals that have periodically beset Northern Ireland, the system of public administration has functioned remarkably smoothly. Transition periods are managed with little fuss. However, its public administration has operated at variance with the traditional notions of the Westminster model such as anonymity. Senior civil servants are pushed into the public gaze. For their part, while having to withstand criticism on two fronts in a bitterly divided society, civil servants have been obliged to show due respect for community sensitivities (something that has not always been achieved). Most recently, some officials have found it difficult to adjust to the new dispensation because they have little or no experience of such pervasive accountability to local ministers.

In policy terms, the evidence conflicts on whether Northern Ireland moves in step with the rest of the UK. Undoubtedly, the NICS is closely modelled on its larger counterpart, the UK Home Civil Service, from which it takes many aspects of its structure and internal procedures, partly because a pervasive *British* Unionist ideology among the upper echelons of the service stressed its affinity with its 'mainland' cousin. Under the glare of international political and media observation, the British state sought political stability, amid sectarian strife in the province, sponsoring a form of 'local corporatism'. During Direct Rule, Northern Ireland might have been expected to conform more readily to UK standards and policy positions given the impetus to integration. However, national UK policy prescriptions had to be tailored according to the exacting conditions of its most troubled and troublesome territory. NICS is a key actor in the forefront of the province's affairs. The government hoped that relatively generous public expenditure settlements might alleviate some of the socioeconomic grievances among disaffected nationalists (and in turn, reduce support for paramilitaries based in these communities). To that end, legislative changes fostered a greater involvement by the minority Catholic community in the policy and administrative process, albeit often alienating a majority Protestant community, wary of mendacious British politicians. Throughout Direct Rule, policy was mediated through a small territorial policy community dominated by administrative interests. The province functioned as a technocratic state. Policy-making in Northern Ireland varies considerably depending on the policy area in question. Certainly, the variegated configuration of departments, several of which are not coterminous with Whitehall, sustains varying degrees of policy divergence perhaps best understood by Gaffikin and Morrissey's (1990b: 144) words which bear repeating: 'adaptation within a standard framework of theories, policies and structures'.

After 1979, the implementation of public sector reform in NICS was partial, delayed and deliberately selective, continuing a pattern established long before Direct Rule. Westminster governments became more systematic, even dogmatic, about introducing reforms from the late 1980s, although their application was often tempered to allow for the idiosyncratic nature of the small and often beleaguered policy community. Hence, while executive agencies were set up in Northern Ireland, their operation has always been subject to the restrictions imposed by their small size and by an in-service culture predisposed to avoid fragmenting the unity and cohesiveness of the overall NICS.

Although devolution has been a faltering process since the Belfast Agreement in 1998, Northern Ireland continues to experience policy and administrative divergence, despite the series of concordat arrangements progressively concluded with Whitehall and the Scottish and Welsh devolved administrations since 1997. These are designed to ensure that the centrifugal forces of devolution do not imperil national (UK) cohesiveness in vital respects (such as clinical standards in health, for example). To accommodate the spectrum of political opinion in the province's new assembly, the executive and its constituent departmental structure have been reconfigured in ways that owe little to administrative efficiency and much to political expediency. Moreover, if and when the provisions of the Belfast Agreement, with its unique form of devolution-*plus*, make themselves felt, the process of differentiation will be entrenched further still.

4

Scotland

Introduction

The most immediate problem that arises when looking at the Scottish civil service is defining the field. There is a natural tendency to think of the Scottish civil service as those who work in the territorial ministry and now in the devolved administration. In fact, the greatest number of civil servants in Scotland work outside these bodies in other UK government departments and agencies. For the purposes of this chapter, the Scottish civil service will be taken to represent non-industrial civil servants employed by the Crown in Scotland. However, civil service representation in Scotland cannot be considered without analysing the history of the Scottish Office and post of secretary of state for Scotland because the civil service became a service through their development.

Of the territorial ministries in the UK, Scotland is the oldest, but this does not mean that the administrative arrangements have been, and are, the most distinct. A brief perusal of the history of the other territorial ministries suggests that:

> Scotland comes somewhere between Northern Ireland and Wales in political status. While possessing neither a government nor a parliament of its own, it has a strong constitutional identity and a large number of political and social institutions.
>
> (Kellas 1984: 2)

With devolution, Scotland departed further from both Northern Ireland and Wales in its constitutional distinctiveness, although it is uncertain whether devolution will increase the distinctiveness of the Scottish civil service.

This chapter traces the history and development of the Scottish civil service through the establishment of the Scottish Office and the development of central departments and agencies in Scotland. It also considers the distinctiveness of the Scottish civil service from that in Whitehall and implications of the new devolved administration.

The Scottish Office and civil service development

[T]here were Scottish *departments* before there was a Scottish *minister*, and a minister before there was a coherent *ministry* to serve him.

(Parry 1982: 4, emphasis in original)

The development of the Scottish civil service was inexorably linked to the development of the Scottish Office. The creation of the Scottish Office did not end wrangling over Scottish distinctiveness in administrative terms. In fact it may be argued that this was only the beginning. The legislation did not detail structure, functions or responsibilities. The first years after creation saw considerable debate at all levels of government, concerning how distinctive 'distinctive' should be. The history of this time confirms that there was little strategic thought given to relationships between the Scottish Office and Home Office and consequently between the Scottish civil service and Whitehall.

Lacking consensus on role and structure, the early development of the Scottish Office depended heavily on the whim of individuals and especially those appointed to the secretaryship. Thus the first secretary, the Duke of Richmond, did very little to develop a distinct Scottish administration, feeling that the secretaryship and Scottish Office were unnecessary creations. Further, the lack of planning added doubts over the possible success of the Scottish Office in providing for Scotland a distinct set of policy solutions.

Before the creation of the Scottish Office the administration of Scotland was carried out through independent boards. These boards covered the main government functions in Scotland and over time were responsible for: agriculture; congested districts; crofts; education; fisheries; health; Highlands and Islands; insurance; local government; manufactures; prisons and poor relief.

The board system provided for the Scottish Office a long-standing administrative system. Board appointments were made on patronage, with the Lord Advocate having considerable influence. Members were often specialists, but importantly were not specialist administrators. However, although problems existed with lines of responsibility and accountability (to Parliament and public), the Scottish board system lasted well into the twentieth century as the scope of government functions meant that duties

> had to be devolved on to subordinate bodies and the Scottish Boards were the time-honoured form which subordinate bodies took in Scotland. Moreover, this structure was given a certain amount of retrospective validity by the not dissimilar structure adopted for the administration of the labour exchanges and national insurance in the years before 1914.
>
> (Hanham 1969: 56)

The role of the Scottish boards can be likened to that of the 'appointed state' today. Criticisms also appear not to have changed in over a century. For the board system, Hanham (1969) draws attention to problems concerning number of appointees, salaries and the levels of public spending in their gift.

Transfer of responsibilities from the administrative boards to the Scottish Office was contentious, and fractious. The prime example here is education, where professionals did not want responsibility transferred to the Scottish Office. Indeed, professional interests lobbied hard for a separate British education board.

After 1885, Scottish administration was split between the boards and the Scottish Office. This system was highly unsatisfactory but the Westminster government did not seem keen to give any more ground to Scottish sentiments. It was only when civil service organization came under scrutiny by organizations with a national remit that any changes were considered.

The transfer of responsibilities from boards to the Scottish Office and the growth of those responsibilities may be explained by three factors: inheritance, performance and demonstration. Inheritance refers to

> the perception that Scotland possesses a historical entitlement to some autonomy of administration . . . from the guarantees of Scottish civil society secured in the Act of Union . . . The result was to check outright assimilation and reassure English political elites that Scottish individuality might be recognised without jeopardising the structure of the United Kingdom.
>
> (Parry 1982: 5)

Inheritance explains the development of several Scottish Office departments between 1885 and 1928. In particular, the Education and Health Departments were directly derived from functions preserved in the Act of Union of 1707 (Parry 1982).

The second factor of performance refers to administrative necessity. In order to perform certain functions of government economically, efficiently and effectively, local (Scottish) administration is required. As Parry notes, there is a historical basis to this reason as well. The performance motive was epitomized by the 'Scottish Manager' who acted as 'the local influential who could interpret between centre and periphery' (Parry 1982: 6).

Third, demonstration refers to the symbolism of transferring responsibility without authority. Parry (1982: 6) suggests that this reason 'has been prominent in the history of the Welsh Office, was the dominant one in the original Scottish Office of 1885, and has proved convenient since'. This motive is closely tied to the development of all departments even where there was a legacy established by the Act of Union. Indeed, when considering the drive behind the transfer of responsibilities and development of departments, all three motives may be identified in all cases to some extent. There is truth also in the statement that, as creation of the Scottish Office was partially an outcome of nationalist pressure, many responsibilities were transferred with a view to 'giving a little, but not too much'.

Writers have categorized the period from 1885 in Scottish Office development in different ways according either to the changing structure, responsibilities and administrative characteristics of those appointed to office, or to chronological periods. What is clear from such categorizations is that structural change has always followed, but not been directly driven by, administrative change. Again there appears no overarching strategy for Scottish Office development. This can most clearly be seen in the work of Parry (1982: 6–8) who identifies three main administrative eras: the 'legatee of Home Rule all round', 1888–1918; 'steady-state administration', 1918–51; and 'administrative decentralization', 1951–99. The first era is characterized by the Scottish Office taking over existing administrative arrangements and assuming responsibilities against the backdrop of Home Rule. The second era sees a break in the trend to decentralize. The central state was strong and the advent of war in 1914 resulted in the recentralization of some functions. Further, as Parry (1982: 7) noted, 'at this time Commons debate often criticised the political weakness and English orientation of Scottish Ministers'. The theme of personal influence on the political status of the Scottish Office is again strong. The third era saw a return to decentralization. The transfer of responsibilities was a means of placating growing Scottish nationalism. Central departments resisted transfer of responsibilities and endeavoured to control those decentralized responsibilities through other means (Parry 1982).

Parry (1982) identified three distinct organizational structures in the Scottish Office. The first is a dual structure that appeared immediately after establishment. This structure was a confusion of the central department and board system. The Scottish secretary had varying degrees of control over different areas of public administration. The dual structure existed from establishment in 1885 until 1939.

The second Scottish Office structure was federal. The change was brought about following recommendations from the Gilmour Committee of 1937. Change took place in 1939 and involved the creation of four departments: Home, Health, Education and Agriculture. The Scottish secretary became the 'head' minister, having the duties of the disparate boards vested in him. The departments carried out the operational duties for their functional areas.

At first glance this system may appear perfect for the conduct of Scottish affairs, but the structure was again flawed. The four departments were created with a degree of autonomy in mind. This autonomy was not from the Scottish secretary but from each other. They were by no means different branches of the same tree. There was no connection between them in, for example, budgeting. Therefore

> establishments, finance, legal and London liaison organisations were all . . . quadrupled so that the 'effective control' of each department might rest with its head . . . and inter-departmental staff transfers and permanent liaison machinery were ruled out as normal practice . . . [The] effect was to impose a fresh structural weakness as others were being rectified.
>
> (Parry 1982: 15)

Further, the strategic role of the Scottish secretary can be questioned: was he a 'guard dog' without any bite?

Problems of the second structure were rectified in 1971, when the Scottish Office's structure was integrated. Under this change, four departments became five through addition and integration (although the Scottish Economic Planning Department was not born out of the Scottish Development Department until 1973). The five departments created were: Department of Agriculture and Fisheries; Scottish Development Department; Scottish Economic Planning Department (1973); Scottish Education Department; and Scottish Home and Health Department. Structural change was required for two main reasons. First, like all government departments in the period, the scope of responsibilities had grown considerably. Second, the overstretching of Scottish Office departments was compounded by the existing structure. Throughout the life of the second Scottish Office, an already bad situation became worse. Change was required if only to improve performance.

The chronology of the Scottish Office is therefore an interesting one: development was not always development; strategy was not always strategy; the public face was not always the private face. For most of its history, little to do with the Scottish Office was what it seemed.

Given the background to the creation of the Scottish Office, there was never any central government intention to make the Scottish Office a major office of government. For most of its existence the Scottish secretaryship has been a minor cabinet post. Given the mismatch of responsibilities and structure, even the strongest Scottish secretaries found it hard to promote the Scottish voice. There is even great debate about what the Scottish secretary's role was in policy-making – a voice for Scotland at the centre, or the voice of the centre in Scotland. The vagaries of an electoral system that can provide a Conservative Scottish secretary when the Conservatives are a minority party in Scotland further compounded the issue.

When the first Scottish secretary took up the post there was no clear idea of what the work of the Scottish Office or Scottish secretary should be. Growth of the Office and development of the role of the Scottish secretary can best be described as ad hoc. There were periods of great activity matched by long periods of stagnation. The Scottish secretary had a 'supervisory' role where responsibility was vested in the boards. The Scottish Office civil service was in a difficult situation about policy inputs: did it leave policy to the boards or did it seek to direct them or did it contest their policy leadership? The practicalities of managing this situation meant that policy was more difficult to formulate and coordinate. Indeed, this situation is a classic example of the lack and confusion of accountability.

The Scottish Office civil service was organized on traditional departmental lines. However, although at first glance it could be said to resemble closely a typical Weberian bureaucracy, it also had federal features, which differentiated senior civil servants from their Whitehall counterparts. The secretaries of departments were directly responsible to the secretary of state and were the accounting officers for their respective departments. This meant that the Scottish Office permanent undersecretary had a narrower role than Whitehall colleagues who were sole accounting officers for their departments. The Scottish Office permanent undersecretary was 'first among equals'.

The distinctive position of the Scottish Office permanent undersecretary was an outcome of the structural development of the Office out of the boards. Although the permanent undersecretaries were the chief advisers to the secretaries of state and head bureaucrats in Scotland, they had greater independence from the minister than their Whitehall counterparts. This structural feature strengthened the strategic vision of Scottish administration. It ensured the primacy of the Scottish Office view in Scotland's polity. The seniority of Scottish Office bureaucrats (by grade and responsibility) meant that they quickly gained influence over the rest of the civil service in Scotland. There was no symbiotic relationship between numerical dominance and administrative dominance:

> [The] fact that Scottish departments are outnumbered by the non-Scottish . . . is not a good guide to the relative importance of the Scottish and non-Scottish parts of the civil service, nor can it be assumed that the non-Scottish bodies do in practice look more to London than to Edinburgh for guidance.
>
> (Kellas 1984: 64)

Administrative dominance was further reinforced by several distinguishing characteristics of the Scottish Office. First, senior Scottish Office civil servants tended to be Scottish or have a strong Scottish heritage. Second, the employment history of Scottish Office civil servants shows that the majority worked within the Scottish Office for the bulk of their careers. Departmental transfers in the main have tended to be between Scottish Office departments rather than between Edinburgh and London. This pattern may be creeping parochialism but it has aided the continuity of influence and therefore strengthened the possibility and ability to look at longer-term strategies for individual policy areas. As Kellas (1984: 75) noted:

> [T]he civil servant can continue to use his specialist knowledge of Scotland in whichever Scottish Office department he serves. Since his clientele is only five million people, with a fairly small number of local authorities and interest organisations, the principal political and official leaders will be known to him already. This is indeed one of the strengths of the Scottish Office as compared to Whitehall: personal contacts with the localities are good, making for frequent face to face contacts between central and local government.

Transfers between Edinburgh and London, however, were not uncommon. Civil servants did not want a wholly regional career, and so transfers between the territorial ministries were unusual. It was more important to work at the centre and gain practical and managerial experience vital to managing links with London after returning to Scotland. This shared background also acted as an informal check on Scottish autonomy because officials sought to stay 'in line' with Whitehall.

Third, the twentieth century has been identified as the era of the technocratic state in Scotland. Brown *et al.* (1998: 55) argue that the politics that mattered were administrative politics, a situation brought about by the desire to use the state as a vehicle of economic redistribution. Politics was taken out of politics and the role of the bureaucrat became central:

> [T]he experts in the civil service shared a culture with similar experts in pressure groups, trade unions or employers' organisations. This common professional outlook was more important in shaping the character of legislation – and, through that, of social development – than the rather amateurish activities of MPs or even of ministers . . . [so] by the middle of the twentieth century Scotland had as much autonomy as could reasonably be hoped for, because it had its own indigenous bureaucracy in the Scottish Office and the other Scottish branches of the bureaucratic state.
>
> (Brown *et al.* 1998: 55)

Thus, civil servants in Scotland, and especially those in the Scottish Office, took on a greater role than those in Whitehall in policy development as well as implementation. Indeed, in this sense, the Scottish civil administration was reverting to type. The similarity to the role of the civil administration in the Scottish boards where administrators had a role comparable to board members in policy-making cannot go unremarked. Clearly, the Scottish civil service has always been somewhat distinctive. This distinctiveness has been heightened over time as powers have accrued to the Scottish Office and also by the lack of checks and balances within the Scottish polity. The Scottish civil service had a degree of autonomy not enjoyed by other regional civil services. The important question is how distinct was, and is, the Scottish civil service. The next section considers this question by looking at the reform of the Scottish civil service.

Civil service reform

One of the longest running debates in British governance concerns the degree of regional autonomy that can be sustained within the unitary (not union) state. Equally, there has been great debate about Scotland's degree of autonomy. The pre-devolution situation was characterized by complexity and a certain degree of confusion (on the part of politicians, officials and the public).

Managerial and structural reform

Although the differentiated polity is an organizing perspective that characterizes recent change, the history of managerial reform of the Scottish civil service shows that regionalization, and therefore differentiation, are not new features of the British 'unitary' state.

The pre-1914 Scottish civil service cannot be considered a civil service by today's understanding of the term. As Hanham (1969: 52) contends:

> [A]dministration in Scotland was very largely left to take care of itself. The Secretary for Scotland and the Lord Advocate had offices in Edinburgh, but they were away at Westminster during the meeting of parliament, or on holiday or on tours of Scotland during much of the parliamentary vacations. Day-to-day business was left to the Scottish boards in Edinburgh, old and new, each of which functioned as a separate administrative unit, subject to frequent consultations with the Scottish Office in Whitehall.

Further, while there was concern with the organization and management of civil administration in Whitehall, such reforms were not translated to the Scottish field, so different were the two systems. There was no administrative class in Scotland and senior civil service posts were the preserve of ministerial patronage. Indeed, the pre-1914 civil service did not approximate to the Weberian bureaucratic ideal.

The MacDonnell Commission (1914) condemned the Scottish system as too remote from the system in Whitehall. In particular, the Commission recommended that career civil servants should carry out senior administrative duties, to counteract the boards' disdain for specialist knowledge. That is, there was a concern that the recruitment methods used for political and permanent appointments were incompatible with the qualities being sought of candidates, resulting in less effective coordination and management of administrative actions.

However, ironically, Scottish separatist sentiment and the threat of Home Rule delayed any management reform until 1939. This reform was driven by pressure from within the UK civil service and not by the disquiet of Scottish people about the quality of public administration. In this reform the Scottish civil service was being brought into a unified civil service system and was in a game of 'catch up' which cannot be interpreted as autonomous action. This management reform was concerned with the relationship between departments, and between departments and the secretary of state for Scotland, and gave Scotland for the first time a civil service based in Edinburgh. The Gilmour Committee's Report on Scottish Administration, which became law in the Reorganisation of Offices (Scotland) Act 1939, perpetuated the autonomy of the Scottish Office departments from each other. However, it strengthened the role of the secretary of state through a final transfer of the powers vested in the Scottish boards. Some responsibilities of the Scottish Office departments were also internally transferred. In responsibility, if not in power, the secretary of state became 'Scotland's minister'.

For the civil service, these changes were pervasive. There were still differences between Edinburgh and London in working relationships between departments. However, the role of civil administration in Scotland became more like the system in England in that civil servants now had a narrower administrative role rather than the broader policy role of the interwar years. The legacy of the board system was clear in the grading superiority of Scottish Office civil servants; however, the distinction in responsibilities between civil servants and politicians was made sharper. The additional powers of the secretary of state for Scotland meant that at the same time as the Scottish Office was being pulled into a unified service, the degree of regionalization and differentiation was being heightened. For example, compared with civil servants in the English regions, civil servants in Scotland had to negotiate with the centre in Scotland (Scottish Office) rather than Whitehall. The lack of a territorial ministry in England helped parent departments to keep their dominance in English governance. Regional civil service structures in England have not provided a voice at the centre for the regions but rather the regional application of central initiatives.

The Scottish Office civil service at this point was still relatively small in numbers. The largest department was Health with approximately 800 staff. The Health Department had been operating on lines similar to those in Whitehall since the employment of graduate generalists in 1928. However, the senior managers of the department were still those who were initially employed by the boards, so that in practice the Scottish Office civil service was still differentiated from that in Whitehall.

Of the other departments, the Scottish Office in London had the smallest staff with less than 100. This department, with various additions eventually became the Scottish Home Department. The Scottish Home Department took on an eclectic series of responsibilities not covered by the other three departments. The Scottish Education Department was the department least in line with the ideal provided by the administrative class. The Schools Inspectorate provided the administrative staff of the department. The department did not develop at the same speed as the others and could not assimilate extra responsibilities. Differentiation was continued through the Gilmour system. With its specialized remit, the Department of Agriculture forged close ties with the Whitehall system. It was a relatively large department of over 500 staff developing independently of the other departments and secretary of state, mainly because of the specialized and specific nature of its work. However, even with a closer working relationship with Whitehall than the other Scottish departments, regionalization was still evident. The department did not follow Whitehall in recruitment of a cadre of young, trained personnel until the mid-1930s.

The structure created by these reforms has changed with various internal reorganizations. However, it did have a lasting influence on the conduct of administration and the experience and careers of civil servants through the separation of departments. Gibson (1985) identifies negative outcomes on administrative performance, both functional and personal. First, the system developed strong departmental loyalties with strategy hindered by past administrative arrangements. Second, civil servants sometimes lacked the breadth and depth of knowledge and experience required to further their careers and to successfully administer cross-cutting issues. These negative outcomes were countered to an extent by the freedom of the secretary of state and permanent undersecretary to take an overseeing role.

After the Conservative general election victory of 1951, the Scottish Office and its work came under close scrutiny. The Royal Commission on Scottish Administration 1953 had been proposed in the Conservative election manifesto. Its general remit was 'to review with reference to the financial, economic, administrative and other considerations involved, the arrangements for exercising the functions of Our Government in relation to Scotland' (Gibson 1985: 124). Significantly, the Commission recommended the status quo for the division of Scottish Office responsibilities and the continuing division between departments under the leadership of the secretary of state. Again, any possible negative influences on civil administration caused by such differentiation were felt to be outweighed by the perceived advantages of departmental autonomy.

Time has shown that the Royal Commission was conservative in its recommendations and the failure to reform the Scottish Office had a detrimental effect on Scottish administration. In the years immediately following the Royal Commission, Scottish economic well-being faltered to such an extent that structural change in the Scottish Office was required to give the coordination that development policy had so long lacked. A more coherent approach to development was aided by the replacement of the Scottish Home Department and Department of Health by the Scottish Development Department and Scottish Home and Health Department. The former took responsibility for industrial and regional development and for the major services pertaining to infrastructure development. However, the failings of the differentiated system were still evident, as structural change did not bring cultural change. Civil servants' deep-set loyalties to the old departments and departmentalism (aided by the system of autonomy) was a major contributing factor in Scottish Office differentiation.

The creation of the Scottish Development Department provides a good example of the problems and tensions underlying the organization of Scottish administration. While the department was an administrative necessity for better coordination, the movement of so many large functions to one department unsettled the equilibrium in departmental size and influence. Internally, there was a desire to avoid any one department dominating because of its size and resources. The departmental heads should be of equivalent rank and influence. Externally, through accountability to Parliament, there was the need to keep departments to a manageable size in terms of staff and functions. The Scottish Development Department provided administrative coordination but accountability was cumbersome. So, almost as soon as it was created, the Scottish Development Department was reorganized, with the Regional Development Division coming under separate management.

The departmentalism of the civil service not only had the outcome of disjointed policy initiatives but also, and perhaps more seriously, often encouraged an inward-looking stance. Policy was based on the perceptions of civil servants. The isolation is demonstrated by the Scottish Education Department: it had little dialogue with the profession until the mid-1960s; it relied on incremental policy development; the culture was self-referential; culture change was not tackled directly but was considered an outcome of changes in structure and removing and reallocating responsibilities. Indeed, the equalizing of departmental influence was an unintended outcome of reforms since the 1950s aimed at strengthening partnership working.

The reforms of the 1970s went some way to ending the preoccupation with equal status of departments and senior civil servants and with administrative differentiation. The driving forces behind this change were external and were outside the realm of influence of administrators. In particular, the development of the Scottish economy around the discovery of North Sea oil was critical. The associated development activities crossed departmental boundaries and undercut the power of individual departments. Structural change also followed with the creation of the Scottish Economic Planning Department. It took responsibility for oil issues and also subsumed the Regional Development Division that had been under the direct control of the secretary of state as his own mini-department.

Counterweights to departmentalism were further strengthened by reorganizing central support systems. Clerical work and human resources were centralized to achieve economies of scale, reduce duplication and centralize organization and management. However, the most significant blow to departmentalism in practical terms was the creation of the Scottish Office Finance Division, which brought together the principal finance officers of the departments. A major power was thus centralized. The emphasis shifted to developing a Scottish Office identity and culture.

The creation of a Scottish Office culture was accelerated by one of the major reforms in civil service organization and management – the reduction in staff numbers. Civil servants perceived strength in 'sticking together'. From the mid-1970s, the civil service was gradually pared to a core. The initial cuts were made in response to a reduction in central government spending overall. However, from 1979, the civil service met with the reforming zeal of Prime Minister Thatcher.

The Thatcher reforms

The Thatcher reforms brought a new level of unity to the 'unified' UK Civil Service. For example, the creation of Next Steps agencies was a major change for the London-based civil service. However, the effects in Scotland were more limited. There is no doubt that the structural change was the same as in other territories, but separating policy and administration did not have the same impact in Scotland because it was already differentiated in this way. From the mid-1950s, the civil service had been withdrawing from direct provision of services through the development of partnership working. In health and education in particular, services were provided by ad hoc and statutory agencies, leaving the departments to concentrate on policy development. So, in Scotland, agencification increased differentiation in some areas of service provision while other reforms eroded the differentiation of departments.

Indeed, some of the initial problems experienced elsewhere in the UK with the establishment of agencies were not as apparent in Scotland. For example, the problem of blurring of responsibility for strategic development between ministers and chief executives was almost a non-issue in Scotland. As Kellas (1984: 79–80) noted, the history of civil service staffing meant that Scotland had

> a bureaucracy derived from, and knowledgeable of, its people and their special needs . . . [T]he type of work they do makes them generalists rather than specialists, although they probably remain within the same department to a much greater extent than do civil servants in Whitehall. This has given the Scottish Office in recent years an overall sense of direction lacking in much of Whitehall, and certainly in any region of England.

Agencification met a Scottish administration that was already relatively modernized along Next Steps lines. There was already considerable experience of working with and through 'agencies' and with the separation of policy and administration. The five departments were already working through partnership and network arrangements. Whether this was fully realized, however, is a different matter. There was some concern that the turbulence of previous decades had stripped the civil service of expertise and that the skills required for agency working were not being developed. However, it was clearly recognized that civil servants in Scotland had to develop expertise in their policy field and have extensive local knowledge. The latter comes with experience on the job, through longevity in the Scottish system. No matter how differentiated the UK civil service has been, the power of the centre has been sustained by transfers. Devolution did not change anything; there is a commitment in the concordat between the Cabinet Office and the Scottish administration to promote interadministration mobility. A cursory examination of the employment history of the senior management of the Scottish Executive reveals both local knowledge and the pull of Whitehall (see Table 4.1).

Before devolution, then, Scotland had a differentiated service. Differentiation was apparent on several levels in spite of the drive towards regional and national integration. The Scottish civil service was differentiated from the wider UK Civil Service, the Scottish Office civil service was differentiated from the wider Scottish civil service, and the Scottish Office civil service was differentiated along departmental lines.

Human resources issues

A significant indicator of the level of regionalization and differentiation is the variation in recruitment and selection, pay and conditions and equal opportunities. Indeed, as an indicator of differentiation, human resources issues have an importance both sides of the devolution settlement as

> [t]he web of relationships with Whitehall has . . . been tilted more to the personnel side. Here, the way that the Scottish and Welsh administrations are treated shows greater similarity to the position of the former Scottish and Welsh Offices than is now the case on the financial side.
>
> (Parry 2001: 56)

The managerialist reforms of Margaret Thatcher and John Major had at their heart the desire to cut costs and improve efficiency by freeing public service managers from the rule-bound nature of the collectivist and universalist provision of services through public bureaucracies. To realize these aims, it was necessary to give managers the power to make human resources decisions locally. Decentralization through delegation from the Crown was required – the vehicle was the Civil Service (Management

Table 4.1 Employment provenance of Scottish Executive senior management as at November 2001

Scottish Executive senior management	Scottish Civil Service employment
Sir Muir Russell KCB, Permanent Secretary	Joined Scottish Office 1970. Four years on secondment from Scottish Office. Appointed permanent secretary 1998 following open competition
Jim Gallagher, Head of Justice Department	Joined Scottish Office 1976. Private secretary to the minister for Home Affairs 1979–80 and to successive secretaries of state for Scotland 1989–91. Seconded to UK Cabinet Secretariat and to prime minister 1999–2000. Current post 2000
Trevor Jones, Head of Health Department and Chief Executive, NHS Scotland	Public finance accountant and chartered secretary. Employment history in local government and NHS. 1995–2000 chief executive Lothian Health Board. Chair of Health Board's Chief Executive Group in Scotland. Current post 2000
John Graham, Head of Environment and Rural Affairs Department	Joined Scottish Office 1972. Private secretary to secretary of state 1983–85. Head of finance 1996–98. Promoted to head of Agriculture, Environment and Fisheries Department 1998
Nicola Munro, Head of Scottish Development Department	Joined Scottish Office 1970. Posts in health, education, arts, criminal justice and personnel. Senior Civil Service 1986. Posts in food safety, hospital services, economic development, education and environment. Current post 2001 following open competition
Eddie Frizzell CB, Head of Enterprise and Lifelong Learning Department	Joined Scottish Office 1976. Undersecretary in Home Department with responsibility for Scottish prison service 1991. Chief executive of the service 1993. Current post 1999
John Elvidge, Head of Education Department	Joined Scottish Office 1973. Seconded to Scottish Homes 1988–89 and Cabinet Office 1998–99. Current post 1999
Robert Gordon CB, Head of Finance and Central Services Department	Joined Scottish Office 1973. Principal private secretary to secretary of state for Scotland 1985. Head of Constitution Group 1997. Head of Executive Secretariat 1998. Current post 2001
Agnes Robson, Principal Establishment Officer	Joined Scottish Office 1985 from Department of Employment. Moved to Health Department NHS Management Executive 1992. Director of Primary Care 1998. Current post 2000
Dr Peter Collings, Principal Finance Officer	Joined civil service 1975 and Scottish Office 1977. Principal finance officer and head of finance 1998

Source: adapted from www.scotland.gov.uk/who/senior.asp

Functions) Act 1992 for which the Management Code (issued under authority of the Civil Service Order in Council 1995) was the engine.

The Management Code provides for delegated powers from 1 April 1997 over a wide range of human resources issues that the centre traditionally guarded. The Management Code includes the Civil Service Code that sets out the constitutional framework within which all civil servants work and the values they are expected to uphold. It is therefore a centralizing influence. Although the Management Code provides for delegation, the level of delegation was not prescribed. For example, in the case of agencies, the level of delegation to a chief executive is for the respective minister to decide. How far civil service terms and conditions can therefore match local circumstances is a moot point and there is great variation between departments.

In human resources issues, it appears that the pull of the centre is pervasive. Overall, the situation in Scotland is that there were, and are, examples of differentiation but these examples are within the centrally set overarching framework. The levels of differentiation are as high as possible consistent with maintaining a unified service. While delegation of power is acceptable, any moves to creating autonomous civil services within the UK are not: the civil service is the glue, the integrating mechanism, in the British unitary state. The Scottish position is well captured in the view of a senior civil servant: 'we are completely independent in our personnel issues as long as we act within the Management Code' (interview).

The position has not changed with devolution. Scotland travels its own route but the end destination is often the same and, in the case of the civil service (as a reserved power), often prescribed. Here the 'partnership of parliaments' so heralded by the Scotland Office does not fully exist if one takes a defining characteristic of partnership to be the ability of the actors to take independent action.

A series of recent policy and position statements provide an interesting insight into the working arrangements in human resources after devolution and indicates the level of regionalization. Scotland Office (as the Scottish Office was renamed after devolution) staff are 'on loan' from the Scottish Executive to which all Scottish Office civil servants were transferred after devolution. The Office is involved in a recruitment campaign and aims to meet its staffing target by the end of 2003. These targets must be met within the running costs set by the centre. All human resources services for the Office are provided by the Scottish Executive and the Executive's Terms and Conditions of Service code applies. This code is the local reflection of the Civil Service Management Code. Thus, for example, recruitment of Scotland Office staff is in accordance with the Scottish Executive policy; this policy is in accordance with the Civil Service Order in Council 1995. Recruitment to the Scotland Office is therefore based on: candidates being given equal and reasonable access to adequate information about the job and its requirements and about the selection process; applicants being considered equally on merit at each stage of the selection process; relevant criteria applied consistently to all candidates; reliable selection techniques; and the application of equal opportunities policies throughout (Scotland Office 2000a). For staff in the wider Scottish civil service, the Management Code is applied by the relevant department and agency (depending on the level of delegation) taking note of local circumstances.

For the Scottish Executive, the centralizing influence of the Management Code means that human resources policies can reflect local concerns on specific matters within a general framework set elsewhere. The concordat between the Cabinet Office and the Scottish administration makes it very clear that the reserved nature of the civil service is total. The Scottish administration is bound by the Civil Service Order in Council 1995, the Civil Service Management Code, the Civil Service Code, the Civil Service Commissioners' Recruitment Code and the Guidance on Senior Recruitment, the Checklist of Processes for Senior Appointment Selection Committee Appointments and the Superannuation Act 1972.

Devolution did not bring any significant additional powers to Scotland in the organization and management of the civil service. Despite transferring powers to the first minister from the minister for the civil service, the powers dealing with terms and conditions of service were already delegated to the secretary of state for Scotland. Therefore, the Scottish administration finds itself in the pre-devolution situation on human resources issues. Differentiation from Whitehall is arguably greatest for pay arrangements. There is supposedly no constraint on what the administration pays staff outside the senior civil service. However, in practice, the level of differentiation is constrained not only by the Management Code but also by the government's policy stance on public sector pay. Further, the concordat between the Cabinet Office and Scottish administration makes it clear that there will be an exchange of information on civil service pay for comparative purposes (Scottish Executive 1999a). Differentiation will continue to be constrained.

Creating the senior civil service in 1996 was a way of recruiting a cadre of managers from outside the public sector. It brought with it a new pay and allowances system replacing the traditional grading pay scale. It gave Scotland no new powers. Control of this system was not delegated (although departments could, according to Job Evaluation for Senior Posts (JESP) score, establish new senior civil service posts) to ensure parity across the senior civil service. Instead, central government responded to recommendations from the Senior Salaries Review Body (SSRB). The SSRB heard evidence from central government and individual departments and made recommendations on pay levels on an annual basis. These recommendations were considered by central government in light of the general UK economic situation and expenditure plans, and its response applied by the Senior Pay Liaison Group. So the role of departments in determining pay levels for the senior civil service is limited to the departmental evidence

Table 4.2 Distribution of pay awards across the senior civil service as a whole, 2001/02

Tranche	Distribution	Award
1	Top 5%	8.2–11%
2	Next 15–20%	5.6–8.1%
3	Next 60–70%	3.0–5.5%
4	Next 5–15%	0–2.9%

Source: Civil Service Management Code, 7.1: Annex A, Senior Civil Service Pay Framework 2001/2002

submitted to the SSRB, which can plead the case for that department's distinctive needs.

The policy of open competition for senior civil service posts means that pay levels have to be attractive to potential candidates outside the civil service. Pay banding replaced graded salary scales. The level of remuneration for individuals within these bands was based on a system of job evaluation (JESP) and progression was performance related. Permanent secretaries were an exception. Their performance-related pay increases were grouped in a single pay band rather than overlapping pay bands as applied to other levels of the senior civil service.

The situation in Scotland reflected the general UK trend. The majority of senior civil servants were in the lower pay bands and, in the individual pay bands, civil servants were clustered at the lower levels. Further, all departments other than those with small numbers, were required in their 2001/02 pay awards to reflect a general distribution laid down by Cabinet Office (see Table 4.2). The Cabinet Office had the task of ensuring that this distribution was achieved.

As part of the Modernising Government reforms for the civil service, a new performance management and pay system was needed to strengthen the link between remuneration levels and competence-based personnel assessment. The arrangements came into effect on 1 April 2001 with the first payments made from 1 April 2002. The specific drivers of change were that:

> almost exclusive use of consolidated pay awards is an inefficient way of targeting resources; the current pay arrangements are one, though not necessarily the most significant, disincentive to movement to a different job or take on more responsibility; and the pay decision is driving the performance management process; an unhelpful dual market between external and internal SCS [senior civil service] appointments is emerging with the increase in open competition and this is set to continue.
>
> (www.cabinet-office.gov.uk/civilservice/
> scs/documents/htm/comp.htm)

More specifically the following problems also prompted reform:

> flexibilities in the current system mean people find it complicated and difficult to understand; there is too much emphasis on individual JESP points and not a sufficiently understood relationship between job weight and pay band; the recommended pay progression is not working in practice – this demotivates staff; and performance related pay is not linked closely enough to performance to be understood or to provide incentives or rewards.
>
> (ibid.)

The main features of the new system include: a lower emphasis on JESP scores; a reduced number of pay bands that are non-overlapping and are tied to specific JESP scores; minima, maxima and target pay rates; and a greater emphasis on performance management through a new competence framework. Recent work by Parry (2001) shows that in the devolved administrations permanent secretaries are taking a hands-off approach to the new system in that they are not attempting to alter the balance of jobs in the senior civil service, instead preferring to maintain the status quo. We will have to wait to see if this is the favoured strategy or merely a pragmatic response to limit change from the effects of devolution and civil service reform.

Equal opportunities policies within the Scottish administration provide an interesting case in human resources management where 'joined up' working is as much an outcome of a command structure as cooperation. The Scotland Office has pledged in its Service Delivery Agreement to

> work with the Scottish Executive in contributing towards diversity in the Civil Service, including increasing the number of women in senior grades and the proportion of staff from ethnic minority backgrounds or with disabilities . . . Implementation arrangements will be set in place in conjunction with the Executive.
>
> (Scotland Office 2000b: 5)

Equal opportunities is a reserved power. The devolved administration can act on equal opportunities policy, but not legislate. It can impose duties on Scottish public authorities and also on cross-border public bodies that operate in Scotland. However, for the civil service, it is constrained by general equal opportunities policy and by civil service policy. Therefore, there is little differentiation from the centre. The equal opportunities priorities of the Scottish Executive civil service are those set out in the UK government's *Modernising Government* (Cabinet Office 1999b). Differentiation is limited to the particulars of Scottish administration.

The current emphasis of equal opportunities reform of the civil service is diversity. Equal opportunities and diversity are terms commonly used interchangeably but there is a difference: diversity builds on equal opportunities.

Table 4.3 Scottish Executive Diversity Strategy targets

Grade Senior civil service	Women (%)		Ethnic minorities (%)		Disabilities (%)	
	Oct. 2000	April 2005	Oct. 2000	April 2005	Oct. 2000	April 2005
JESP[a] 13[b]	11.4	20.0	No target set		No target set	
All SCS	22.0	30.0	0	1.7	–[b]	3.0
Band C	31.6	43.0	–[b]	1.7	1.1	1.6
Band B	40.0	48.0	0.4	1.7	2.0	3.2
Band A	No target set		0.6	1.7	3.4	5.0

[a] Broadly represents most senior grades from head of group up to permanent secretary
[b] Figures confidential to preserve anonymity
Source: Scottish Executive 2000a

> [E]qual opportunities management . . . concentrates on issues of discrimination, particularly in relation to the law, whereas managing diversity concentrates more on valuing all employees regardless of their background and on helping them to achieve their potential . . . [I]n the civil service there is an observable shift of emphasis towards the latter.
>
> (Cunningham and McMillan 2000: 6)

The Executive's interpretation of *Modernising Government* (1999), *21st Century Government for Scotland* (Scottish Executive 1999b), follows the diversity theme. The programme has four main aims. Government should: work in partnership; be open and accountable; be inclusive; and deliver on its commitments. In order to achieve these aims there should be reform of the civil service in the Scottish administration, and with this in mind, the Executive launched its five-year Diversity Strategy in November 2000 (Scottish Executive 2000a). The Strategy provides for specific diversity targets (see Table 4.3). These differ from the centre only in that the targets reflect local circumstances.

Policy case studies

Economic development

Economic development in Scotland has a long but disjointed history. For the Scottish Executive (2000b), economic development covers: securing economic growth through integrating the Scottish economy within the global economy; ensuring that all regions of Scotland enjoy the same economic opportunities; ensuring that all in society enjoy the same economic opportunities; and the integration of sustainability considerations –

economic, social and environmental. The background to economic development is driven by the political goals of efficiency and equity.

The Executive is trying to provide an integrated and coherent framework within which the promotion of Scottish economic development can
move forward. The main drivers of economic development are said to be:
a supportive macroeconomic environment; supportive national physical,
human and electronic infrastructures; and competitiveness of enterprises
and economic policies to secure favourable social, regional and environmental outcomes (Scottish Executive 2000b). The Executive's definition
does not vary greatly from that held centrally, for example in plans for
regional development agencies outlined in *Our Competitive Future: Building the
Knowledge Driven Economy* (DTI 1998) and *Regional Development Agencies:
Regional Strategies* (DETR 1999).

Two of these drivers to economic development are outwith the direct
responsibilities of the Scottish administration. First, macroeconomic policy
is a concern of the UK government, which in turn is influenced by EU
policy. Second, there is now considerable consensus that private enterprise
should be the primary driver of economic growth, but the competitiveness
of enterprises is not wholly within the gift of public policy (Scottish Executive 2000b). So, the influence of the Scottish administration on outcomes appears limited.

Yet, by the mid-1980s the Scottish Office had accrued considerable
powers in economic development issues, not least in the administration of
grant aid. Control of economic development was as much within the gift
of the territorial ministry as could be expected in a unitary state. The civil
service worked with and through other actors (public and private) to
deliver economic development opportunities. Network administration has
also been a feature of Scottish Office working more generally. In this way,
Scottish civil servants already have the skills that are now highlighted by
Whitehall as crucial to the modernizing agenda. Network administration
for economic development is clearly a successful governing structure. The
approach and policies helped reinvigorate the Scottish economy and, while
there have been hiccups in some policy outcomes, the fact that well over
100,000 jobs have accrued is testament to its success. Network administration of economic development continued after devolution. In the devolution debate of the 1970s, one fear was that devolution would lessen the
capacity to manage the economic development network and lessen Scottish
Office influence in Whitehall. There is no doubt that the Scottish civil
service did have considerable influence not only on economic development
policy in Scotland but also on the definitions, understandings and policy
initiatives of Whitehall.

The impact of civil servants on policy formation and implementation did not dissipate with devolution. Continued network working was
an operational necessity if nothing more. The current network arrangements for economic development are partly an outcome of the pre-existing

administrative arrangements. Along with the new Department for Enterprise and Lifelong Learning and Scottish Executive Development Department, the core network consists of Scottish Enterprise and Highlands
and Islands Enterprise. These two non-departmental public bodies became
operational in April 1991 (see Figure 4.1).

The enterprise bodies operate through contractual arrangements with
local enterprise councils (LECs). There are 22 LECs in Scotland, 12 linked
to Scottish Enterprise and 10 to Highlands and Islands Enterprise. Of the
two enterprise bodies the Highlands and Islands board probably most closely
reflects the all-encompassing definition of economic development. Not only
does it act in the belief that the Highlands and Islands is a distinct area with
specific issues but, unlike Scottish Enterprise, it is also concerned with
social well-being, so it has a broader remit and can support projects that
will bring social as well as economic improvement.

Here it is useful to distinguish between the enterprise network and
economic development network. The former may be considered the implementation network and the latter the administrative network. The administrative network includes local authorities and private sector businesses
and organizations. The implementation network includes the organizations
formally charged with responsibility for economic development initiatives.

Herein lies a problem. The Framework

> provides the approach of the Executive in answer to the questions
> 'What are we seeking to achieve through economic development?'
> and 'What are the key channels through which this can be achieved?'
> It provides a vision and the Framework within which the primary
> objectives will be approached. It does not address the next set of ques-
> tions that are of critical importance: namely, 'What are the specific
> initiatives that need to be designed and promoted to achieve these
> objectives?' and 'Who is best placed to drive forward the policies and
> programmes that are needed to bring sustained progress?'
>
> (Scottish Executive 2000b: 75)

Scottish economic development is delivered through a network that
has a mish-mash of accountabilities and reporting relationships. The split
between policy formulation and implementation raises the question of
whether a coherent approach is possible at Executive level. Also, there is
still scope for civil servants to play a significant role in formulation and
implementation, exacerbating the problem of strategic control. Scottish economic development continues to be characterized by vagaries in political
control in two ways. The first concerns the organization of the function at
Executive level, and the second the level of political control that can be
exerted on the implementation and administrative networks.

Evidence suggests that devolution may bring a subtle shift in the
role of the economic development network. This change is precipitated
by the Executive's wish to be more inclusive in policy development and

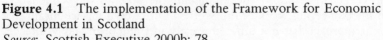

The Scottish Executive

Framework for Economic
Development in Scotland

Thematic work on specific objectives

Within the Executive and beyond:

- Skills for employment in schools, further education and higher education
- Rural Scotland
- Sustainable development and the environmental challenge
- Support to business: the creation and nurturing of enterprises
- Commercialization of knowledge and innovation
- The demands of the information age, including e-commerce
- Export promotion
- Inward investment

Sectoral work on specific objectives

Within the Executive and beyond:

- The provision of integrated transport services
- Cluster policy and of other sector-specific initiatives
- The promotion of tourism

The champions of economic development

The institutional roles and responsibilities in driving development:

- The Scottish Executive
- Scottish Enterprise
- Highlands and Islands Enterprise
- Other economic development bodies
- Local authorities

Figure 4.1 The implementation of the Framework for Economic Development in Scotland
Source: Scottish Executive 2000b: 78

implementation. It is also shaped by Labour's Modernising Government agenda. As a senior civil servant remarked:

> [S]ince Labour came in in '97 the emphasis has been on joining up, pulling policies together. It is hard to say if we had not had devolution this would not have happened anyway. But what is true is that the people on the street are more aware of the Scottish Parliament than they were of the Scottish Office and there is more expectation to be joined up from the public.
>
> (interview)

The subtle shifts brought about by devolution concern degree rather than direction. For the implementation network, there is a move to strengthen political control. This is not aimed against the network but to give clearer direction so network actors achieve their aims. There is still considerable scope for the network actors to put the flesh on the bones of policy initiatives. This scope extends to the administrative network. The economic development network may not be driving the agenda but neither are the politicians. Mutual steering is the dominant operating code through partnership working, for as a senior civil servant confirmed, 'even if the minister had a particular hobby-horse policy, I am not sure how far this could be articulated and implemented without full support of the network' (interview).

For civil servants, influence is now more closely tied to the style of the ministers responsible for economic development matters. There is a perception that ministers are now closer to the action. In some instances, this perception has brought a partnership approach between politician and administrator, but where the minister has no clear preference for policy initiatives then the civil servant retains considerable influence in policy development and implementation. It is the civil service that takes the lead in network management by identifying key actors for any specific economic development policy initiative. Such network management is critical as 'there is always consultation before political decisions are made' (interview).

The influence of the civil service on differentiated economic development policies for Scotland is not a recent development. The Scottish Office civil servants influenced the definition and understandings of economic development for many years. Scotland was always ahead of Whitehall in developing strategies that delivered economic development rather than the somewhat narrower concept of industrial development. A good example is in the definition of economic development as covering planning and regeneration (the work of visionary Scottish civil servant Robert Grieve, chief planner in the Scottish Development Department).

However, in economic development, the take-up by Whitehall of some of the pioneering work of the Scottish Office civil service meant that the overall approach has not differed greatly in Edinburgh and Whitehall. Whitehall's aspiration to control economic development is long-standing.

For example, the 1953 Royal Commission on Scottish Administration concluded that:

> industrial development in Scotland must remain primarily the responsibility of the Board of Trade though that department's Scottish presence should be strengthened . . . London control had to be the way of steering industry northwards.
>
> (Gibson 1985: 125)

In this way the centre wanted to rein back Scotland and maintain the idea that economic development was best served by strategies controlled by Whitehall because it could play the overseer role whereas that territorial ministries could not.

Although there are examples of policy differentiation and the influence of the civil service, the critical point for economic development may come with different governing parties in Edinburgh and Westminster.

Community care

Community care policy in Scotland is distinctive and has been since the NHS and Community Care Act 1990 carried special provisions to reflect the Scottish local government system and previous specialist legislation. The special provisions cover: the power of the secretary of state to give directions; local authority plans for, and complaints in relation to, community care services; inspection of premises providing accommodation; inquiries; duty of local authorities to make the assessment of needs; and residential accommodation with nursing and provision of care and aftercare. Under the terms of the Act, local authorities and the NHS (through district health authorities, family health service authorities and health boards) were identified as the main agencies. Local authorities were identified as the lead agency in terms of provision, planning and needs assessment.

Initially, community care policy was concerned with health and housing, and the respective Scottish Office ministers led policy area developments. Its administration was multifaceted. The development of community care after 1993 was expeditious. For the civil service the results were perverse. As a senior civil servant confirmed:

> [E]arly on in community care we tried to do too much too quickly. In 1993, there was a lot of ambiguity about community care at all levels – providers and policy-makers. This took us the wrong way initially towards a needs-led service and worse still a needs-led service with no cash limits. It was misleading. It's hard to explain why people can't have services when there's no money left in the overall budget. We had no HRM [human resources management] strategy for changing residential carers into home carers.
>
> (interview)

Civil service influence partly reflected the fact that policy was split between three departments and a territorial overview of community care provision and no single minister or department had overall responsibility. First, the Scottish Development Department was responsible for housing and local government organization and finance, in particular, sponsoring Scottish Homes. Second, the Department of Health was responsible for health policy and all matters to do with the NHS. Third, the Home Department was responsible for social work services. As a major policy area, vesting community care policy in one department would unbalance again the long-cherished departmental equilibrium of the Scottish Office. The fact that community care was a 'new' policy area compounded the problem.

However, the problem of community care administration was not unique to the territorial ministry. There were also problems in the parent departments in Whitehall. There was a lack of 'joined-upness'. Also, the civil service had to build a network and choose its members. Initially, the civil service struggled to identify a small representative sample of all actors and interested parties to develop policy initiatives. The policy area was subject to piecemeal change by individual actors rather than strategic policy development. Of the constituent nations of the UK, England has suffered most from the 'Whitehall' factor. There is no England mechanism, only a UK mechanism within UK departments.

In Scotland, within the civil service, the fragmented administrative arrangements resulted in a negative way of looking at policy. Civil servants started from the premise of what cannot be done rather than what can and needs to be done. Nonetheless, too much was attempted too quickly, resulting in the belief that the policy area was just too big, too complex and too unmanageable (interview). Such negative views helped to create the impression among all the major actors that community care was failing. After five years of community care, the transfer of people from hospital care to residential care was slow, hindered by clearly identifiable organizational and managerial constraints.

The history of civil service involvement in community care policy shows two major influences: the modernization agenda and devolution. Evidence suggests that both have had an impact on the relationship between the civil service and politicians but on different facets of that relationship. The modernization agenda in community care reflects UK developments. The joined up government part of the agenda has had an impact on civil service workings and influence. *Modernising Community Care: An Action Plan* (Scottish Office 1998) (a Scottish Office leap into the modernization dark) gave a parochial twist to joining up by promoting a 'tartan' of services. To create such a tartan, community care actors had to consider carefully their role and what community care represents. A new way of approaching community care emerged, in essence involving a move from a top-down approach to a bottom-up approach. The emphasis moved from civil service concern with the administrative structures of community care to what makes sense at local level. The drive for change now comes from the community care network through the public's experiences of community care policy. The civil service has become more pivotal because emphasis is on network management through consultation and negotiation. Thus, the civil service legitimizes network members when it invites them to join the new inclusive modern policy-making process (interview).

The reforms of *Modernising Community Care* were expected to continue after devolution. As the authoring minister stated:

> [T]his action plan is very much a response to the particular circumstances of Scotland. We recognise that the Scottish Parliament may want to look again at the wider range of options, including structural change. But our emphasis in this action plan is on improving results in the short to medium term using existing structures.
>
> (Scottish Office 1998: 7)

This leap into the dark was therefore a stop-gap measure in community care reform.

With devolution, the priority given to the policy rose considerably. Although there are now eight ministers with an impact on community care provision, the policy area has been given a dedicated department and senior and junior ministers. The Scottish Executive Health Department has responsibility for social work policy and community care, and the minister and deputy have community care named in their official titles. Although there is still, by the nature of the policy area, a division of influence on community care, there is the structural capacity within government to provide the strategic leadership that has been lacking for so long.

There has been a discernible policy shift since devolution. Along with the modernization agenda, the Scottish administration has also introduced structural reform. Structural reform was presaged in a White Paper, *Aiming for Excellence: Modernising Social Work Services in Scotland* (Scottish Executive 1999c). The most important structural reform is the regulation of care services, where the main problems highlighted were lack of independence, consistency and integration (Scottish Office 1998). Reform included the proposed creation of a Scottish Commission for the Regulation of Care (SCRC), Scottish Social Services Council (SSSC) and a National Care Standards Committee. The SCRC would deal with regulation of care services whereas the SSSC would deal with regulation of staff. The National Care Standards Committee would develop standards for the services regulated by the SCRC. The Scottish Administration announced this change in policy focus with the position paper *The Way Forward for Care* (Scottish Executive 2000c). The Regulation of Care Bill was enacted by the Scottish Parliament in May 2001. The SCRC became operational on 1 April 2002 and the SSSC on 1 October 2001.

So, devolution has not yet led to great policy differentiation between Scotland and the other nations of the UK, though change is imminent.

Several examples are in the pipeline, such as the joining up of community care regulation. However, the reality of service provision means that there will be an interface between devolved and reserved powers that will limit the distinctiveness of Scottish policy. As a senior civil servant commented:

> [I]t may not be centralisation as such but there will be times, depending on circumstance, where the centre will have to take the lead. A recent example concerns those living in unregistered accommodation and access to benefits. This is a UK issue.
>
> (interview)

Initial indications suggest that there has not been a great change in the role of the civil service in policy development and implementation. Where there appear to be changes, they are of degree rather than direction. First, ministers exercise greater scrutiny over the civil service:

> [T]here are now 29 ministers as opposed to 5 before devolution. They are also better informed from outside the civil service so we have to be on our mettle. But this can also be down to general change in government. It's also true for Whitehall.
>
> (interview)

Second, the community care network in Scotland is changing. The internal dynamics have not bedded down after the changing organizational structures. Within the network, the role of local government is being affected by the 'ad hockery' of performance management. Local government organizations are struggling to find the information to fit the new measures that have not been part of the traditional system of performance management through the annual report and accounts (interview). The civil service has continued to have the prime rule in the network and, post devolution, is setting up the new network by deciding who will be consulted, although there is evidence of inputs from the Scottish Parliament and its relevant committees. Third, and related to the above, influence of the civil service on policy implementation is maintained through the change process. However, the genesis of such change may be linked more to the modernization agenda than to devolution. So, after devolution, the role of the civil service in policy development and implementation is changing and the distinctiveness of Scottish government continues to evolve.

Devolution: where are we going?

On devolution, Scottish Office civil servants transferred to the new parliamentary structures. However, simultaneously, they remain part of a unified UK Civil Service. A confused situation currently reigns. The operational position of the civil service was not considered in great depth in the negotiations about the Scottish administration's roles and powers. Although concordats have been developed for day-to-day relationships between Edinburgh and London, they cannot possibly cover every eventuality.

The problem of who does what was illustrated by Angus MacKay MSP, the then deputy minister for justice, when on the morning of 24 July 2000 he gave a press statement on the Register of Child Sex Offenders vowing to aid central government in its development. The reason given: the Register is a reserved power. By the afternoon of 24 July 2000, Mr MacKay was again in front of the press explaining that in fact the Register is a devolved responsibility. Whichever argument you favour, minister leading civil servant or vice versa, on this important issue it is clear that on the morning of 24 July neither knew their responsibilities.

The failure to anticipate possible problems in relationships with Whitehall post devolution is best shown by the proposed non-solution to the accountability of civil servants. In an attempt to clarify the 'regionalness' of the civil service, a 'loyalty' solution has been put forward (Scottish Executive 1999a). This solution means that civil servants will have to delineate between 'practical loyalty' (to the minister they serve) and 'ultimate loyalty' (to the Crown). Although the concordat between the Cabinet Office and Scottish administration states that duty to the Crown is owed through the administration that the civil servants serve, the reserved nature of civil service policy means that practical loyalty and ultimate loyalty may not be seen as the same thing, with ultimate loyalty being linked to Whitehall. And how to define practical and ultimate loyalty?

The modernization agenda and 'joined up government' have important implications for the civil service in the devolved administration. It will be hard to promote the 'joined up regionalness' the government seems to favour. We have seen that some policies are already regionalized, and with devolution it may be expected that this regionalization will be strengthened. In Scotland, 'joined up regionalness' will require integrating mechanisms that may, first, reduce regionalness and, second, add to the number of mechanisms to be coordinated. The centre's preferred solution to problems of governance may thus breed more problems.

With recent reform the civil service may become less unified. It is increasingly being touted that a break up of the unified civil service is the likely outcome of the devolution agenda. For example, Hazell and Morris (1999: 19) argue that:

> the conventions of a permanent, anonymous and apolitical service operating in a confidential relationship with whichever government is in power have themselves been the products of a particular constitutional arrangement. The more the arrangement is altered, the more the conventions themselves come under stress . . . [The] unified civil service is likely to divide into a separate civil service in Scotland and Wales, similar to the Northern Ireland Civil Service.

Further, they add that:

it is not difficult to see how the new dynamic released by devolution will, together with the demands of the rest of the programme of constitutional change, amount to a fundamental shift in the way that Whitehall works – and provide the context for Sir Richard Wilson's next review.

(ibid.)

It is too early to draw conclusions about devolution project but the desire to achieve 'joined up' government in Scotland has various likely outcomes. First, the civil service could maintain its current level of 'regionalness' (echoing a concordat commitment to maintaining a unified service). Second, the civil service could pull away from central control. To go down this road is to raise the spectre of independence. This concern may explain the 'reserved' powers and Joint Ministerial Committee, which are clearly bulwarks against further separation. The 'reserved' powers of the civil service and EU relations are critical. Thus, the first minister was not delegated any more powers pertaining to the civil service than those that were previously vested in the secretary of state for Scotland.

There is a third possible outcome: that the civil service in Scotland will not remain as a *civil service* either unified or separate but will become part of a unified *public service* in Scotland. Such a move would bring together central and local government, the NHS and a range of other public bodies (Ryan 1999). Scotland would be modernizing government and achieving a 'joined up' public service. This 'joined-upness' will be limited to Scotland, help to create a territorial polity, and so may fuel fears of a break-up of the UK.

Hazell and Morris (1999) argue that, post-devolution, civil service scrutiny will increase substantially, bringing with it fears of creeping politicization. In the Scottish case there is evidence that while the number and type of scrutiny measures may not have changed dramatically thus far (other than in, perhaps, the presence of an official national opposition in Parliament), the fact that ministers are 'on the doorstep' means that civil servants perceive there is a higher level of scrutiny. Further, that perception may carry through into a greater desire to 'please someone now sitting across the table from you' (interview). Such fears of politicization are, it seems, also felt at the highest level, as the concordat between the Cabinet Office and Scottish administration highlights cooperation as a way of maintaining impartiality (Scottish Executive 1999a).

Devolution in Scotland brought with it the feeling that 'devolution must work' (interview). The civil service and Scottish Executive appear keen to cooperate towards this end. How far such cooperation will continue when roles are more firmly set remains to be seen. If and when politicians become more dominant in the policy process and challenge the traditionally strong role of the civil service in the Scottish polity such a collegiate attitude may dissipate. There is obvious room for conflict as there is also a desire on the part of civil servants to remain as part of a UK service. Even in devolved systems the pull of the centre is strong.

Conclusions

The Scottish civil service has several distinctive characteristics. The Scottish civil service was differentiated from the Whitehall-based unified civil service. The Scottish Office civil service was differentiated from the other branches of the civil service in Scotland, and the Scottish Office civil service was itself differentiated by long-held departmental autonomy. Such differentiation is not a new feature of the operational realities of Scottish government. The degree of differentiation has grown in recent times but the evidence is contradictory. If devolution sustains differentiation, then Labour's modernization agenda is a centralizing influence. However, the fact remains that civil service differentiation has been and remains a feature of the operation of UK government.

5

Wales

Introduction

Y Ddraig Goch, the Red Dragon, was brought to Wales by the Romans over 1800 years ago, and was adopted by the British kings. It was, so tradition says, the flag of Arthur and Cadwallader from whom the Tudors claimed their ancestry and the right to the throne . . . As a point of entry into understanding the complex nature of Welsh identity, the Red Dragon is, perhaps, as good as any other. For a country whose identity has for so long been virtual, rather than institutionally or politically meaningful and real, the mythical beast is a somewhat appropriate symbol to represent Wales. The dragon exists as a state of mind, rather than as an actual living, breathing creature.

(Parsons 1998: 25)

The Government of Wales Act 1998 changed all that. It followed the 1997 referendum vote in favour of devolution, gave political and institutional form and substance to the Welsh dragon. In order to understand a nation's public administration it is necessary to understand its politics. In order to understand its politics, it is necessary to know the institutional, cultural and historical context in which it is situated. For more than a millennium, the Cymru (or 'compatriots') represented the surviving remnants of the native Celtic British nation, language and culture. Linked to, but distinct from, the Scottish Gaels, and the Celtic peoples of Ireland, Cornwall, the Channel Islands and Brittany, the Welsh retained a linguistic and cultural separateness while experiencing political absorption following their annexation by the Norman-English king Edward I in 1282–83. Indeed, the name 'Wales' means 'stranger' or 'foreigner' and is taken from the Saxon 'welisc' or 'wealh' (Parsons 1998: 25–59).

The Tudor Acts of Union of 1536 and 1543 provided the Welsh with equal political and civil rights with the English, but at the expense of their continuing political dependence on England. Although never a unified and independent country like Scotland, the gradual search for ways to protect and enhance their nationhood led the Welsh along a tangential route to devolution. The extension of administrative devolution, represented by the Welsh Office, through to political devolution has important repercussions for the arguments of this book. The implementation of political, or what is sometimes called 'democratic', devolution

> significantly enhances the notion of the 'differentiated polity' because it adds a territorial dimension to what tends to be a largely functional conception of governance. In fact it is possible to discern the beginnings, however tentative, of a multi-level polity in the European Union that straddles local, regional, national and supranational levels of governance. In this polity, one of the key issues is the application of subsidiarity, the principle that commends the devolution of power to the lowest level that is capable of executing it effectively.
>
> (Morgan and Rees 2001: 163)

This chapter explores some of the more recent imperatives towards institutional and political devolution; discusses the implications of these trends for the UK's national unified civil service; and finally provides case studies of economic development and community care.

The context of devolution

The impact of devolution will take many years to work through to some kind of conclusion. The one thing that may be asserted without fear of contradiction is that the UK's civil service will be irrevocably changed by it. The move of the Welsh Office and other civil servants to Cardiff represented more than a geographical relocation, it also established a new locus of accountability. Whatever the Government of Wales Act 1998 may say about sovereignty and power remaining in London, the reality is that Welsh civil servants, like their Scottish colleagues, now have a dual allegiance: an amorphous one to the Crown, and a practical day-to-day allegiance to Cardiff and Cymru.

The ripples and eddies formed by the settling down of the constitutional settlement seek 'to reconcile two seemingly conflicting principles, the sovereignty or supremacy of Parliament and the grant of self-government in domestic affairs to Scotland, Wales and Northern Ireland' (Bogdanor

1999: 1). The product of this settlement is a developing quasi-federal relationship in which any attempt to impose their will and vindicate their
power by the Westminster-based ministers will be deemed illegitimate and
resisted in Scotland and Wales (pp. 287–93). The observation of Madgwick
and Rose (1982: 1) that 'territory is important politically' seems almost a
truism when applied to the discussion of Welsh devolution, in that:

> The land contributes to national identity and images and symbols of
> community. Politicians demand equitable treatment of all regions of a
> country, and institutions of governance must be able to deliver the
> benefits of public policy to all of its parts.
>
> (Madgwick and Rose 1982: 1)

An understanding of the background to devolution and the impact it has
on the Home Civil Service, must begin with recognizing the territorial
context.

We have entered the era of intergovernmental diplomacy and governance through persuasion, an era that will witness increasing constraints on
Westminster and a time where Whitehall's writ will not run automatically
beyond Offa's Dyke and Hadrian's Wall. In seeking to secure agreements
for policy formulation and implementation, senior Whitehall officials will
now need to cross the domestic borders as emissaries, not as proconsuls.
Devolution and attendant redefinition of the role of the British civil service
represents the most substantial addition to the process of the hollowing out
of the state since Britain signed the Treaty of Rome in 1972.

Background to devolution: the civil service tradition in Wales

Nationalism is an atavistic elemental movement (Rokkan and Urwin 1982:
1–19, 19–74). If the Red Dragon represents the fiery element of a cultural
and historical dynamic towards Welsh national consciousness, rather more
prosaical considerations concerning land (or land use) and water provided part
of the wider political context. Certainly the attempts of previous English
(and Welsh) political leaders to eradicate the Welsh language were motivated by a misguided notion of seeing Britishness as Englishness. They
backfired spectacularly, leading to the establishment of Plaid Cymru in
1925 (Madgwick and Rawkins 1982: 67–100; Parsons 1998). In the fifteenth
and sixteenth centuries the Tudors had defined Wales as a part of England
because, as a partly Welsh dynasty, they sought to undermine any alternative
power bases, but Elizabeth Tudor's insistence on having the Bible translated
into Welsh provided a solid foundation for the preservation of the language
and culture. It was the insensitivity of the late Victorians' imperial and
unionist perspective that led to the resurrection of demands for institutional
recognition of Wales's separateness (Davies 1993; Parsons 1998; Bogdanor

1999). Unionist politicians and Whitehall's civil servants stressed the benefits of a unified civil service, resenting any division of authority and arguing that the situation in Wales was not sufficiently unique to justify a separate administration 'merely' to recognize a Welsh national identity (Randall 1972: 335–72).

The Industrial Revolution transformed South Wales. Its coal mines provided raw material for the furnaces of its iron and steel mills and these in turn built the heavy industries of the principality, exporting to England and the Empire. Welsh prosperity was dependent upon the economic integration of Wales into the wider British and imperial economy (Parsons 1988; Davies 1993). Large numbers of immigrants moved to industrial South Wales from other parts of the UK (and beyond) in the latter half of the nineteenth century. This established what Chaney et al. (2001: 4) described as Welsh Wales, the industrial heartland. The other parts they describe as the linguistic heartland of the West and North Wales (Y Fro Gymraeg) and an eastern, more Anglicized border (2001: 4).

The Welsh defined themselves as Welsh through their Britishness, but successive Welsh politicians sought to obtain a voice for Wales in London, and through that in the wider world in order to protect and advance Wales's economic well-being. It was this unspoken policy of the Welsh political elite that had been pursued from the time of the first Tudor king, Henry VII (r. 1485–1509). These politicians included the nationalist-minded David Lloyd George, who eventually forsook the cause of Cymru for the imperial residence in Downing Street (Parsons 1998). For much of the last century-and-a-half, therefore, successive Welsh political leaders in the Liberal and Labour parties have been opposed to Home Rule, seeing it as weakening the UK as a whole and thereby weakening Wales (Randall 1972; Parsons 1998).

It is no accident that Plaid Cymru was formed during the depressed interwar years. The massive economic dislocation, indeed industrial reversal, led to the permanent emigration of over 400,000 people, out of a population of under 3 million (Parsons 1998). The decline of heavy industry has never been reversed. In fact, it accelerated throughout the 1970s and 1980s. As the British economy restructured during the 1980s, the heartland of heavy industry, both manufacturing and extractive, were hardest hit (Gamble 1988; Parsons 1988), while unemployment and poverty in South and central Wales soared. At the same time, first hill farmers and then agriculture generally, entered an economic depression that profoundly damaged the economy of North and West Wales.

The earlier benefits of integration with England now bore a high economic cost. There was no institutional representation for Wales that could be used to mitigate the costs. From the Great Depression onwards there began an agitation for some kind of political recognition of Welsh separateness. In other words, a mechanism was sought to allow a greater measure of self-determination over the economy and land use (Randall

1972). The behaviour of certain utilities and quangos, especially the water authorities and railways from the end of the First World War, exacerbated Welsh sensibilities. The closure of much of the Welsh rail network caused discontent in rural areas. The decisions by essentially English utilities to dam Welsh valleys in order to provide water for English conurbations was deeply resented and led to calls for a Welsh Office along the lines of the Scottish Office (Randall 1972; Rowlands 1972).

Welsh political leaders saw the need for establishing a method of control over Welsh affairs in order to prevent the continued subordination of Welsh interests to those of England. Influential sections of the Welsh political elite sought greater control over the officials who made and implemented policies in Wales. Instead of simply seeking to influence events by representation in London, they now additionally and successfully sought to have those officials institutionally located in a Welsh Office. On occasion, commentators have dismissed the Welsh Office as a Raj style of governance, at once attempting to be the voice of Wales in Whitehall and the eyes and ears of Whitehall in Wales (Morgan and Rees 2001: 130). However, the 'real historical significance of the Welsh Office was that it furnished an institutional framework within which a Welsh system of governance could develop' (Morgan and Rees 2001: 131), thereby illustrating the political importance of institutions, and imbuing them with a significance beyond their simple administrative structure and organizational role.

Wales gained its first secretary of state, James Griffith, in 1964, when the incoming Labour government of Harold Wilson established the Welsh Office (Kellas and Madgwick 1982: 7–34). Previously, there had been a gradual institutionalization of Welsh public administration. In 1907, a Welsh Department of Education had been set up and, in 1919, a Board of Health in Wales, to be followed in 1946 with the establishment of Welsh Regional Hospital Boards (Parsons 1998; Griffiths 1999: 800–3). Both Education and Health were reluctant to devolve, despite the fact that, from the beginning, these quasi-departments were given a great deal of devolved administrative power to deliver services within the broad framework of policy set out by the parent department in London. 'Indeed the latter was a microcosm of the Whitehall department, exercising within Wales the full range of administrative tasks of the central department' (Rowlands 1972: 334).

These administrative developments were followed in 1948 by the establishment of the Wales Gas Board and the creation in 1951 by Winston Churchill of a minister for Welsh affairs in the Home Office (Parsons 1998: 28–50). In 1955, Cardiff was established as the capital city, although its historical rivals fiercely contested its claim to this honour.

It must be emphasized, however, that these were institutional changes, a decentralization of public administration, not devolution proper. Subsequent events, however, demonstrate the importance of institutions for acting as a focus and catalyst for radical change. Even though the 1949 campaign for a Welsh parliament, launched by Undeb Cymru Fydd, was largely ignored, Plaid Cymru took up the refrain, gaining their first seat in Parliament in 1966, taking the Carmarthen constituency away from Labour at a by-election.

Part of the reason for the growth of calls for Home Rule in the 1960s was a perceived weakness of the Welsh Office in its dealings with Whitehall. Although Labour's 1964 manifesto envisaged executive responsibility for the Welsh Office over housing, local government, health, education and agriculture, the large Whitehall spending departments sought to restrict the role of the Welsh Office to that of a watchdog with 'a general oversight function over all government activities as they affect Wales' (Rowlands 1972: 334). The shock engendered by Plaid Cymru's victory at Carmarthen enabled Griffith and his successors to extract some real executive power from Whitehall. Even so, it still took nearly four years for the secretary of state for Wales to assume significant responsibility for education and health in Wales. Even then the secretaries of state for education and health based in London retained ultimate control for policy-making in these fields, regardless of Welsh interests or perceptions.

A large part of the difficulty experienced by the Welsh Office to establish itself in its early days reflected the fact that it found itself in the midst of an old-fashioned Whitehall turf war. The UK's civil service, far from being unitary and centralized, has long been fragmented between rival departments. The explosion of agencies and quangos since 1980 has exacerbated the process of fragmentation. The governance of Wales and Northern Ireland acted as a precursor to this recent development. Discrete parts of departments were split off to oversee the implementation of policy in the principality and province. They were left to their own devices, provided they did not intrude on the 'high politics' practised in London. These administrative fragments behaved in similar ways to the Next Steps agencies that were to be set up in the 1980s and 1990s; indeed, many of them went on to become agencies, while others were formed into or amalgamated with quangos.

The (often quite junior) officials in charge of these decentralized units were reluctant to devolve because their distance from London and the autonomy given to them allowed them to exercise a great deal of discretion. In the case of education, for example:

The Welsh Secretary (Assistant Under-Secretary rank) and his staff have enjoyed an enormous influence over educational policy in Wales. The Secretaries have been able to report directly to the Secretary of State for Education. They have also been major public figures in the Principality. The department did not volunteer to be taken over by the Welsh Office and, until the major transfer of functions in November 1970, had always attempted to keep a good arm's length distance from the expanding Welsh Office.

(Rowlands 1972: 335)

In other words, the establishment of the Welsh Office looked set to curb the autonomy of the principality's fragmented public administration and begin a process of restoring a degree of day-to-day accountability through the responsibility of the new secretary of state. In fact the Welsh Office never successfully carried out this role of what later became termed 'joined up government' (Morgan and Rees 2001: 138–71).

Such a move would have been viewed as a retrograde step by the officials and professionals involved, individuals who would have been motivated to seek professional autonomy and to seek to minimize their accountability to politicians (Massey 1988: 93). It does seem, however, that the attempt to coordinate the delivery of services in Wales with Whitehall's central policies was responsible for the resurgence of an older deference to Whitehall. This permeated the new Welsh Office. Rhodri Morgan, the Assembly's second first minister, explored this issue after devolution when he sought to establish some independence for Welsh civil servants. He recalled:

> In the Scottish Office, which had been around for 100 years, they had developed a tradition of independent policy. The Welsh Office had no capability of policy making at all in the late 1960s. Likewise you promoted staff in the Scottish Office on the basis that they had put one over Whitehall. You promoted staff in the Welsh Office on the basis of whether they had kept their noses clean with Whitehall.
>
> (Morgan, cited in Osmond 2000: 13)

Successive Welsh secretaries of state (with some notable exceptions) had to overcome this cultural hurdle in order to be effective. They did so by slowly creating a new culture, one that emphasized the distinctiveness of Wales and the 'Welshness' of their policy objectives: they cultivated allegiance to Cymru (Walker 1991; Griffiths 1999: 793–808).

By the 1980s and Peter Walker's tenure as Welsh secretary, it was claimed that Walker was able to act within the principality almost as prime minister, chancellor and cabinet rolled into one (Griffiths 1999). Walker claimed he had a free hand to carry out a range of interventionist policies denied to his colleagues in other departments. Research into the claims for this Welsh policy exceptionalism, however, tends to suggest it has not been as pronounced as Walker and others (such as Griffiths (1996)) have claimed. Recent studies of education and housing illustrate more convergence than divergence between England and Wales (Griffiths 1996). Those in favour of devolution argued the need to make those policy-makers responsible for Wales more directly accountable to the people of Wales rather than to the Westminster MPs (Parsons 1998; Rhodri Morgan, quoted in Morgan and Rees 2001: 130–70). In other words, the decentralization of administrative activities to Welsh-based institutions provided some autonomy and flexibility in the administration of public services, but this did not extend to policy formulation, or even to policy variation to any great extent.

By 1970, an extensive range of public sector activities were supervised or coordinated by the Welsh Office. In addition to health and education, they included agricultural issues, economic and industrial planning, energy, trade, transport and forestry. Rowlands (1972: 27) argued that these activities enabled the secretary of state to prevent overexploitation of Welsh water resources in favour of thirsty English conurbations, as well as to ensure Welsh representation on all important policy matters relevant to the principality. But the fact remained that the line of accountability was to London. Furthermore, the 'quangoization' of Welsh public administration buttressed the patronage power of ministers, including the secretary of state for Wales, but it did not address the call to make Welsh governance accountable to the Welsh people. A series of notable scandals regarding the Welsh Development Agency exacerbated this situation (Chaney *et al.* 2001). The 1997 referendum, followed by the Government of Wales Act 1998 were designed to address (though not redress) that grievance.

After devolution

From the perspective of Plaid Cymru and many of those in favour of devolution, the whole purpose of establishing the Welsh Assembly was to secure autonomy in domestic policy matters. Such autonomy implies ensuring the civil service is directed according to Welsh interests and is therefore accountable to the Assembly. The traditional basis of accountability, however, is to secure the redress of grievance before the granting of supply. Without the power of the purse there is no funding for grand policy designs, and the Government of Wales Act 1998 made it clear that London would retain ultimate power over national policy-making and all power over taxation. The Assembly has the power of subordinate legislation, that is statutory instruments, while primary legislation remains the prerogative of Westminster (Bogdanor 1999: 209–10).

As with the provisions for Scotland under the *Scotland Act 1998*, the civil service remains under the formal control of the Cabinet Office in London and the secretary of state for Wales, who retains responsibility for primary legislation. However, there is a radically changing perception of the public sector and civil service. Although London retains responsibility for enacting primary legislation, its implementation and most secondary legislation are now the responsibility of the Assembly. Consequently, the oversight and accountability functions to which public officials are subjected must now include the Assembly for those officials based in Wales engaged upon Welsh business. This latter point is of course distinct from those carrying out UK business having been simply geographically relocated, such as the people employed by the Driving and Vehicle Licensing Agency in Swansea.

Part two of the *Concordat between the Cabinet Office and the Cabinet of the National Assembly for Wales* (Cabinet Office 1999d), attempts to clarify the management of the Home Civil Service under the new conditions pertaining to it. Paragraph eleven states:

> Staff at the National Assembly for Wales are Crown servants and part of a unified Civil Service. The Prime Minister as the Minister for the Civil Service is responsible for civil servants, advised by the Head of the Home Civil Service. The Minister for the Cabinet Office discharges, on a day-to-day basis, the responsibilities of the Minister for the Civil Service. As servants of the Crown all civil servants owe a duty of loyalty to the Crown.

Paragraph twelve proceeds to labour the point by stating:

> The management of the Home Civil Service is therefore a matter reserved to the UK Government. The National Assembly for Wales is bound by the legislative framework governing the Home Civil Service.

This includes compliance with the various orders in council and codes governing recruitment and conduct. Yet the *Memorandum* (Cabinet Office 1999e) does recognize the reality of the transfer of functions to the principality and the attendant need to accept flexible structures within the UK Civil Service, noting that the

> Minister for the Civil Service has, however, delegated to the National Assembly for Wales the responsibility for a wide range of terms and conditions of service for staff of the National Assembly for Wales.
>
> (paragraph 113)

Further, it notes that 'both parties mutually affirm their mutual commitment to working together to maintain a unified Home Civil Service and their recognition of the collective benefits derived from it', benefits which include the interservice mobility of officials building their careers (paragraph 14).

Career mobility has only ever been a fact of life for senior civil servants and those recruited into the fast stream (Farnham and Horton 1996). For most civil servants, certainly those employed outside of London and below the old principal (grade 7) level, there were few opportunities to move across departments and around the UK. Within Wales there were early signs of the Balkanization of the Home Civil Service. From at least 1972, it was observed that there was a gradual process of 'indigenization' of the civil service, a process long established in the Northern Ireland Civil Service and increasingly so in Scotland too. Rowlands (1972: 338) notes that by 1970 some 70 per cent of the old administrative class in the Welsh Office were of Welsh background, and of these one-quarter were Welsh speakers, with about 10 per cent of the department as a whole being reasonably fluent in Welsh.

Such institutional traits, evolving long before the *de jure* establishment of devolution, no doubt fuelled concerns about a unitary service.
Thus, Prime Minister Blair's speech to senior civil servants in October
1998 expressed the 'great importance' he attached to a unified civil service
and the need to prevent anybody working in Scotland or Wales feeling that
they had been 'cut adrift' (quoted in Parry 2001: 56). Blair's comment
recognized the institutional impact of devolution on the civil service. It was
an attempt to secure the allegiance of the permanent bureaucracy to the
new structures of accountability:

> The Civil Service is listed alongside the Crown and the UK Parlia-
> ment as one of the reserved matters under the 'Constitution of the
> United Kingdom'. A theme of the devolution transition planning was
> the note of reassurance given to officials from senior management
> that their traditional values and positions in the Constitution would
> not be overturned.
>
> (Parry 2001: 56)

The indigenization of both policy and institutions, however, reflects the
gap between ministerial intentions and their ability to deliver given the
new structures.

The announcement of a 'coalition government' between Labour and
the Liberal Democrats in October 2000 put the Assembly onto a new foot-
ing. Secretaries in charge of portfolios had the nomenclature changed and
were henceforth referred to as ministers, although this earned a mild, but
impotent, rebuke from the Speaker of the House of Commons in London
(Osmond 2000: 1–20). The Assembly and Welsh politicians generally sought
to expedite devolution and enhance the Assembly's status. A logical corol-
lary was a desire to ensure the allegiance of Welsh civil servants to the
Assembly and its Welsh 'ministers', rather than to British ministers and
Whitehall. The *Partnership Agreement* drawn up by the Labour and Liberal
Democrat coalition partners provided an undertaking 'to move the Welsh
civil service in a more autonomous direction' (Osmond 2000: 13). The
agreement boldly stated:

> We will review the existing structures and workings of Assembly
> officials to ensure they are in tune with the reality of political devolu-
> tion. We seek to move towards an increasingly independent and Welsh-
> based civil service – investigating ways of introducing an Assembly
> 'fast-track' programme to attract and retain high quality staff.
>
> (Osmond 2000: 13)

Compared to the wishes of the British prime minister to retain a unified UK
Civil Service, this separate Welsh aspiration displays a remarkably frank ad-
mission of the different path devolution has taken and will continue to take.

The work of Morgan and others has charted the change in allegiance
displayed by civil servants of all ranks within Wales. A change promoted

by the new administration and implemented by the officials, as one former senior civil servant stated:

> There was a very noticeable sea-change very quickly . . . when people, and I think that they responded to it, mostly, with great enthusiasm, had a set of ministers who were giving them a different agenda and were saying . . . 'Well actually, we want you to do this in Wales.' I really think that . . . [this] had an enormous impact on morale and on . . . the priorities that officials here saw for themselves . . . there was almost a revolutionary change – that's a big word – a radical change in the relationship between Cardiff and Whitehall.
>
> (cited in Morgan and Rees 2001: 138)

This assertiveness is a prerequisite to much greater political, or democratic, devolution. It represents a strengthening of the 'Team Wales' approach to policy-making and service delivery. As the case studies below seek to illustrate, it permeated through to the establishment of new policy networks and the reformulation of older ones.

Devolution combined with management changes to reinforce the role of the Cabinet Office and Treasury as UK central coordinating departments. However, at the same time, and paradoxically, it reduced the power they have to coordinate. Fragmentation forced them to shift even further from a hierarchical command role to one of being senior partners in a continuing series of negotiations over policy and administration. While the senior civil service remains reasonably assured of career mobility and protected national pay and pension schemes, it makes up only a small part of the overall service in Wales (Cabinet Office 1999d: paragraphs 8–14), and all other officials are subject to local conditions of service. A welter of guidance notes and memoranda have been published by the Cabinet Office, Treasury and spending departments to attempt coordination with the devolved regions and the Home Civil Service working there (HM Treasury 1997; Cabinet Office 1999b,c,d; Lord Chancellor's Department 1999; DSS 2000). Like Mr Gladstone's struggle with the inherent contradictions of Irish Home Rule, much of this information and guidance is an attempt to reconcile the goal of the maintenance of a unified civil service (replete with 'joined up government') with the reality of a devolved polity intent on following a separate path.

These tensions run through the relations between the executive and the Assembly, and between London and Cardiff. The permanent secretary at the time of devolution clearly attempted to pursue the Whitehall line of a unified UK Civil Service, making decisions that reflected past practice under the old Welsh Office. In appearing to treat the Assembly as a kind of advisory add-on and clashing with the presiding officer over his powers and those of the elected Welsh members, a minor constitutional crisis was provoked (Osmond 2000: 15–22). The result was a greater clarification of the independence of the presiding officer and the Assembly members in

their favour. Given the day-to-day realities of power and the political soci-
ology of the personnel concerned (including the equal status given to the
use of the Welsh language for official business), the first call on the loyalty
of officials in Wales is increasingly less likely to be Whitehall.

The executive and legislature: new roles and rules

The 60 members of the Welsh Assembly are elected in two ways. The first
40 are elected by the traditional simple plurality method, one for each of
the parliamentary constituencies. The remaining 20 are taken from the
political party lists on a regional basis (Government of Wales Act 1998, Chapter 38). The five electoral regions are based on the European parliamentary
constituencies and each of these returns four members to the Assembly.
The Assembly has powers and responsibilities to develop and implement
policy over:

- agriculture
- ancient monuments and historic buildings
- culture
- economic development
- education and training
- the environment
- health and health services
- highways
- housing
- industry
- local government
- social services
- sport and leisure
- tourism
- town and country planning
- transport and roads
- the Welsh language (Government of Wales Act 1998, Chapter 38; see
  also www.wales.gov.uk).

As a result of this transfer of power, the Assembly makes decisions
over areas such as appointments to and funding of NHS bodies in Wales,
the National Curriculum as it is applied to the principality, the administration of European structural funds, and agricultural and environmental
issues.

In the Assembly, the Cabinet is the main decision-making body and
represents the executive. The Assembly elects a first secretary who serves
as leader of the Cabinet and who then appoints Assembly secretaries,
most of whom are responsible for discrete policy areas, such as education
or health. Since establishing the coalition, the Assembly has referred to

secretaries as ministers, ostensibly to prevent confusion with the civil service use of the term 'secretary' to mean a senior official. In reality, this *de facto* (but not *de jure*) change of label signals the political aspirations of Welsh politicians.

All members of the Cabinet are accountable to the Assembly as a whole. Under the Act, the secretary of state for Wales must transfer to the Welsh Assembly the Welsh budget from the Treasury, consult and debate the UK government's legislative programme with the Assembly and participate in plenary sessions of the Assembly, but without the right to vote. The Welsh Office itself ceased to exist on 1 July 1999 when its powers and responsibilities were transferred to the National Assembly for Wales. The much smaller Wales Office, under the responsibility of the secretary of state for Wales, replaced it. Although it would be unfair to describe the office of the secretary of state for Wales as a cipher, it does appear that, shorn of its executive functions, it is an office that could be carried out by a competent individual on a part-time basis. In any event, it is clear that the locus for administrative accountability has passed from the Office of the Secretary of State for Wales to the Cabinet of the Assembly. The Assembly has been quick to respond to this and become jealous of its newly acquired rights and prerogatives.

One of the goals of those in favour of devolution to Wales was the perceived need to ensure that the growing number of quangos exercising power over public administration in Wales were made accountable to the people of Wales. Charter 88 (1997) estimated that there were as many as 214 national and local Welsh quangos involved in Welsh public administration. Members of the Assembly have sought to ensure that their jurisdiction does indeed extend, wherever possible, over all public bodies operating in the principality. In answer to a question to him in the Assembly, the then first secretary noted that there are

> 35 UK bodies that have a member appointed to represent Welsh interests and where the Assembly has a role in the appointment process. There are many other appointments on which the Assembly is consulted, and members from Wales can be, and often are, appointed because of their expertise and knowledge of Welsh interests. We have inherited a mixed bag of arrangements and over time, I hope that we can achieve some consistency through a series of bilateral discussions.
> (Official Record of the Welsh Assembly
> 9 November 1999, Question 1)

The subsequent supplementary questions illustrated the depth of feeling many Assembly members felt over the issue and their belief that the Assembly should have a decisive impact on the selection and ratification process for public appointments.

Welsh legislation is secondary not primary law, that is it is in the form of statutory instruments (SIs) passed by the Assembly following the passage of primary enabling legislation at Westminster. Despite the term 'secondary' denoting a certain hierarchy of administrative precedence, in Wales SIs comprise the bulk of day-to-day regulations governing public administration and life in the principality. For example, there are several thousand SIs passed by Westminster each year, and this devolved power is central to British policy-making, since it gives ministers (and their officials) the flexibility to deal with changed circumstances and unforeseen events. During the first six months of the Assembly's operation (July to December 1999), there were 34 Welsh SIs. They dealt with everything from new schools in Wales (The Education (New Schools) Regulations 1999 (No. 2242)), through to local government Acts commencement orders (No. 2815), an SI dealing with home repair assistance (No. 3084), and housing renewal grants (No. 3468). All dealt specifically with Wales and Welsh issues, varying the previous situation inherited upon devolution. Some brought the Welsh situation into alignment with England, but many did not.

The largest transfer of executive function came with the order in council (No. 253) made on 8 February 2000. This was the National Assembly for Wales (Transfer of Functions) Order 2000. Schedule 1 transferred responsibility for the enactment and continued implementation of a large number of SIs relating to housing, transport, fisheries, food regulations, health and safety, education, local government, land use planning and agriculture, to the Assembly. Schedule 2 transferred 'enactments subject to constraint on ministerial exercise of functions', such as the Disability Rights Commission Act 1999, Chapter 17, which was transferred in amended form to state:

> The function of the Secretary of State under paragraph 2 of Schedule 1 of making appointments to the Disability Rights Commission shall be exercisable only with the agreement of the Assembly so far as necessary to ensure that there is at all times one Commissioner who has been appointed with the agreement of the Assembly.

Schedule 3 of the order varied the 1999 transfer order to provide greater coherence and responsibilities in the field of mental health, the Building Act 1984, Town and Country Planning Act 1980, Water Industry Act 1991 and the Nurses, Midwives and Health Visitors Act 1997. There is a total of six schedules to this order, representing a substantial transfer of functions and an attempt to ensure a greater degree of coherence to the role and responsibility of the Assembly. The devolution of public administration, therefore, has been substantial. As a result, despite the codicils in the legislation and the subsequent memoranda, there has been a cultural change in the civil service: it is based in Wales employed upon Welsh business.

The senior civil servants and ministers based in London have found themselves beset by a problem. Their desire and stated intention to retain a unified Home Civil Service is undermined by the fatal flaw that, in Wales, as elsewhere, the local officials have acquired another focus for their loyalty, and a new hierarchy to hold them accountable. In short, Wales has acquired its own civil service in *de facto*, if not yet *de jure*, form.

Policy case studies

Economic development

Economic development policy in Wales begins in the 1930s, when, as a depressed region of the UK, the Welsh Valleys were designated as Special Areas, later renamed Development Areas in line with the Barlow Report on the Geographical Distribution of the Industrial Population (Barlow 1940). Unlike Scotland, responsibility for the policy and its implementation in Wales was vested with the Whitehall-based Board of Trade (Wood 1987: 234). After the war, while some additional measures were taken, it was not until the 1960s that an active regional policy emerged. During the 1964 Labour government, major organizational adjustments were made. The new Welsh Office's responsibilities included implementing economic development policy, though Wales remained essentially in step with the rest of Great Britain. The Welsh Development Agency (WDA) was created in 1976 to succeed the Development Corporation for Wales (Griffiths 1996) because

> it was felt that what was needed in the market place was an arm's length body with a high degree of operational autonomy. Major private sector players had largely disappeared from the radar in the 1970s.
>
> (interview)

Concurrent with the WDA, the Development Board for Rural Wales (DBRW) was also set up in 1976, being akin to Scotland's Highlands and Islands Development Board. In addition, the Labour government's Inner Urban Areas Act that established the Urban Programme made local authorities the principal local agencies of economic development.

Rees and Morgan (1991) contended that a regional consensus exists in Wales that promoted cooperation by business, labour and government to a degree exceptional in the UK. It was 'a kind of 1960s corporatism', according to Thomas, former president of Plaid Cymru, who added that it 'is a feature of the scale of Wales' (Hansard 28/11/91, col. 1131). Regularity of high-level contact is ensured (Griffiths 1996). It ought to be noted that the community role of the private sector has been conspicuously lacking throughout modern Welsh history, in that big business simply did not engage with civic society on anything like the scale seen in England (Morgan and Rees 2001: 130–70).

The principal administrative body, until devolution in 1999, was the Welsh Office based both in London and in Cardiff. The latter was the principal centre. Over time, the Welsh Office expanded its functions. For example, in 1979 the newly elected Conservatives

> carried through an important extension of the Welsh Office's powers in relations to bargaining with other Whitehall departments. In 1980, the Welsh Office was given a block grant for the expenditure on most Welsh Office programmes. The two main components of Welsh Office expenditure outside this block were expenditure on agricultural support and aid to industry.
>
> (Griffiths 1996: 53)

While the Conservatives were retreating from active regional policy, their policy changes were against a backdrop in which the recession in Wales (1980–81) was deeper than in the rest of the UK, the recovery being less impressive.

Such was the depth of that recession that the government felt compelled to act. Thus, economic development policy itself was amended. Alarmed by spiralling costs and a policy with only modest achievements, the first Thatcher government cut regional assistance grants and suspended Industrial Development Certificates in 1981.

The 1983 White Paper on regional policy stated that:

> incentives must be made much more cost effective than at present with greater emphasis on job creation and selectivity, and less discrimination against service industries. They also need to focus on encouraging new and indigenous development in the assisted areas rather than simply transferring jobs from one part to another.
>
> (DTI 1983)

Harrison (1990a) noted that one of the White Paper's principal recommendations was a shift from automatic to selective forms of assistance. The WDA had actively pursued that policy. However, when UK regional aid was cut substantially during the 1980s, the WDA was forced to reassess its strategy. Moreover, other European regions were becoming more active in pursuing inward investment. Thus, the WDA had to alter its traditional three-pillar strategy of land reclamation, advance factory building and inward investment. The new policy placed more emphasis on developing business support services, technology transfer, skills development, and the needs of small and medium-sized enterprises.

Interest in the Welsh experience is given added piquancy by the role of the Welsh secretary and his allegedly considerable leeway to pursue 'experiments' at variance with the stated policy of the government, especially during the period of the Thatcher administrations. Griffiths (1999) observed that, provided the arrangements in the 'territories' did not impinge on the 'high politics' of London, they were left to their own devices.

The period in office of Peter Walker, the 'great survivor' of the Tory 'wets', has often been associated with a proactive policy of localized state-directed regeneration in Wales, and an anathema to the free-market neo-liberalism of a cabinet otherwise increasingly dominated by the Thatcherite Right. It attracted 20 per cent of all foreign inward investment to the UK (Gaffikin and Morrissey 1990a). Walker (1991: 123) boasted that he was able to implement policy in Wales as he wished and not as the prime minister commanded. The WDA (and Scottish Development Agency) 'were instruments of interventionism – "caring capitalism" and the last vestiges of corporatist tripartism' (Gaffikin and Morrissey 1990a: 87). 'Wales has been described as an enclave of "relative Keynesianism" where government intervention is still practised' (Griffiths 1996: 20).

Certainly, policy variations existed, but as noted above, a number of myths have emerged, too. For Griffiths (1996: 20), the selection of secretary of state for Wales

> owes more to the desire of the Prime Minister to balance the left wing and right wing of the Conservative Party around the Cabinet table than reflecting a desire to maintain Wales as a relative haven of 'wet' Conservatism.

Whatever evidence exists of experimentation (for it is highly contested), some facts are beyond doubt. Griffiths (1999) remarked that impressions about the Walker–Hunt era as a period of 'wetness' in Wales probably owe more to the fact that both politicians were not Thatcherites. But to infer that this implied soft peddling is mistaken. As Bradbury (1998: 126) noted also, successive Conservative governments displayed a 'cavalier attitude' and moved to marginalize local government, bolster the power and budgets of quangos and showed general insensitivity to Welsh needs on many occasions. Moreover,

> Conservative governments after 1979 sustained much distinctiveness but they essentially worked on the assumption that a special approach to governing Wales had definite limits, meaning that arrangements built up over time were open to testing as to their utility and level of importance.
>
> (Bradbury 1998: 137)

Specific references to a 'Welsh Keynesian oasis' ignore the fact that the policy tools of the Welsh Office did not include the prime levers of fiscal and monetary policy. No matter how ingenious the deployment of its chiefly supply-side measures, the actions of the Welsh Office and its ministers remained firmly bound by the externally imposed parameters set by the Chancellor of the Exchequer and the vagaries of the international global trading system. Moreover, even on a practical everyday level,

> Despite the centrality of regional financial assistance to economic regeneration in Wales, it would appear to be an aspect of policy over which the Welsh Office had relatively little control. Payments to firms

through the government's regional development policies did not become part of the Welsh Office Block, over which the Secretary of State for Wales has some discretion to vary expenditure between different programmes according to his interpretation of the needs of Wales, until 1994/95.

(Griffiths 1996: 99)

As noted near the start of this chapter, many commentators have concluded that 'the claims of Welsh exceptionalism (certainly in terms of policies) have been much exaggerated' and that 'the "centre", Westminster and Whitehall, was able to impose its preferred policies, whatever appearances to the contrary' (Griffiths 1996: 793). Nonetheless, Jones (2000: 16) maintained that the Conservatives made no attempt to denigrate the Welsh Office, 'arguably a constitutional aberration in a unitary state, or to integrate Wales administratively with England'.

In 1992, the Welsh Office acquired responsibility for training from the Department of Employment as well as funding for further and higher education. A new department in the Welsh Office was created, responsible for training, education and enterprise, to coordinate the work on the training and enterprise councils (TECs), local enterprise agencies and the local careers services within Wales (Griffiths 1996: 54). Also during the 1990s, each part of the UK developed its own distinctive small and medium enterprise (SME) support network. In Scotland, for example, Scottish Enterprise (SE) and Highlands and Islands Enterprise (HIE) are legally required to decentralize much of their operations and budgets to the 22 Scottish local enterprise Councils (LECs). In England, the idea of a one-stop shop, known as Business Links, emerged in 1992, funded principally by the Department of Trade and Industry (DTI). In Scotland, the one-stop shop principle was followed in 1993 with the introduction of the Scottish Business Shop Network (SBSN). According to Bristow and Munday (1997), the one-stop shop has been slower to emerge in Wales. Only in 1996 did the Welsh Office introduce Business Connect, an advice and support network for SMEs modelled closely on its Scottish counterpart, the SBSN. The Welsh Office and participating partner organizations that include the TECs, local authorities, local education authorities and the WDA, jointly fund Business Connect. The Welsh business support infrastructure may have benefited from having learned some of the lessons of both the English and Scottish experience.

Lovering (1996: 6–7) argued that 'the consensus that the Welsh economy should be regarded as a triumphant case of regeneration has little basis in fact'. As Brand et al. (1997: 219) noted, for all the talk of economic miracles, 'the regional economy entered the 1990s, as it had the 1980s, as the poorest region of the UK mainland in terms of key indicators of personal economic well-being'. Wales was further behind the UK average in 1994 than in 1974. Brand et al. contend that the causes of GDP per capita disparities are often interrelated, making it virtually impossible to ascribe causality accurately. Given the success in attracting inward investment, it is paradoxical that Wales has remained stubbornly at the foot of the economic league table within the UK.

Griffiths (1996: 11) considered that:

> Modest as it has been up to now, devolved bureaucracy has given the Celtic nations the capacity to develop structured economic development powers. Both Wales and Scotland have been able to develop a regional governance capacity, so far as economic development is concerned, which the proposals for the Regional Development Agencies (RDAs) in England do little to compensate for.

Nonetheless, the historical antipathy among the Welsh to calls for a greater measure of home rule waned. By the 1990s, the Cardiff University Devolution Group remarked:

> [As] currently structured there exists a number of disparate internal Welsh Office Divisions dealing with 'economic development'. However, instead of being organised to effectively deliver regional development, the internal organisation of the Welsh Office seems to be modelled on the different Ministries found in Whitehall. For example, there are different 'Ministries' awarding funds for the environment, transport, regional selective assistance, the WDA, DBRW, Business Connect, the Unitary Authorities, the TECs, enterprise agencies and a host of other local bodies (public, private and voluntary) all concerned with 'economic development' . . . [The] present system is best described as a confused mixture of good intentions and conflicting objectives delivered by poorly co-ordinated agencies. However, it must be stressed that the Welsh Office has been at the centre of this confusing structure for many years.
>
> (Welsh Affairs Committee 1998: 67)

As such, accountability flowed through Whitehall and Westminster.

Osmond (1998: 6) quoted one senior civil servant as arguing that:

> Currently we are working for one Minister whose preoccupations are London rather than Wales centred. But once the Assembly is in being collective responsibility will go out of the window. We are very close to being released from the straight jacket of thinking that Britain is a homogenous community where policy diversity is a dangerous activity.

Since devolution, the National Assembly for Wales (NAW) has assumed responsibility for all but a handful of Welsh Office functions. Within the NAW's competence, there are a series of Assembly committees, one being Economic Development, based on the portfolio of the Assembly secretary for economic development. The Assembly secretary's portfolio embraces regional development, including indigenous and inward investment; European economic policy, including structural funds; industrial policy and business support, including demand-side employment issues (minimum wage, working time); tourism and urban development and regeneration. The main public bodies covered are the WDA, Welsh Tourist Board (WTB), DBRW, and the Cardiff Bay Development Corporation (CBDC) although the WDA has since subsumed the functions of the DBRW and the Land Authority, with a widened remit that includes social development. Civil servants report to the economic development secretary, while there is also interface with the Assembly's Economic Development Committee.

When the National Assembly for Wales was created, although economic development policy was a transferred matter, other Whitehall departments remained involved since various relevant functions are either reserved or excepted. On links with other departments, one senior official commented:

> We have close links but their influence on us is very limited. [Moreover,] the concordats ensure a degree of civility and that we don't speak at variance with one another. There are both formal and informal links. For example, there are six-monthly meetings around the UK (though usually in London for ease of access but we do rotate). Also, all the English regional directors meet regularly . . . On policy learning we try to benchmark ourselves by reference to similar bodies. Our arrangements with the IDA [Irish Development Authority] (in the Irish Republic) are stronger than with the IDB [Irish Development Board] (Northern Ireland). We are seeking to learn lessons from them.
>
> (interview)

One example of how other departments are involved with economic development in Wales is that the then Department for Education and Employment (DfEE) was responsible for the New Deal initiative, Labour's programme for securing employment for the young and the long-term unemployed.

Another complicating factor stems from the financing of the economic development heading of the Welsh Office Public Expenditure Budget, known as the Welsh Block. Since there is no direct equivalent Whitehall departmental block, the money assigned to this budget heading for Wales cannot automatically expect to benefit from any change in the national UK budget, unlike, say, education or health (through the Barnett Formula). Consequently, the economic development element of the Welsh Block emerged over the years, largely without reference to the UK budget. As a result, it has to compete with other policy areas in the Welsh Block. Given the pressures from such highly salient policy areas as education and health, there is an inevitable limit on what can be achieved. As one senior official remarked:

> On budgets, my focus is internal. I compete with my colleagues in education, health etc. but it is more advantageous. The Regional Development Agencies (RDAs) by contrast in England draw their budgets from three, four, five departments, with a finite budget. In Wales, it is open-ended. The pattern is one of incremental growth with a variance of plus or minus 5 per cent year on year. We account for about 8–9 per cent of the Welsh Block (while education and health swallow 75 per cent between them).
>
> (interview)

It is important to recognize the limited role of civil servants. 'We have some 120–130 staff, so, for every one civil servant involved in economic development, there are ten times as many involved in delivery and implementation' (interview).

Despite the relatively low number of staff within the department, however, one official commented:

> [W]e don't just monitor. We advise the NAW Committee on strategy and give advice to the various agencies that deliver policy. With the WDA, for example, they have a three-year rolling (corporate) plan. We negotiate targets with them. If you are going to have an arm's length agency, you have to allow them to produce a business plan.
>
> (interview)

The WDA is an all-Wales body. Under the terms of devolution, the WDA remains a strictly non-civil-service body but it is officially designated as an Assembly-sponsored public body. As an arm's length organization, outside the core area of government, its employees are public servants rather than civil servants. As to the merits of this status, one official observed:

> [I]n a quango like the WDA, we have people with all manner of skills (surveyors, accountants, engineers, lawyers etc.). I don't have that range of expertise at my disposal. The current head of the WDA happens to be a former civil servant. If these functions came in-house, I am not sure that we would have the same powers.
>
> (interview)

There are conflicting views on the extent to which there are differences in policy between the different parts of the UK. One senior civil servant believes that:

> as for policy variation, there wasn't really any under the Welsh Office. For years, we've been topping and tailing Westminster and Whitehall. The big difference was that the agencies in Wales, Scotland and Northern Ireland were streets ahead in resources. In England, it is still

only potential. These bodies were in the marketplace and rather than having a distinctive policy agenda in their patch, it was their resource advantages that counted.

(interview)

The reason for confusion about the scope for variation stems from a failure to appreciate that:

there is a clear division between devolved and non-devolved areas of activity. The economic agenda of Wales is coloured by issues over which we have no control. Bank of England decisions, for example. Some parallels exist between Wales, Scotland and Northern Ireland but comparisons in other ways would be unfair. Resentments have occurred between adjacent areas although no one has really begrudged Northern Ireland its special level of funding. In England, resources and impact are dissipated. You have the DTI and the Treasury. Then there are the RDAs – another tier but with nothing else changed. The TECs still continue also. In Wales, the TECs are going. There is more budgetary flexibility as a result of having only one department.

(interview)

Since devolution is a recent development, it is too early to reach firm conclusions about how it has affected economic development policy and administration. But it is the clear intention of Welsh politicians to set a distinct Welsh course. In this they are greatly helped by the switch in allegiance of the civil servants away from London and towards Cardiff.

Community care

In most policy areas, Wales is often appended to England in UK legislation. The NHS and Community Care Act 1990 is one such example. We may, then, expect little policy differentiation from the centre.

Community care is a 'new' policy area. Also, Welsh administration does not have much experience of dealing with related issues. The secretary of state for Wales took over formal responsibility for local government and housing in 1965, and for health and welfare services (formerly administered by the Department for Health and Social Security) in 1969. Most childcare responsibilities were transferred from the Home Office only in 1971. Probably most importantly, however, the secretary of state was not given powers of direction in respect of social services functions until enactment of the NHS and Community Care Act itself.

Community care in Wales has a structural administrative history similar to that in Scotland, with a further complicating issue: community care in Wales has generally been subsumed under the more general heading of social care. The definition of social care is broader than that of community care and concerns the delivery of personal social services and support to vulnerable groups within society in any setting. Indeed, community care is not even clearly defined in the NHS and Community Care Act. The government left it to local authority social services departments to define care management.

Pre-devolution community care in Wales reflected a major difficulty with the policy area, namely, its cross-cutting nature. Thus, when community care was fully introduced it fell between several divisions/groups in the Welsh Office. Somewhat ironically, however, the earlier incarnations of the Welsh Office divisions would have better suited the administration of community care policy. By 1974, one division was responsible for a vast array of community care functions, being responsible for social and health services for the physically disabled, the elderly, the mentally ill and children. The division was the responsibility of an undersecretary of state along with three other divisions. In 1976, the division was reorganized, losing its health responsibilities; the remaining division became the Local Authority Social Services Division which, in 1985, was renamed the Personal Social Services Division. The Welsh Office went through several reorganizations, and future community care functions were amalgamated and split.

In 1987, the Housing, Health and Social Care Policy Group was created, with three divisions. This structure was probably suitable for administering community care. However, another reorganization in 1994 split responsibility again. Most importantly, all health matters were amalgamated under the Welsh Office Health Department. The following year the Social Service Policy Division was created in the Local Government Group. Responsibility for the two main agents of community care was therefore split between departments and groups. On devolution, community care responsibilities were shared by the Welsh Office Health Department, the Local Government Group and the Health Professionals Group. The administrative history of community care before devolution is not merely an exercise in describing the allocation of functions but also had important implications for strategy, policy development and the role of the civil service. By 1990, the Welsh Office had accrued a vast number of responsibilities with a small ministerial team to cover them. Therefore, the Welsh Office civil service had a considerable influence on policy – a direct consequence of the lack of political leadership. The broad notion of social care meant that community care was often hidden from view and the split nature of administration meant that no minister had sole responsibility.

The lack of political leadership from the Welsh Office was officially highlighted in a House of Commons Report *Lost in Care* (HC 201) which, although concerned specifically with child care 1974–96, considered the criticisms that the Welsh Office

> failed . . . to play a sufficiently interventionist part in the management and operation of county social services departments to ensure that appropriate standards were observed; . . . failed to plan the development

of social services by setting clear aims and objectives and ensuring that they were understood; . . . failed to collect and disseminate adequate information about the services that were being provided on the one hand and the needs that ought to be met on the other; . . . failed to monitor adequately the performance of county social services departments in such a way as to promote the achievement of aims and the maintenance of standards; . . . failed to provide sufficient practical guidance to social services departments in a readily accessible form; failed to provide adequate resources to enable those responsible in the Welsh Office itself and the county councils to discharge efficiently their respective wide and onerous duties.

(HC 201, 2000, 47.47)

Such failings also occurred in the community care policy area. As a senior civil servant confirmed:

there was a political push to community care implementation then there was a hands-off scenario. From 1993, the civil service had to push through because there was not the political will to do it. The political line on non-intervention was strong so nobody picked it up to run with, it sort of fumbled along. In the Welsh Office some politicians thought that it was for local authorities and other agencies to work out so anything prescriptive was frowned upon. Prior to '93, care could be hidden by pushing onto the social security budget. There was a boundary between health and social care and this became a problem. The civil service and one individual in particular had to drive community care until '97–'98 when, with a new government, the cracks started to show.

(interview)

The influence of the civil service on community care policy in Wales appears to have gone through several phases. On institutions, the civil service was strong in all areas. It set up the Welsh community care network by identifying both necessary and preferred actors in provision. These actors included the statutory providers plus, from an early stage, inputs from the private and voluntary sectors. Representative organizations such as the Welsh Local Government Association were also included. Owing to a lack of political leadership from the Welsh Office, this stage in policy development saw considerable reliance on the parent department in Whitehall for policy steering. Thus, initially in community care policy in Wales, there was little divergence from the centre. This link to the centre was also identified in the *Lost in Care* report and is an outcome of the structure of the Welsh Office and the range of responsibilities covered. It seems, then, that structural weaknesses in the Welsh Office negated its function.

A second, more recent, phase in civil service influence on community care policy concerns the re-emergence of politics as a major driving factor.

This phase began with the transition to a new central government and new political agenda in 1997. Labour's emphasis on improving public services through its modernization programme brought community care onto the agenda in Wales. While the modernization programme affected each territorial ministry, the state of social care in Wales had reached crisis point. Not least of these was the failing of the care system for children in North Wales that eventually led to the judicial inquiry into child abuse in council homes that was the basis of the *Lost in Care* report. Further, there was no overall strategy development: solutions were plucked from research for community-care-related issues in Wales that was conducted before the NHS and Community Care Act 1990 was passed (interview). All aspects of social care services came to the top of the political agenda at a time when Welsh politicians were bedding into a new government regime:

> [T]he political pressures suddenly escalated. There were problems in the workings of the policy, nobody was talking to each other, and we had a new government with new politicians wanting to make a name for themselves. Community care was politically up for grabs.
>
> (interview)

The political and the politician had been put back into community care policy.

The emergence of the modernization agenda for community care was heralded by the White Paper *Modernising Social Services* (Cm 4169) published in 1998, that helped alter the balance of power in the relationship between politicians and civil servants. In 1999, the secretary of state for Wales, Alun Michael, introduced a major reform programme for social services in the White Paper *Building for the Future* (Cm 4051). This gave a Welsh twist to *Modernising Social Services* and put in train reforms similar to those instituted in Scotland in *Aiming for Excellence*. Here again, the lead was coming from the centre in policy development but the politicians had the impetus rather than the civil service.

Building for the Future concentrated on standards and efficiency and included proposals to create a Commission for Care Standards in Wales, a Care Council for Wales, statutory standards of service and a new performance management framework. These reforms mirrored those in Scotland. There was also an initiative to improve social services management information systems. A limit on the initial strong position of the civil service in developing community care policy was the lack of evidential-based information. Graham Williams, chief inspector of the Social Services Inspectorate for Wales gave a flavour of the problem:

> [T]he present Research and Development Strategy for Social Care was published by the Welsh Office of Research and Development (WORD) in January 1998 following the work of a Planning Group and wide consultation. It was considered that at a time of significant

reported pressures on the budgets for social care there is a need to identify which features of social care delivery are effective and cost effective. More generally there is an impression that social care has suffered from not having a cumulative body of evidence to support policy and practice.

(Williams 2000)

As with Scotland, there was an acceptance that reforms in *Building for the Future* would necessarily impact on the devolved administration.

Devolution signalled a third phase in civil service influence on community care policy. As highlighted by a senior civil servant:

[C]ommunity care was beginning to get the attention it deserved but then the creation of the Assembly did for this. I have not met a civil servant who wanted devolution, we certainly didn't hold any hopes for the calibre of person we'd get in the Assembly. We were quite happy to work away under the old system.

(interview)

Under the devolved system, responsibility for all community care policy transferred to the Social Policy and Local Government Affairs Section of the Assembly Senior Management Team. This section in turn is divided into eight directorates/groups, four of which have a direct impact on community care policy, namely the Social Care Group, the Local Government and Housing Group, the Social Services Inspectorate of Wales and the NHS Directorate. Community care is again subsumed under social care, and so the lead within the civil service is taken by those in the Social Care Group and within that the Social Care Policy Division. Unlike in Scotland, community care is not separated from the more general social services. The main Assembly committee shadows the Assembly minister responsible for health and social care.

The Assembly minister's portfolio covers a wide range of areas, including health and the NHS in Wales, food safety, social care and social services, children and the voluntary sector partnership. While the priorities of the minister and committee are similar to those in Scotland and centrally (and include joined up working, regulation and primary care), there is little identification of community care as a distinct policy area. This has had an influence on the relative power relationship between politicians and civil servants in community care. One official observed:

[W]e now influence planning and strategy in community care and we can do this without politicians' support. Through evidence-based research we have a better handle on what the balance of care should be and on matching resources to needs. We need strategy that is not wholly medical in approach. We're getting groups to agree but we need to operationalise.

(interview)

The civil service does not need the support of politicians to influence policy as the civil service has maintained the community care network, through the transition to the Assembly. Three phases of civil service influence are identifiable. Indeed, the Assembly's lack of interest in community care means that the civil service's role in community care policy will remain undiminished. Divergence from the centre in this area is not as great as may be expected under a devolved system. Civil service influence means the ends of policy have not diverged and, given the current legislative powers of the Welsh Assembly, divergence is less likely to occur.

The main thrust in policy development since devolution was highlighted by the Assembly secretary Jane Hutt AM, in an address to the Developing Partnerships Conference – Research and Development for Health and Social Care (Hutt 1999). The secretary outlined a set of guiding principles around: the primacy of the patient or service user; the importance of joined up thinking; planning and service delivery; the need for evidence-based effectiveness; best value and affordability; and the need to promote and recognise high quality staffing in services which have status and public value (Hutt 1999). The secretary made little mention of community care specifically, preferring to see it as part of social care. Such considerations allow the civil service some leeway in policy development. Welsh priorities reflect the concerns of *Building for the Future*. On 12 July 2000, a statement by the secretary entitled 'A healthier future for Wales', reviewed policy developments. The secretary confirmed that:

> we are making very good progress in delivering the 42 commitments in . . . *Building for the Future* . . . [T]he modernisation agenda is being taken forward vigorously through an innovative approach, with the full involvement of the voluntary and private sectors, as well as the statutory partners.
>
> (National Assembly for Wales 2000: 19)

More specifically for community care, the secretary reported progress on a series of reforms introduced in October 1999 for NHS Wales. These reforms included: rapid development of joint working and the reduction of barriers to care; increased support to allow additional contributions from the voluntary sector, users and carers; and an attack on inequality of access. All these are 'in hand' (National Assembly for Wales 2000: 16). The coalition policies inaugurated under the new ministerial regime in October 2000 sought to deepen and extend these policies and included the stated intention to create the new post of Children's Commissioner for Wales (Osmond 2000). However, for any radical departure, primary legislation would be required in the British Parliament.

For community care, then, there has been no major deviation from the centre's ends. Its hidden nature compared with social care has allowed the civil service influence. The civil service will continue to influence community care because of its expert knowledge of the network and, as in

Scotland, its role in setting general frameworks for community care actors to measure and monitor their own performance.

Conclusions

Wales is no longer a country that possessed an identity and a culture but lacked institutions. Devolution recognizes that the UK is a union of territorially distinct nations, something of a novelty for the Welsh who have never been a unified and independent nation. The lessons of Northern Ireland and Scotland suggest that separate political entities, whatever their size, develop separate identities and grow apart. The lessons of the managerial reforms of recent years in the public sector, from Next Steps onwards, suggest that there may also be an organizational imperative to this phenomenon. It is the informal networks of the differentiated polity that will ensure the success or failure of policy coordination, of joined up government and whatever succeeds the unified Home Civil Service.

6

England – government offices for the regions

Introduction

The purpose of this chapter is to explore devolution in England through a study of the establishment of the government offices for the English regions (GOs). The chapter explores their provenance, their structure and the aims they were set up to achieve. The chapter first traces the background to the regional debate in England. It then explores the origin of the government offices and debates the governance of English regions (Smith 1964, 1965a,b; Mackintosh 1968; Banks 1971; Parsons 1988; Rhodes 1988). The chapter also explores the institutional setting of GOs and discusses the impact of managerialism and performance. Finally, we discuss regional development agencies and their impact on English regionalism, the devolved civil service and the GOs.

The concept of the English regions

The genesis of the English regions lies deep in Saxon history. The *Anglo-Saxon Chronicles* for AD917 record:

> All the people of the area around Huntingdon who had survived bowed to King Edward, and sought his peace and protection . . . Still after that in the same year, before Martinmas, King Edward went with troops to Colchester, and repaired and restored the borough

where it had been broken down. Many people submitted to him,
both from East Anglia and Essex, which had been under Danish rule.
All the force in East Anglia swore an agreement to do all he wished,
to keep peace with all the King kept peace with, both on sea and on
land. The force belonging to Cambridge chose him especially as lord
and protector, and affirmed it with oaths as he determined it . . .
Aethelflaed, lady of the Mercians, . . . obtained the borough that is
called Derby, with all that belonged to it.

(Phillips 1982: 118)

The tumultuous end to the first millennium in England witnessed an abiding
struggle over the resources of land and the taxes it generated.

The powerful earls and barons gradually submitted to the central authority of the king seated at Winchester and then London. But the regions (and
constituent counties) carved out by the invading Germanic tribes during the
Dark Ages were largely accepted by the Normans and successive regimes,
surviving into the twenty-first century. A glance at a map of the English
county boundaries on New Year's eve AD999 and again on New Year's eve
AD1999 displays more similarities than dissimilarities. The regions of Mercia,
Northumberland (Bernicia), Essex, Wessex, Sussex (with Kent) and East
Anglia, remain recognizable entities. While the interregional rivalries of previous generations are no longer settled by the deployment of twibil[1] wielding
warriors, the issues erupting into the political arena as a result of the onset
of devolution will increase in their intensity and need addressing. As with
their Saxon forebears, the current regional leaders are concerned with the
issues of power relationships, resources and taxation. They seek to maximize the resources inwardly invested into their areas, while minimizing
both centrally levied taxes and centrally devised controls.

Regionalism revisited

Setting up government offices for the regions and the regional development agencies (RDAs) represented the latest phase in a continuing process
of regional change. The hegemony of central government in England had
not been seriously challenged for centuries, and the impact of two world
wars left a legacy of general public and official support for functional decentralization (Gamble 1988). By that it is meant that planning and strategic
policy-making were located in Whitehall, while the implementation of day-
to-day administration was decentralized to regional structures for the majority of government organizations, including the nationalized industries.

[The] origins of British regional policy are to be found in the interwar years: in what came to be described as the 'devil's decade', the
'hungry wasted thirties'. Alongside the maintenance of 'treasury
orthodoxy' in the main thrust of economic policy governments made

small, but nonetheless significant moves, in the direction of economic
management and state intervention in industry.

(Parsons 1988: 1)

The intense debates of that period, followed by wartime coalition and
Labour's postwar command of the economy, pushed the concept of regional political devolution in England out of the political consciousness,
although a great deal of attention was paid to administrative decentralization (Smith B.C. 1964: 65; Smith, T.A. 1979). Wartime and postwar planning concentrated on regional development and balanced employment,
influenced (among other things) by the Barlow Report and Hugh Dalton's
Distribution of Industry Act 1945 (Parsons 1988: 57–65). The 'cult' of the
economist followed the perceived successes of Keynesian economics during
this period. Both government organizations and public and private sector
industries were organized to secure dynamic economies of scale, as well as
to manage demand and secure balanced full employment throughout the
different regions (Beer 1965; Gamble 1988; Parsons 1988).

This pursuit of the 'best' regional structure for different organizations
and industries combined with the federal nature of Whitehall ensured that
there was no generally accepted regional structure across England; that is,
there was a lack of geographically coterminous boundaries. Certainly, the
general regional areas were respected in the sense that London, the northwest and the south-west were recognized as separate entities, but there was
no general recognition of regional boundaries. For example, there were standard Treasury regions, but these were different from the Gas Board regions,
which in turn were different from the Electricity Supply Industry's regions,
as determined after the Electricity Act 1958 (Massey 1988). The NHS's hospital regions were different again in that they had a Wessex region that did
not include the south-west, while the regions of the Advisory Councils for
Further Education called 'Wessex' its southern region and included Oxford
and a large part of the Thames Valley. All had different boundaries from
the so-called Industrial Development Associations (Smith 1964: 92–6).

Even central government departments had different regional boundaries from each other for their field operations. For example, in 1965, the
Ministry of Town and Country Planning regions were significantly different from those of the Ministry of Transport's divisions. Dorset was part of
the south-west for one but not the other, and the concept of what con-
stituted Greater London and the metropolitan region varied considerably,
as did the boundaries in the north of England (Smith 1965: 112–13). A
steady flow of academic and official proposals over the years had sought
to rationalize these sub-national government structures, beginning with
Cole's 1921 opus and including the work of Self (1949, 1964), Hall (1963),
and Mackenzie (1963). The work of George Brown's short-lived Department
for Economic Affairs and the reports by Redcliffe-Maude Commission
(1969), Bains (1972) and Kilbrandon (1973) among others, all contributed

to the debate and had varying degrees of impact. But it was not until 1994 and the establishment of the GOs (followed shortly after by the absorption of the Merseyside Government Office into the North West Government Office), that proper standardization of regional boundaries could be said to have begun. At the time of writing it remains unfinished, although the GOs and RDAs together make a formidable case for finally agreeing on coterminous regional boundaries and the Regional Coordination Unit's (RCU's) *Action Plan* (RCU 2000a) and *Summary of Progress* (RCU 2000b) are explicit about the need for coterminosity. 'For the bulk of the post-war period, sub-central government (SCG) could be described as the government of Britain "beyond Whitehall". This phrase captures the mutual insulation of central and local government' (Rhodes 1988: 12).

Establishing the government offices: the institutional background

Throughout the 1980s, the realization grew in Whitehall, Parliament and the regions themselves that there was a need to improve the coordination of the delivery of central government policy (across departmental responsibilities) within the regions. The original commitment to set up GOs may be found in the Conservative Party's 1992 election manifesto pledge to strengthen the central government's field offices in the English regions (Spencer and Mawson 1998: 5). The impetus for the change came from several sources. Among the more influential ones were observations by the House of Commons Civil Service Select Committee, which noted 'the lack of disaggregation on a consistent basis of public expenditure information for the English regions' (House of Commons 1989, cited in Spencer and Mawson 1998: 5). These comments, combined with critical reports from the Audit Commission and National Audit Office and pressure from the business community, encouraged the government to strengthen the regional coordination of Whitehall departments. There was especially strong pressure for change emanating in the Cabinet from those ministers with responsibilities for specific (depressed) regions and cities. The then deputy prime minister, Michael Heseltine, was especially vocal in support of a regional initiative. It was an early attempt at what the Labour opposition was to call 'joined up government', a term it later amended, when in power, to 'modernizing government' (see Cabinet Office 1999b).

The Departments of Trade and Industry, Education, Employment, and Environment and Transport established the GOs in April 1994. The primary purpose of the GOs was to address those needs, but they began their institutional life in a typically minimalist way. With so few departments involved, the GOs originally appeared to be a trial run with the rest of Whitehall looking on to assess its success. This limited start proved useful, as the problems of meshing a few departments together in the GOs

may have proved insurmountable had there been more to begin with. There
was a gradual extension of the project, with the siting of other departmental staff in GOs. There followed its formal, indeed statutory, recognition
through the adoption of the GO regions as the basis for English regional
boundaries, as defined in the Regional Development Agencies Act 1998, a
recognition that has demonstrated their growing importance in the process
of English governance.

Subsequent structural changes implemented in Whitehall first witnessed
the merger of the departments responsible for education and employment,
while the Department of the Environment and Transport became the Department of the Environment, Transport and Regions (DETR). Following the
report of the Cabinet Office's Performance and Innovation Unit on regional
government in February 2000 and the restructuring of central departments
after Labour's election victory in 2001, the participating departments became:

- the Department of Trade and Industry
- the Department of Transport, Local Government and the Regions
- the Department for the Environment, Food and Rural Affairs
- the Home Office
- the Department for Education and Skills
- the Department for Culture, Media and Sport.

The new Regional Coordination Unit was located in the Cabinet Office. This
last change was designed to signal the government's intention to ensure greater
oversight and inclusion of the regional perspective in policy-making.

The changes that took place between 2000 and 2001 recognize the
government's determination to integrate four key areas of policy-making.
The government wants:

- to ensure better coordination of area-based initiatives;
- to bring the regional perspective to bear on central initiatives, both in
  their formulation and delivery;
- to act as the key representative of government in the regions;
- to establish the RCU as the unified head office for GOs, hence its symbolic
  as well as practical location in the Cabinet Office. This move took the old
  Government Office Central Unit (GOCU) away from the former Department of the Environment, Transport and the Regions, where it could be
  seen by the other departments (rightly or wrongly) to have a partisan
  approach to issues of interdepartmental coordination (RCU 2000a, 2000b).

The review by the Cabinet Office's Performance and Innovation Unit
(PIU) (February 2000) confirmed the growing importance of GOs for the
delivery of government policies. It recommended that the Regional Coordination Unit be established in the PIU. The deputy prime minister, John
Prescott on behalf of the government, accepted this proposal, and Lord
Falconer, a Cabinet Office minister, was appointed its first head. The process
of extending and strengthening the work of the GOs to other departments

in the regions was a logical progression of their earlier success in integrating government activity at regional level as they sought to operationalize the 'joined up' government. The main conclusions of the PIU report were:

• Stronger and higher-profile GOs in the regions covering all government policies, with the GOs accountable for ensuring effective coordination of policies.
• Better ministerial and Whitehall coordination of policy initiatives and coordination with GOs through the creation of the RCU.
• Greater focus on the strategic outcomes of central government initiatives affecting local areas, with success judged against these.
• Government spending reviews to explore the linking of area initiatives as a priority.
• A closer working relationship between GOs and regional development agencies (Cabinet Office 2000a: 1–2).

The analysis of the PIU report clearly confirms the intransigence of the problems identified by the Conservatives in their 1992 election manifesto. The report also stresses the need to reinvigorate the mission of the GOs if they are to deploy the national government's considerable resources in the fields of education, welfare and criminal justice issues effectively. The regional policy actors similarly report their frustrations when confronted by Whitehall in its guise as a hydra, rather than Leviathan.

The almost federal nature of Whitehall (Massey 1993; Campbell and Wilson 1995; Smith 1999) is replicated in the regional structures of England. Indeed, prior to the creation of GOs, the regional offices often resembled a disparate and isolated collection of field stations, working in close proximity to each other but seemingly unaware of each other's existence. Sometimes, they even appeared to be working against each other, such was the lack of coherence across policies (Smith 1964; Mackintosh 1968). Thus:

> it was recognised that the centralised and departmentalised nature of decision making in Whitehall had historically presented considerable difficulties in securing effective policy co-ordination at urban and regional levels. This was partly because government departments with a regional presence did not readily relate their separate regional offices to each other.
>
> (Spencer and Mawson 1998: 6)

In addition to Whitehall's historically disjointed approach to policy implementation, the central departments, their agencies, non-departmental public bodies (NDPBs) and publicly owned corporations, did not have common regional boundaries. There was also no 'goodness of fit' with local government boundaries, hindering attempts by local authorities, often acting in concert with private sector interests, to maximize take-up of European funding. The then deputy prime minister, Michael Heseltine, drew on his previous experience as minister for Merseyside to press successfully the case for setting up GOs (Spencer and Mawson 1998: 6). The government announced the launch of the network of ten (later nine) integrated regional offices (subsequently to be known as the government offices for the regions) in November 1993 and they came on-stream in April of the following year. In 1998–99, the integration of the Government Office for Merseyside with the Government Office for the Northwest was completed. At the same time as the GOs were launched, the government established a Single Regeneration Budget (SRB) which drew together 20 separate programmes from the original 5 parent departments. It was initially set at £1.4 billion for the fiscal year 1994–95 (Mawson and Spencer 1997: 73–5).

Each GO was launched with a set of local objectives, which were refined over the first five years of their existence. These were set in the context of a sextet of national objectives common to all GOs (see, as an example, Government Office for London Annual Report 1996/97: 12). These common objectives are:

- To meet the operational requirements of Departments and Ministers;
- To contribute local views and experience to the formation and communication of Government policy;
- To promote a coherent approach to competitiveness, sustainable economic development and regeneration using public and private resources and through the exercise of their statutory responsibilities;
- To develop the skills of staff and methods of working to achieve these objectives and to demonstrate their success in doing so;
- To develop partnerships with and between all local interests to promote and secure these objectives;
- To provide a single point of contact for local people and deliver high quality services on Citizen's Charter principles.

The local objectives have been structured to fit these broad central objectives and to ensure that there is also an attempt to address local requirements. For example, some of London's key objectives for 1997/98 included:

- To develop proposals for the planning and transport responsibilities of the strategic authority for London, for consultation;
- Liaise with the Millennium Commission and the London Borough of Greenwich on Millennium Exhibition transport access issues and Greenwich's World heritage Site application;
- Represent London's interests in the revision of planning guidance for the south-east;
- Consider London's future housing requirements in the context of projected household growth;
- Define a viable package of river crossings for East London and continue with the development of the East Thames Appraisal Framework model.

(Government Office for London Annual Report 1996/97: 2–3)

The aims for the comparatively economically disadvantaged north-east of England for the same year included:

- Encouraging the growth of existing companies, securing inward investment, the creation and survival of new businesses;
- Secure the regeneration of the most deprived areas and their communities.

(Government Office for the North East
Annual Report 1996/97: 19)

Meanwhile, Merseyside concentrated on a mix of urban regeneration, inward investment and crime prevention objectives (Government Office for Merseyside Annual Report 1996/97: 10–13) and the south-east was concerned about coordination with neighbouring regions. Their plans included policies to manage the potentially damaging effects of unchecked economic growth on the environment, the housing market and an overburdened transport system (Government Office for the South East Annual Report 1996/97: 2–13).

At no time, however, were the senior managers in the GOs under the illusion that they were to act as the champions for the region in Whitehall. On the contrary, at all times they were to lead the arguments to implement and coordinate Whitehall's policies in the regions, a role stressed by the RCU after the winter of 2000/01. As one senior official in a GO explained:

> The objective is to actually deliver the national programme in a reliable and cost effective way . . . I am there to explain local policy to the centre, and to some extent to lobby in a non-conformist way. But at the end of the day the Government Office is there as an agent for Central Government.

(interview)

It is this 'district commissioner' role which precludes the GOs acting as a consistent lobby for their region, but which ensures that their senior officials adopt a coordinating role on behalf of their parent departments, coaxing, coercing and coopting sub-national governments, agencies and businesses into implementing national public policy. Where they do represent regional preferences, it is in the form of feeding back to the parent departments the practical experience of implementing policy at sub-national level. Generally, they aim to ensure business and local government have one point of contact. To facilitate this, they have staff seconded to them from departments other than their parent ministries.

The Labour Party's regional agenda

The Labour Party's 1992 manifesto first mooted the idea of regional development agencies (RDAs) at about the same time as the GOs policy was being formulated by the Conservatives. In this early draft, Labour saw RDAs mutating into 'the basis for elected regional governments' (quoted in Wood 1998: 9). The wording of the 1997 manifesto is clearer, but toned down:

> We will establish regional chambers to co-ordinate transport, planning, economic development, bids for European funding and land use planning. These will build on the tier of regional government created through quangos and government regional offices, and the coming together of local authorities to create a more co-ordinated regional voice.
>
> (quoted at www.number-10.gov.uk)

The background to this lay in Labour's criticism while in opposition that the GOs were not democratic. While Scotland and Wales were to be accorded varying measures of devolution under a Labour government, the party also said it would address the perceived democratic deficit in the English regions. The elected chambers of the RDAs were to do so. It is worth recording that the manifesto also recognized the need to take due cognizance of the GOs. The Labour Party consultation paper *A Choice for England* (1995: 9) proposed:

> The creation of indirectly elected regional chambers of local authorities representatives that would have two main purposes:
>
> – Strategic co-ordination; and
> – Democratic oversight.
>
> Rather than being in competition with local government, the chambers would be their regional voice. The democratic element would be developed in time by the creation of elected regional assemblies 'where public demand existed'. A precondition for these would be the establishment of a predominantly unitary system of local government. The assemblies would not have tax-raising or legislative powers.

On the whole, the manifesto took a similar ad hoc approach, noting it was up to the people of England to decide region by region whether they wished to have regional government. By the time legislation was passed (with the Regional Development Agencies Act 1998), this policy had mutated into a call for voluntary arrangements by local interests to form voluntary local chambers 'and use these as a mechanism through which RDAs can take account of regional views and give an account of themselves for their activities' (Labour Party 1995: 11). The Act 'does not give the Government powers to create regional assemblies, or even to hold referendums on the creation of assemblies' (p.13). It is clear that, by the time of their establishment, the RDAs had come to represent some kind of decentralization rather than an attempt at devolution. Yet the principle of a *potential* for devolution remained, especially in the north-east and south-west of England.

Establishing the GOs is an example of decentralization, not devolution, because there was no transfer of policy-making power and scrutiny to a devolved government with a separate assembly. However, the government did look for some of the benefits of decentralization. For example, it sought increased efficiency with greater scope for consumer choice in the provision of public goods and services. For the Major administration (1990–97), GOs fitted with the managerialist reforms of the Next Steps agencies, and Citizen's Charter because all these reforms sought to facilitate greater public sector responsiveness and accountability to consumer demand (Mawson and Spencer 1997; Spencer and Mawson 1998).

Establishing RDAs did not change fundamentally government policy. The provisions of the 1998 Act, which allowed RDAs to be established across the UK coterminously with GOs on a region-by-region basis, ensured that they are another form of functional decentralization. An unintended effect of the RDAs is that they gave new meaning to the role of the GOs. There is now an increased need for coordination at regional level and a greater focus on regional requirements. In an administrative and broadly, though not party, political sense, the GOs are able to act as the interface between the role of the RDAs as champions for their region and the policy requirements of Whitehall as represented by the GOs.

Some senior officials in GOs have so argued. They welcomed the continued transfer of their Single Regeneration Budget to the RDAs in 1999, because it freed them from parts of their regional remit and made their position as agents of central departments unequivocal. As one senior GO official argued: 'My job, if there is a national policy with which local government doesn't agree, is to persuade local government to fall into line' (interview). One of his colleagues in another GO similarly remarked:

> GOs have a lot of other business that isn't RDA, so they are not under immediate threat. The passage, if it is to be a passage, between what they have now and eventual regional government, is the broad path that the government hasn't yet set; they have high hurdles to achieve. Along that path Government Offices are needed in a lot of local roles, those budgets will not be handed over lightly and there will always need to be some liaisons to set Government policy. Departments might emerge more on a French model where there is a tiny staff.
>
> (interview)

While obviously agreeing with this observation, another official, this time from a central department, took the even more hard-line *dirigiste* view that, with the emergence of RDAs, GOs have

> a role as kind of sponsors of RDAs and they will need to produce a Government view on whether the Government agrees with what the RDAs are saying. They are independent of the RDAs but the Government is bound to have to comment on what the RDAs are doing. And therefore, in a sense, the Government Offices are an

interface between central departments and the RDAs and I think that's not a particularly difficult role for them to fulfil. That's in some ways an easier role for them to fulfil in a slightly more proactive intervention as well as in relation to the impact of governments on a local level.

(interview)

It seems, then, that the continued development of GOs is linked with that of RDAs in order to:

- develop the process of administrative and political decentralization within the unitary polity of England;
- provide an administrative coherence to the cross-cutting policies of central departments such as that identified by various taskforces and to coordinate those and other policies with the sub-national governments and agencies in England;
- engage in the kind of intergovernmental diplomacy inherent to systems of governance characterized by a hollowing out of the core executive.

Even though the RDAs have the potential for acquiring devolved powers, they lack clear statutory authority for doing so. Although they may establish regional assemblies, the assemblies will be advisory only and they will have no fiscal authority. The 1998 Act that established the RDAs was heavily influenced by Labour's experience of power and the government's often stated wish to coordinate or 'join up' government. The dynamic for the RDAs had been the belief by (mainly northern) Labour MPs that the regions of England deserved a measure of self-government, a degree of freedom from the distant oversight of Tory-dominated London. The reality of power led to a softening of the approach and a realization that in order to achieve many of their other manifesto commitments, the party required a degree of centralized coordination that the establishment of truly devolved regional assemblies would be unable to deliver. A compromise that left a great deal of administrative authority in the GOs began to appear more desirable.

As a result, the Regional Development Agencies Act 1998 established a statutory framework that allowed the deputy prime minister and his successors to retain a tight fiscal and administrative grip upon the RDAs. Section 1(2)(1) of the Act established that '[A] regional development agency shall consist of not less than 8 nor more than 15 members appointed by the Secretary of State. The Act gives the secretary of state the power to appoint the chair and deputy chair, but:

A regional development agency shall not be regarded as the servant or agent of the Crown or as enjoying any status, immunity or privilege of the Crown and its property shall not be regarded as the property of, or property held on behalf of, the Crown.

(s.1(3))

In other words, RDAs are statutory corporate bodies with less status and authority than many other public bodies, less even than local councils. Their purpose is statutorily defined. Each RDA acts:

- To further the economic development and the regeneration of its area,
- To promote business efficiency, investment and competitiveness in its area,
- To promote employment in its area,
- To enhance the development and application of skills relevant to employment in its area, and
- To contribute to the achievement of sustainable development in the United Kingdom where it is relevant to its area to do so.

(s.1(4)(1a–e))

These goals are so vague as to be meaningless. Assuming these goals are more precisely defined from time to time, the financial and administrative powers bestowed upon the RDA and its toothless chamber are all at the discretion of the secretary of state and may be varied or amended at his or her discretion. Even the acquisition of land (a function essential for the success of the former London Docklands Development Corporation in the 1980s) requires the 'consent' of the minister. The chair of the RDA could not even be said to rank as the minister's proconsul. That honour belongs to the director of the GO in each region, by virtue of his or her position within the administrative hierarchy of Whitehall.

It is clear that the purpose of GOs, and of their senior staff, is that of implementing the predetermined policies of the centre. The sole purpose of channelling local demands and responses up through the hierarchy is to ensure efficient and effective compliance. GOs are not designed to allow or to facilitate the free expression of distinct regional identities and cultures. Their job is to encourage regional and local institutions to fit national policy as designed and interpreted by ministers and senior officials in London. The field personnel of GOs are part of the administrative hierarchy of their parent departments. They are sent on short-term postings to carry out the duties of their London headquarters in the regions. In any conflict over administrative needs and the political demands of Whitehall versus the region, GO officials will inevitably deploy their considerable skills and experience in the service of the minister in London; to do otherwise is to invoke the spectre of dismissal.

Government offices for the English regions in practice: implementing managerialism

In what ways, if at all, do the GOs deviate from Whitehall when carrying out their administrative activities? To answer this question we examine the following topics.

- The way in which the GOs sought to establish an integrated team from disparate departments with different traditions and organizational perspectives.
- The relationship with the parent departments and difficulties in coordinating both with the centre and with the region.
- What have been the managerial developments in terms of budgeting and hard-charging within the GO (often different departments and agencies use different budgetary systems, each designed for a specific, if limited purpose (Massey 1995)).
- How the GOs seek to implement the *Modernising Government* (or 'joined up government') agenda.
- The impact of the RDAs on the GOs.
- Officials' perspective on what they saw as the success of the GOs as well as the main areas of disappointment/weakness.

The starting point for this was the operation of the Civil Service Management Code and the original Government Office Central Unit (GOCU) advice notes relating to the code. GOCU's functions, and responsibility for these documents, were moved to the Cabinet Office after the election of 2001.

These advice notes run to 28 papers and are in excess of 100 pages in total (unpublished documents).[2] They deal with:

0. An introduction to the advice note series	Sept. 1996
1. Interim advice on vacancy filling (revised)	Aug. 1996
2. Integrated personnel management in GOs (revised)	Feb. 1998
3. Staff development in GOs	Nov. 1995
4. Leave allowances for staff in GOs (revised)	Dec. 1997
5. Attendance in GOs	Nov. 1995
6. Equal opportunities	Mar. 1996
7. Harassment (revised)	July 1997
8. Variable working patterns	Mar. 1996
9. Gifts and hospitality	Mar. 1996
10. Data protection	Apr. 1996
11. Special leave	May 1996
Plus supplementary note	Feb. 1996
12. Human resource planning	May 1996
13. Resignation and reinstatement	July 1996
14. Citizenship	Aug. 1996
15. Recruitment of establishment staff	Aug. 1996
16. Overtime	Sept. 1996
17. Sick leave	Nov. 1996
18. Employment of casual staff	Nov. 1996
19. GO staff annual report appeals procedure	Nov. 1996
20. Fixed-term appointments	Dec. 1996
Plus supplementary note	Jan. 1998

21. UK and overseas travel and subsistence	Mar. 1997
Plus supplementary note	Apr. 1998
Plus supplementary note 2	June 1998
22. Positive action for people with disabilities	Mar. 1997
23. Age retirement, retention	Nov. 1997
24. Stress at work	Dec. 1997
25. Deputizing and temporary promotion	Jan. 1998
26. Health and safety at work	Apr. 1998
27. 'Gazetteer' of GO personnel policies	May 1998

This impressive and comprehensive list of documentation implies a high degree of standardization. The aims are to:

• supplement the Civil Service Management Code and give guidance and interpretation thereof; and
• to act as an aid to the integration of GOs owing to the fact that the employers of GO officials are at least four and often five separate Whitehall departments, each in possession of devolved pay and grading structures for their staff.

Having Treasury guidance on devolved pay and conditions has resulted in greater disaggregation of structures and conditions of service than existed prior to the changes of the 1980s and 1990s. Partly as a result of this, the GOCU advice notes are formidably comprehensive; but interviewees suggested that most officials rarely read them in full. That said, GOCU was a small servicing and coordinating unit that lacks executive power over individual GOs. The PIU reforms implemented in 2001 were designed to address these issues of management and policy coordination, especially as they relate to service delivery.

Officials responsible for harmonizing pay and conditions have tended to approach the issues involved on an ad hoc and local basis. One resources manager remarked that:

The index to the GOCU guidance alone is frighteningly long, so too from my perspective, is referring to the GOCU guidance notes. The difficulties that concern me most are those areas where we don't yet have harmonised terms and conditions for the staff and in particular where one of our parent departments brings forward a new initiative and how that might affect one part of the GO staff.

(interview)

Another senior GO official from a different region affected nonchalance and disdain for the advice notes on the grounds it was simply a 'gruesome exercise'. Her view was that so far as the Civil Service Management Code was concerned:

Most people have to remember that it exists. I shouldn't worry too much about that. The one thing about the code is that it has been absorbed into the skin, so if you were to ask me what was in it I would probably gag horribly and fail the exam question. But in a sense that is the way we operate, it has been around for so long, that it is the way we do things. I would also be hard put to list what are the GOCU amendments to it, it sounds like a piece of bureaucratic exercise that will touch almost nobody, but there may be some great heaving issue in that . . . God knows who commissioned that lot! I can't believe anybody in a Government Office would take it seriously.

(interview)

A senior official in a GO with a slightly different structure and regional priorities argued:

I do pay attention to them and I am slightly dispirited that we haven't got further than we have. I think in any good organisation if you are going to create a coherent sense of an integrated team, it is awfully helpful to have people operating with a similar management framework, similar performance management system say in terms and conditions of pay and travel and subsistence, same disciplinary procedures, same arrangements for managing surpluses and so on. You don't have to [though]; the Cabinet Office has succeeded as a department for a very long time with between a third and a half of its staff being on loan from other departments.

(interview)

In other words, the approach taken within each of the GOs reflects the requirements of that office and the perceptions of its senior managers, and as such, interpretation of these management issues is a good example of bureaucratic decentralization. It is unlikely the organizational tinkering that took place after the 2001 election will make a difference to this perspective.

With regard to attempting to create a single entity and identity for the officials of several departments, nearly all of whom (at senior level at least) are on time-limited secondments, most senior officials had similar views regarding their problems. In summary, the problems are seen to be grounded in the fact that each of the parent departments continues to set separate terms and conditions for its staff. One senior official argued that:

When the Government Offices were set up, I was certainly one of those who thought it would be sensible to try to move them to common terms and conditions and common management practices and that has proved to be fearsomely difficult. And the main reason why it is fearsomely difficult is to do with their constitutional structure. They are not independent departments and at one time there were up to six parent departments . . . [also] there are quite a lot of Home Office people now, so that has grown . . . I would argue that pushing through the standardisation of the management practices ought to have been pretty straightforward. Standardising some of the terms and conditions was always going to be a bit more difficult, because changing people's terms and conditions, unless you can persuade them all to agree, is a bit tricky. And it is almost by definition the case that if you are bringing three or four pools of people together and you are going to standardise something, some are going to feel that they have ended up with something less good than they had before . . . There is still quite a lot that isn't harmonised . . . It doesn't stop things functioning, it just makes it a bit ragged. When you want to fill jobs you have got to scratch your head and think which promotion system are we going to use for this job? Well, having to have a personnel function familiar with the promotion system of three parent departments is the sort of thing that one only expects to see these days in a *Yes Minister* skit; to find it in real life is rather silly.

(interview)

It is the small changes (such as travel allowances or leave entitlements) that can cause disruption to the working life of individuals who are members of the same team, perhaps at the same grade, but who are treated differently regarding benefits and remuneration. As another senior GO manager argued:

Everyone in the office is on the books of one department or another, so people see themselves not only as GO staff, but also as DETR staff and so forth. I come from [department] and am on [department's] books, because I am on Senior Civil Service terms and conditions. But if there are any little quirks then I would be subjected to [department's] quirks, like for example performance pay, where [department] runs a slightly different way of writing up bonuses from the other departments.

(interview)

The Treasury and Cabinet Office's experiment with devolved pay and grading, was designed to allow managers greater flexibility in delivering public services. It has some obvious drawbacks at regional level. The main difficulty is that the policy has to be reversed within the GOs, where senior managers need to integrate their team into a single entity. Regional integration is hindered by the Whitehall departments slowly drifting apart and away from any notion of a unified national civil service (see also Parry 2001). The gradual extension of devolved pay and conditions therefore creates and exacerbates institutional mechanisms and dynamics that hinder and prevent 'joined up' government. The GOs are an attempt to achieve continuity of policy delivery, but are hampered by the tectonic shifts occurring in Whitehall.

The process of achieving civil service reintegration generally takes place at GO level, especially as each GO is structured slightly differently in order to meet the specific requirements of its area and its unique set of circumstances. First GOCU, and now the responsible Cabinet Office unit provides coordination and guidance, and seeks to draw the elements together in order to set national standards and examples of best practice, but most work is done in the offices. It can be a difficult process, as confirmed by a former senior official:

> It is amazing how people start fighting over ridiculous things and say, 'Oh no! We can't give up an inch on this!' And it becomes an incredibly tedious grinding committee process to reach agreement on something that will work for all government office staff, regardless of who is involved in each department. And in my time . . . they did not complete that task. In my office, though, it mattered not at all . . . all the things that really mattered were sorted quite quickly, and all the rest was just going through the grind.
>
> (interview)

In other words, the major managerial, organizational and strategic policy issues were settled at high level quite quickly; the rest, because it was mundane administrative and personnel business, was sidelined to be sorted out if and when it became an important issue.

Another GO manager observed that, with regard to these issues:

> There are two rather different points we are debating here. One is, do you want to harmonise arrangements across the Government Offices? To which my answer would be, 'Yes'. And it is rather a pity we haven't been able to complete on that rather more quickly. The second issue is, do you want to delegate to a local level decisions on certain aspects of terms and conditions and management practice? To which my general answer is, 'Yes, as much as possible'. But I am prepared to debate [whether] some of those component parts and pay might be . . . worth debating. But either you have a national system that applies to the policy core of the civil service or you delegate. And if you are going to delegate you delegate to Government Offices as separate operations. I say the policy core because I think there is a very powerful case for executive agencies having delegated pay and bargaining structures, but there is actually quite a lot of homogeneity between the nature of work undertaken and the policy cores of the various departments. The lesson of pay and grading reviews generally in Whitehall, I think, is that we have secured more change that is beneficial at the executive end of Whitehall . . . The variations between the different bits of the policy core don't seem to be very great and we do create a certain amount of smoke.
>
> (interview)

In other words, the benefits of the flexible system are often outweighed by the contradictions inherent in it, but managers would not wish to lose the advantages provided by those flexibilities, even when they create institutional barriers to GO integration (and 'joined up government').

The way in which the new regional directors began to set up their teams and the structures adopted were often designed to reduce the barriers erected by parent departments between their officials. Most directors sought to integrate their team rapidly rather than continue as a collectivity of officials from disparate departments. In the Government Office for the South East for example, a matrix system was established whereby the entire staff was first moved to a high quality office in Guildford, disposing of several older, less well appointed buildings. It was important to provide better quality facilities so that people immediately were aware that their move to a new organization and a new office was an improvement in their working conditions; it also helped to ensure that everyone began in new (neutral) territory.

The second reason for this radical approach was that the south-east, although large both geographically and in terms of population, is not as easily identifiable as a region in the way that the south-west or north-east are. Neither the officials nor the client groups could readily identify with it (interviews). The client groups, such as county chief executives and so forth,

> were telling us we were pretty remote . . . and there was a lack of coherence in government presence generally and there was a lot of feeling that . . . the south-east wasn't a region. Above all we did not have that loyalty. They wanted to know what you were going to do about Kent or what you were going to do for Hampshire.
>
> (interview)

In order to address these issues they created a geographically structured team in the Guildford headquarters. But in addition to this, although there were directors in charge of area teams, each was 'double-hatted' in that each official also retained a functional responsibility, for example for transport or planning, that cut across the area and sometimes the region as well. The GO also retained two functional teams: regional Strategy and Finance, and Corporation Management (interviews; Annual Reports 1996/97, 1997/98). Despite its innovative nature, or perhaps because of it, the matrix system set up in the South East did not prove popular elsewhere, or with the GO management board in London.[3]

Some officials in other GOs sought to deny the existence of a matrix in the south-east, simply referring to it as a geographical structure, while one manager went so far as to say:

> I hate matrix structures actually, I'm with those OD [organizational development] theologians who say that the matrix is for organisations that are changing very fast or don't know where they are going.
>
> (interview)

That is perhaps a view that South East's advocates of a matrix system would in part share. They opted for the system in order to cope with rapid change in a region that lacked coherence or identity. Most GOs opted for a more traditional management structure, in which functional directorates deliver a service or provide a contact point across the region as a whole. Some regions, for example South West, did opt to establish and retain sub-regional offices that have sometimes acquired a geographical identity, that is the customers identify with them in area or geographical as well as functional terms (see Annual Reports 1996/97, 1997/98).

'Joined up government' and issues of coordination

The *Modernising Government* White Paper (Cabinet Office 1999b) sought better coordination across the web of central services and interests, looking for greater coherence in policy implementation not only at an interdepartmental level but also across the country. The experience of the GOs demonstrates the difficulties inherent in achieving this goal, as each regional office fought to secure coherence within its own functional field as well as across the region. At best this coherence could be uneven:

> It is uneven in two kinds of ways. First of all, some bits of departments are more committed to using Government Offices than others. Don't let's beat about the bush, the education side of DfEE has never quite brought into being part of the Government Office sponsoring framework in the way the employment part has. Post-16 may be an example of that, but Education wasn't part of the original family, and it only came in at the merger . . . The Department of Transport was always very hesitant and it didn't really give the Government Offices very much strategic role in relation to transport . . . it means that the GO interface of transport issues looks a bit thin at times.
>
> (interview with senior GO official)

From the perspective of the Whitehall-based officials, especially those in the central departments, the opportunity afforded by the GOs to establish some kind of coordination of regional and functional taskforces and zones is important. In some quarters they are even being talked of in terms of an English version of the French prefectures (various interviews).

This notion may appear fanciful. However, new emphasis on 'one-stop shops' for government services, and greater commitment to improved service delivery, depends on better coordination for its success. The organizations best placed to deliver these results 'on the ground' are the government offices for the regions. Taskforces and coordinated policy formulation teams at the centre of government in the Cabinet Office are a start in terms of 'joined up' government. The goodwill has always tended to unravel during the delivery phase because of old-fashioned Whitehall 'turf wars', or squabbling over resources (Smith 1999). The establishment of the GOs and their gradual evolution into something resembling a departmental prefecture would go some way to ameliorating these problems.

The evolution of *government* into *governance* has further reinforced the need for this kind of approach. The hollowing out of departmental functions to a plethora of agencies, non-departmental public bodies and private sector entities has placed a new emphasis on the need for government organizations to engage in intergovernmental diplomacy and coalition-building in order to deliver their own priorities. An unexpected outcome of the atomizing of government has been the corresponding recognition by officials of the need to counter its effects through networking and their willingness to engage in this activity.

Such behaviour is not always admired, but its utility is recognized. The case of the slow merger of budgeting systems is a case in point. When Next Steps agencies were established, a raft of amalgamations and restructurings occurred, and it was sometimes found that, within a single agency, more than one budgeting system was being used (Massey 1995). This odd state of affairs reflected the fact that different departmental divisions had been set up to run and report for slightly different stakeholders and slightly different reasons. It took some time to iron out these difficult administrative obstructions. In the case of the GOs, similar problems occurred, indeed they were sometimes worse. As one senior official observed:

> All I can say is, it is a morass. It is no way to run any kind of operation, and it comes back to this question of the constitutionally bizarre nature of the Government Offices, and having to negotiate with a whole lot of parents around funding. And it goes back to the unevenness. Some bits of some departments are very positive in supporting coherent plans, others don't get frightfully interested, and the whole thing ends up as a horse trade. So the skills you need in the Government Office finance function are not classic accountancy skills and that sort of thing. You need superior barrow boys who can go off and fix things and spot when departments are beginning to underspend a bit during the year and persuade people they can let you have a little bit more in this year. A great deal of effort has to go into this kind of activity.

> (interview)

These same diplomacy skills are much in evidence when the GOs take the lead in seeking EU money for their regions. One of their aims is to coordinate inward investment of EU funding. It is clear that those GO officials who displayed a talent in this area are those who put together a case based on a coalition of regional interests and then made that case in Brussels (various interviews).

The positioning of the GO on inward investment from the EU varies, even between counties in the same region. Likewise, the interrelationship between GOs and RDAs can become complex, straining the diplomatic and networking skills of the officials involved. As an example, one official argued that, in his region,

The Government Office is seen by its local authority partners as an asset and they are keen to keep us involved. The attitude to the RDA rather varies. [One county] has got off to a rather good start with the RDA on the whole, [another county] is rather suspicious of the RDA. [It] would quite like to run its own Objective 1 programme by itself, but knows it can't quite manage it. It's not very keen on a new 'big brother' on its patch. So the idea of having a Government Office around as a kind of neutralised broker is rather appealing. And the way that the 5B and Objective 2 programmes have been run has left people reckoning that they get a reasonably proactive entrepreneurial contribution from the secretariats in the Government Office, rather that just people explaining why you can't do things. And actually I don't want to run it in that kind of way, and I want to grow a partnership resource to do a lot of the management. I don't want to do it all out of the secretariat. I don't want to bid to have a lot of civil servants in the Government Office to manage the programmes. What I want is to have under the monitoring committees, a core strategy group to project-manage the programmes in a series of taskforces in different competitive parts of the division.

(interview)

So the expertise provided by the GOs in this kind of example will be as a kind of 'honest broker' between the RDA, the counties, the EU and other private sector interested parties. In short, the GOs will fulfil a brokerage and auditing role, with audit including financial and administrative oversight.

To pull together some of the issues raised in earlier sections of this chapter, it is clear that although the role of the GOs (and the perceptions by other agencies of that role) varies over time and place, GOs have the potential to evolve several key functions in English governance:

- to develop the original coordination functions for which they were originally established and extend them to include central government departments and agencies, the RDA, local authorities, non-departmental public bodies operating in the region and important private sector organizations involved in the delivery of public services;
- to monitor and audit the delivery of central government policies and intervene when and where appropriate using a range of fiscal and executive powers to encourage compliance with national strategies, as defined by the national government;
- to use their privileged position straddling the national and regional arenas, to act as neutral brokers between the different actors involved in the policy networks at regional level, as well as to facilitate their access to supranational (EU) level on relevant issues.

The continuing managerial revolution, with benchmarking, performance measurements and so on, also aids intergovernmental diplomacy and reinforces its importance. However, there is also a certain 'weariness' in the GOs, as in departments and agencies generally. Partly this is due to the perception that there is a constant process of change that never allows the successive waves of reform to bed down sufficiently before the next upheaval (Massey 1995). Partly it is due to the poor quality of forethought that had gone into some of the earlier reforms, especially the use of performance indicators and other forms of performance measurement. While most senior officials accepted, and even welcomed, the need for the auditing of their performance, there was a near universal dislike of performance indicators. As one official commented:

> I'm afraid Michael Heseltine has a lot to answer for in terms of his obsession with oversimplified performance indicators and people not understanding them. You have to have a basket [of them] and you have to interpret them.
>
> (interview)

Senior officials seek a flexible and robust set of measurements but this holy grail of performance measurement remains some way off.

Conclusions

One of the main reasons for decentralization is to provide flexibility and to allow government bodies to meet the needs and aspirations of regions and the other constituent elements of a nation. A concomitant of this, therefore, must inevitably be that organizational structures, priorities and operating procedures will diverge. The central contradiction of GOs is that, in promoting regional divergence, both in their own structures and in the performance of other organizations, they also have the responsibility of harmonizing the implementation of central priorities and policies.

As the new regional structures such as the RDAs develop, they will increasingly come to reflect the nature of their individual regions. In some cases this will mean acquiring a more political role, while in others it will mean eschewing all but a business orientation. In the case of those that opted for this latter option, there is the danger that in seeking technocratic solutions to their regions' problems, they will forget to remain vigilant about the political nuances of their position. Any such political insensitivity could lead to conflict with the elected politicians in Westminster. One GO official warned:

> Junior officials in the RDA have said quite explicitly in my hearing, 'We are not a political organisation.' And that is quite an interesting statement for a quango, and it didn't mean, 'we are not a party political organisation,' it meant, 'we are not a small "p" political organisation'. They said, 'we are a business-led organisation'. And I have to say I

don't know what that means. And I worry about it because I think there is a risk that we will repeat some of those early problems with Next Steps agencies where people like [an official who was later disciplined] in his early days did believe the rhetoric that they had been brought in to run their organisation as though it was a private company. And that is not what anybody is asked to do when they are running a part of the public service. They are asked to bring in the private sector skills and apply them to running a part of the public sector.

(interview)

In this context, with each region approaching links to the RDA on an individual basis, the problem for GOs will be to make RDAs a success by keeping them out of trouble and ensuring they conform to central government expectations.

A further probable development will be the full-scale integration of more departments into the GO set-up. Many senior GO officials believe it was a mistake not to have brought in the NHS, Ministry of Agriculture, Home Office, Department of Culture, Media and Sport and Department of Social Security at the start (interviews). It may have been politically and administratively easier to integrate the first four departments, but the coordination of government policy, especially the goals of *Modernising Government*, cannot be achieved without a regional element. That is now most effectively achieved through the GOs by extending their role and increasing the number of participating departments. The accountability line of command for the GOs (as well as the source of money) is from the region directly to Whitehall. As such, there can be no overt conflict of loyalties. The GOs, therefore, look set to be the key administrative players in England's regional politics. If they are denied that role, then an essential lubricant for easing the new machinery of English *governance* may be lost, with damaging consequences for effective *government*.

Notes

1 A battle-axe with two cutting edges.
2 This list of documents is not published and the documents are not readily available. The researchers are grateful to (the then) GOCU for providing access.
3 A group of deputy secretaries (grade 2) from the parent departments.

7

The differentiated polity revisited

Introduction

We draw the strands of our argument together in three ways. First, we summarize our main conclusions for each country. Second, we give summary answers to the questions posed at the end of Chapter 2. Finally, we discuss the strengths and weakness of the differentiated policy approach.

Summary

England

Government offices for the regions (GOs) illustrate the problems of enforcing the writ of Whitehall even when there is no devolved government for the English regions. There is a paradox at the heart of them: by seeking to implement 'joined up' government the GOs demonstrate the lack of coordination in regional and local policy implementation in the differentiated polity. This problem will be exacerbated as regional development agencies (RDAs) develop their role. GOs are one cause of the fragmentation they seek to coordinate. They are responsible for joining up at the regional and local levels; they are the node of regional networks, linking central and local government, special-purpose bodies and the voluntary sector. But they institutionalize fragmentation because their organization is functional, paralleling the parent department, and each department has a different degree of autonomy from its Whitehall parent. It is amazing how people start fighting over ridiculous things and say:

> 'Oh no! We can't give up an inch on this!' And it becomes an incredibly tedious grinding committee process to reach agreement on something that will work for all government office staff, regardless of who is involved in each department. And, in my time . . . they did not complete that task.
>
> (private information)

GOs are unable to speak either with a single voice to local actors or with an authoritative voice to Whitehall where, when heard, they may not be heeded. GOs will continue to develop because they will: be a part of the process of administrative and political decentralization in England; join up the cross-cutting policies of central departments; and engage in intergovernmental diplomacy, managing the networks of public, private and voluntary bodies so typical of networked policy systems.

The dynamic for the RDAs, and to a lesser extent GOs, has been the belief by (mainly) northern Labour MPs that the regions of England deserve a measure of self-government. The 'new' Labour government wanted a degree of centralized policy coordination that devolved regional assemblies would undermine. So, deconcentration to RDAs and GOs prevailed, but the policy remains a compromise and the call for devolution to the English regions has not been stilled. For the foreseeable future, uncertainty and instability remain the lot of regional civil servants.

GOs also show the limits to managerialist policies. The Treasury and Cabinet Office's ambition to devolve pay and grading to allow managers greater flexibility had some obvious drawbacks at regional level. For the most part, this policy was not implemented in GOs because senior managers needed to integrate their team into a single entity. Whitehall departments, which slowly drifted apart and away from any notion of a unified national civil service for pay and conditions of work, hindered the GOs' search for integration. Whitehall-based officials see GOs in terms of an English version of the French regional prefectures. However fanciful this notion may appear, it is the case that there is a new emphasis on 'one-stop shops' for government services, and a far greater adherence to improved delivery of service demands upon the improvements in coherence and coordination for its success. The central contradiction of GOs is that in recognizing and articulating regional distinctiveness, both in their own structures and in their work with other organizations, they also have the responsibility of enforcing the priorities and policies of central departments.

Scotland

Scotland is part of a unified but not a unitary civil service. It is important to distinguish between members of the UK Civil Service in Scotland (e.g.

Ministry of Defence, Department of Social Security) and the Scottish Office (now the Scottish Executive) civil service. The Scottish Office civil service was in the unusual position of dominating the Scottish polity while part of the unified civil service. The Scottish Executive civil service confronts local political masters and the imperative to stay in step with Whitehall.

Experience in Whitehall is the 'done thing' and advantageous to those seeking promotion. There is little evidence of transfers between territorial departments and no evidence of civil servants seeking a territorial career through work only in the territorial ministries. The civil service was not considered in detail in the Scottish devolution settlement beyond the general injunction that the 'ultimate loyalty of civil servants will remain to the Crown'. However, 'in practice, the loyalty of individual civil servants will be to whichever administration they are serving' and they 'will continue to take their instructions from their departmental ministers' (Cabinet Office 1998b: Note 2). There was limited change, with existing Scottish Office traditions and patterns of organization prevailing. The Scottish Office 'carried on'.

In Scotland, there is a feeling that 'devolution must work' so the civil service and the Executive are keen to cooperate. Such collegial attitudes are likely to dissipate as politicians strive to show that Scottish government is distinctive and effective and as they become more dominant in the policy process. Political scrutiny has grown: ministers are now on the doorstep. Working relationships are more direct. There are worries that the civil service may become more politicized because civil servants will be keen to please their local masters. Conversely, they remain part of a unified service and, even in devolved systems, the pull of the centre remains strong. These tensions will be played out in the process of devolution.

For both economic development and community care, relations with Whitehall after devolution are marked by coordination. Both policies already had distinctive Scottish characteristics and little has, therefore, changed. The UK government remains dominant but hands-off, even benevolent, in managing intergovernmental relations. However, in Scotland, policies are subject to greater scrutiny than occurred under the Scottish Office. Ministers and their departments are now more visible with an opposition in parliament looking at their decisions.

The policy process changed after devolution, in part to keep in step with changes in Whitehall – for example spending reviews, accrual accounting – but also reflecting Scottish policy reviews (community care) and the need to build Scottish implementation networks. Scotland is now embedded in a changed and changing set of institutional links. A Joint Ministerial Committee (JMC) provides central coordination. A senior civil servant observed, 'we have a knack of taking decisions under anaesthetic, and it hasn't worn off yet'; a cute way of noting that the consequences of devolution could be dramatic. His subsequent, if more prosaic, observation that 'the first meetings of the Joint Ministerial Committee was an extraordinary constitutional event which nobody remarked on' seems accurate in all respects.

Wales

The civil service did not welcome devolution. There was concern about quality of members and acute awareness that Wales was the least distinctive territorial unit. 'A lot of my staff have a strong desire to remain part of the UK higher civil service' but there is a growing awareness that 'in a sense it is a contradiction in terms'. So, the Welsh departments seek to keep their existing links with their Whitehall counterparts.

Political scrutiny of the civil service is greater since devolution. As with Scotland, ministers are now on the doorstep, and working relationships are more direct: 'that has pulled all sorts of pressures on the civil service'. Top officials work closely, and in private, with the presiding officer and the Cabinet. So, 'we are perceived as part of the Cabinet – it puts us in a different position'. 'There is a concern among members that they are not getting the service they deserve'.

In economic development and community care, Welsh civil servants did not consider themselves part of a Welsh service but part of a UK service with distinctive interest in Wales. So, they remain 'in step' with Whitehall's policies but seek to apply them in their own way.

The breadth and depth of responsibilities allocated to the Welsh Office meant that its civil servants were experts. Now ministers are becoming as expert as their civil servants. The 'professionalization of politics' is under way. The civil service is strong and policy networks are weak in the policy-making process; for example, community care policy was driven by the civil service. The civil service fears small town politics, politicians with axes to grind, and sees its role, in both policy development and policy implementation, as mitigating the worst excesses. 'Partnership is more rhetoric than reality.'

Northern Ireland

The Northern Ireland Civil Service (NICS) is closely modelled on its larger counterpart, the Home Civil Service, from which it takes many aspects of its structure and internal procedures, partly because civil service beliefs stress its affinity with the mainland cousin. To promote greater stability amidst sectarian strife in the province, successive governments have presided over a form of 'local corporatism' in which the civil service is a key actor. NICS's small size (30,000), and violent intercommunal strife over the province's constitutional status, both ensure that there are important differences between the two civil services. Despite Direct Rule, Northern Ireland has been governed differently from the rest of the UK and senior figures in NICS have 'enjoyed' a far higher public profile than their Whitehall counterparts.

Policy-making in Northern Ireland varies considerably depending on the policy area in question. The variegated configuration of departments – they have long been not coterminous with Whitehall – sustains varying degrees of policy divergence. It can be described as an 'adoption or adaptation' continuum, although most policies are variations on the UK framework of policy. Financially, the fiscal regime in the province has remained relatively slack, at least in comparison with that in the rest of the UK. Public expenditure, having risen rapidly under the Labour government of 1974–79, was maintained under successive Conservative governments and has now levelled out. Since 1997, it has moved in line with Great Britain's spending levels.

For economic development and community care, there is considerable scope for variation from the rest of the UK. The Department of Health and Social Services (Northern Ireland) appeared to adopt a line that is much closer to the UK position than was the case of the Department of Economic Development.

The implementation of public sector reform in NICS has been partial, delayed and deliberately selective. Westminster governments became more dogmatic about introducing the reforms during the late 1980s and early 1990s but, even then, the application of the reforms was often tempered to allow for the idiosyncratic nature of the small and often-beleaguered policy community. So, while executive agencies were set up in Northern Ireland, their operation has always been subject to the restrictions imposed by their own small size and by an in-service culture predisposed to avoid breaking up the unity and cohesiveness of NICS. Devolution after the Belfast Agreement of 1998 has led to further policy and administrative divergence, despite the concordat arrangements developed since then.

Addressing our research questions

The fact that the UK was differentiated before devolution is simply and clearly illustrated by the empirical sections of this book. To return to the questions posed in Chapter 2, we have found distinctive civil services with their own ways of working, servicing territorially specific policy networks. Most of the civil service lives and works anywhere except Whitehall. And location matters. The civil services of Northern Ireland and Scotland have distinctive histories. It borders on overstatement but, for periods, for many policy areas, NICS was the government of Northern Ireland. The territorial departments can and do act as the executives for their countries and initiate territorially specific policies, although clearly there are important differences between the territories. It is useful to adopt, in a slightly modified form, Davis's (1995: 28) distinction between the politics of elections, the politics of policy and the politics of implementation. For all the territories, the discretion of territorial ministries is greatest over the politics of implementation; all modify UK-wide policies when they implement them. In Northern Ireland and pre-devolution Scotland there was discretion over policy, which grew in both cases post-devolution. Only in Northern Ireland and post-devolution Scotland was there any territorially specific influence on the politics of elections. For Great Britain (not the UK), the dominance of the major political parties and of prime-minister-led media campaigns was clear.

The degree of territorially specific discretion may be high in Northern Ireland but it is less in Scotland and lower still in Wales and the English regions. Devolution has already induced significant change. The policy may presuppose a unified civil service, but many wonder whether this expectation is realistic. Scotland is the paradigm case and, within a year, the Scottish Executive civil service has to balance the demands of local political masters with the imperative to stay in step with Whitehall. Even the English regions can go native and all too often occupy the uneasy halfway house of speaking for the region to the centre and for the centre to the region. Reforms seek to create 'joined up' government, and this search for uniformity in the politics of policy implementation attests to the unevenness of yesteryear.

Recent reforms reinforce the existing pattern of functional differentiation with decentralized political authority, and increasingly the centre has to manage packages of services, packages of organizations and packages of governments. Managing intergovernmental relations is the new skill, and distinctions between types of organizations and levels of government become blurred as the centre seeks to manage a seamless web.

So, *initially*, devolution will reduce the tension between territorial and functional politics within the constituent territories of the UK because the devolved governments will be able to 'match' policy to expectations more closely. The new consultative machinery, allied to the tradition of keeping in step with the Whitehall departments, will minimize conflict between the constituent territories and the centre. However, the lesson of our case studies is that this equable climate cannot be sustained because the rationale for devolution lies in difference, not homogeneity. The pressures on a unified civil service will intensify, therefore, and civil servants may become more politicized because they will be keen to please their local master. In the words of the head of the Home Civil Service, Sir Richard Wilson (1998), the civil service is 'going to have learn skills that we haven't learned before'. In future, the pattern of intergovernmental relations in the UK may well increasingly resemble those of other states (like Canada) with Westminster systems. In the new dispensation, the institutions of central state public administration, most notably the civil service, are pivotal. As Rhodes (2001a: 31) remarked, 'even in devolved systems, the pull of the centre remains strong'. So, the oscillating tensions on and in a unified civil service will be one of the central characteristics of the evolving process of devolution.

The case against the differentiated polity

There are various criticisms of the notion of the differentiated polity. We want to discuss five lines of criticism because they will help us to suggest new avenues of exploration. First, some critics insist that Britain keeps its strong core executive and has not been hollowed out (Weller *et al.* 1997; Holliday 2000; Marsh *et al.* 2001). Second, others comment that networks have not spread and insist that hierarchy pervades central–local government relations (Davies 2000). Third, some non-academic critics comment adversely on the 'patois' of the approach, or its language of core executive, power dependence and the differentiated polity (Riddell 2000). Fourth, the approach pays insufficient attention to the role of ideas (Marsh *et al.* 2001). Finally, the approach is neo-pluralist and 'politicist', ignoring the influence of socio-economic structures (Marsh *et al.* 2001).

Rescuing the strong executive

Ian Holliday (2000) concentrates on the hollowing out strand in the argument that Great Britain is becoming a differentiated polity and asks three questions: How big is the core executive? What role does it play in policy networks? And how does it run more distant parts of the state?

First, he argues that the core executive has grown, as if size equates to effectiveness. It seems obvious that this growth is a response to perceived weakness. However, as Holliday acknowledges, the numbers directly involved in supporting the prime minister are still small compared with both core executives in other countries and the tasks to be carried out. Arguably, the Cabinet Office performs key coordinating and conflict resolution functions but the following quotes perhaps best capture its inexact roles:

> [The Cabinet Office is] a collection of previous prime ministers' pet projects.
>
> (Cabinet Office official)

> It is a dumping ground for issues they don't know what to do with.
>
> (political adviser)

> The Cabinet Office brings nothing with it. Other units, with the backing of the prime minister, can do something. (departmental official)
>
> (all the above quotes are private information)

The increase in size illustrates the centre's sense of its own weakness. It is a power grab, a reaction to felt weakness, a response to baronial power, a frustration with the inability to pull effective levers; it is evidence for, not against, hollowing out.

Second, Holliday argues that the core executive is the nodal point of 11 networks – for example domestic policy, overseas policy – that produce effective coordination. He concedes that the core can lose control and that there are failures. He notes the great variation between policy areas. He agrees that 11 networks make for problems of overall coordination and integration. He argues that coordination is at times partial. Nonetheless, he insists that core actors are effective and 'enhancement of core executive capacity has been considerable'.

It is hard to accept his judgement. There are two limits to central steering. First, the centre has rubber levers; pulling the central policy lever does not necessarily mean something happens at the bottom. Such frustrations lead to colourful language. So, for the Department of Health, instilling financial discipline in doctors is likened to 'herding cats'. Despite several attempts over the years to strengthen central control over such departmental policy silos, the problem persists. Second, ministerial or baronial government is a long-standing feature of British government. Power dependence characterizes the links both between barons and between the barons and prime minister and forms the fault line at the heart of the machine. So, 'new' Labour criticizes central departments for acting as iron cages frustrating action on the wicked issues. It calls for a corporate approach, stronger horizontal policy-making, reforms of the Cabinet Office and a prime minister's department. These calls are not new. For the umpteenth time, a government confronts the problem of the centre's strategic capability. Coordination is a central theme not only of the *Modernising Government* White Paper but also of the prime minister's search to control government policy-making.

This endless search for coordination is a search for the holy grail. As Wright and Hayward (2000: 33) concluded, core executive coordination is in practice modest. It has four characteristics:

(i) It is largely negative, based on persistent compartmentalisation, mutual avoidance and friction reduction between powerful bureaux or ministries.

(ii) Even when co-operative, anchored at the lower levels of the state machine and organised by specific established networks, co-ordination is sustained by a culture of dialogue in vertical relations and of integration at the horizontal level.

(iii) It is rarely strategic, so almost all attempts to create proactive strategic capacity for long-term planning . . . have failed.

(iv) It is intermittent and selective in any one sector, improvised late in the policy process, politicised, issue-oriented and reactive.

(p.33)

Reforms to strengthen the core executive reflect the strength of the barons and the core's past weakness, not its current strength (for we do not know if these reforms will work, only that previous reforms did not). Wright and Hayward (2000: 34) also argue that core executives lack political will, time, information, cohesion and effective instruments. The weight of 'urgent' political issues needing attention and multiple constitutional and administrative constraints further limit the capacity of the core executive to coordinate effectively. So, 'building capacity' and 'overcoming the structural weakness at the centre', to use two of today's catchphrases, both illustrate power dependence and the ever swinging pendulum between the barons and the core. It does not illustrate the power of the centre. Rather it justifies the contention at the heart of the hollowing out thesis that the power of the British centre is all too often overstated. Holliday's claim that the argument about prime ministerial power, whether in the guises of presidentialism or Bonapartism, was about steering, and not about command and control, takes the breath away. It is the hollowing out thesis that substitutes steering for command and control and power dependence for the strong executive in our understanding of British government.

Third, Holliday concedes that the 'operating environment of the contemporary core presents with many challenges' but concludes 'it is hard to see that the changes of the last thirty years have made any dramatic difference to the co-ordinating capacity of the core'. Many would consider the problems of steering an ever more complex, devolved government machine evidence of a dramatic difference, but the most obvious example is membership of the EU. In Chapter 2, we cited Menon and Wright (1998) to show that the UK was bypassed for the history-making decisions, scarcely evidence of the core executive's ability to act effectively. In the same vein, Bulmer and Burch (2000: 61) argue that British government has neither established a planning capacity on European policy nor developed a constructive engagement with EU policy processes. It is a failure that stems from intraparty disputes and an absence of political leadership; but whatever the causes, it is implausible to interpret it as evidence of central capacity.

In sum, Holliday suggests that the 'analysis of resource and power dependency within the multiple policy networks that characterise the contemporary British state is a powerful corrective to traditional institutional accounts, but it does not provide a complete picture'. Exactly so. Rhetorical flourishes to one side, we do not argue the state was disabled or that it had broken up. Rather we present a corrective to the Westminster model and that corrective is still necessary because we still talk about Blair presidentialism and Bonapartism using minor institutional changes as supporting evidence.

These comments on Holliday apply with equal force to Marsh *et al.* (2001) and Taylor (2000). Marsh *et al.* subscribe to the strong executive model of British government and treat the differentiated polity as a series of qualifications to the power of the executive. As a result, they pay too little attention to the sour laws of unintended consequences. They do not deal with such questions as 'Why does the strong centre fail?' and 'Why is coordination so elusive?' Taylor (2000) examines the use of taskforces, especially the Social Exclusion Unit (SEU) as a mechanism for policy coherence. Selective, focused attempts to coordinate have always been possible, even effective. That conceded, the Labour government's reforms of the core executive are as much evidence of the ineffectiveness of yesterday's efforts to coordinate as they are of today's effective coordination, especially when it is too early for an authoritative analysis of the outcomes of SEU interventions. We would argue, as Taylor recognizes, that such attempts at selective coordination are evidence of felt weakness by the centre and an attempt to assert more control over less. We agree that taskforces are an equal and opposite reaction to hollowing out but see the filling in as putative.

The ever changing mix

Davies (2000) argues that 'the world of governance . . . does not exist in the realm of local politics'. Rather, it resembles 'vertical networking' with central government 'rowing' rather than 'steering'. Networks are not pervasive. He compares markets and hierarchies with networks and sees hierarchy as the defining characteristic of central–local government relations.

There are several important qualifications to this argument. First, 'it is the mix that matters' and 'no one service will deploy only one resource allocation mechanism' (Rhodes 1997b: 51). Second, the argument was never restricted to local government. Central government's bypassing of local authorities for special-purpose bodies, and contracting out to the private sector, fragmented service delivery systems and created the imperative to build networks if only to coordinate service delivery. Third, networks are found not only in central–local government relations. They are locality based, spanning public–private and voluntary sectors. They pose acute steering problems. Fourth, the power relationship in central–local relations is asymmetric (Rhodes 1986) and a high degree of dependence does not leave the dependent partner powerless. Fifth, networks are characterized by trust, and the failure of central departments to recognize that networks have such characteristics means their interventions fail to have the intended effect. The lack of trust does not invalidate the claim that networks proliferate, rather it explains why central interventions fail. Finally, the emphasis on networks aims to redress an imbalance. Conventional accounts of the 1980s and 1990s stress the power of the centre and the decline of local government. This Westminster model stress on the strong executive is the fatal conceit in British government because it overemphasizes the power of the centre and fails to see the limits to its power. Network governance is one of those limits.

New ideas and everyday language

We need a new language to capture the changes that have and are taking place. We quoted Peter Riddell in Chapter 2 and his criticism of the 'private patois' of the differentiated polity. We remain convinced that the old vocabulary for describing Westminster and Whitehall is at best a partial description of how British government works. Also, it matters how we understand British government. Such understandings are not the privilege of the chattering classes. If our existing map of our institutions and how they work is faulty, we mislead citizens and undermine representative democracy. Such maps are about how we are governed, and politicians with faulty maps will make promises they cannot keep, not because they are venal but because, unwittingly, they travel in the wrong direction. We are trying to make corrections to the existing map of British government so citizens and politicians alike know what journeys they can and cannot take.

The notions of core executive, hollowing out and the differentiated polity provide a more accurate and fruitful map of British government than the more familiar concepts of the Westminster model. Yet Riddell rejects a new language less because he thinks it inaccurate than because it lacks the familiarity and the clarity of that of earlier political scientists such as Bagehot, whose own metaphors were new in 1867. To respond to his concerns, we have to examine the nature of concepts.

What makes ideas familiar? Familiarity obviously comes from use. Here lies a puzzle; the new vocabulary is not acceptable until approved by everyday use but it cannot be so approved until we start using it. Clearly, then, a lack of familiarity cannot be a serious objection to new concepts. We must be able to translate our ideas into ones that other political scientists and practitioners recognize, but this translation must not entail a slavish adherence to the existing, mainstream language of the Westminster model because it would restrict debate and innovation in political science.

What gives concepts clarity? Any concept gets meaning in large part from its place within a body of concepts. In isolation, all concepts are vague. Just as the differentiated polity gains clarity when filled out with ideas such as the core executive, so the Westminster model gains clarity when filled out with ideas such as cabinet government. No doubt people unfamiliar with concepts such as the hollowing out of the state might need an explicit link to processes such as the erosion of the authority of the state by international interdependences. Equally, however, people who are unfamiliar with the concept of a unitary state might need us to contrast it with federal systems. Although concepts such as the hollow state can sound like metaphors, that too need not be a matter of concern. After all, they are metaphorical only in that they apply novel names to processes and practices that we can unpack in more literal terms, such as international pressures and organizations eroding the authority of the state. What is more, all concepts begin as metaphors in this sense. They start out as novel names, such as 'loyal opposition', to describe a set of parliamentary practices, only later to acquire familiarity. Over time, our new concepts might become as much a part of the everyday language of practitioners and commentators as the terms embedded in the Westminster model.

Taking ideas seriously

Marsh *et al.* (2001) argue that the differentiated polity does not take ideas seriously and stress that an elitist, conservative British political tradition underpins Westminster institutions. We agree with the general comment that the differentiated polity narrative, and the policy networks literature in general, pay too little attention to ideas (Marsh and Rhodes 1992: 257–61;

Rhodes 1997a: 12–13). We further believe that the notion of tradition plays a central role in explaining changing patterns of governance in the UK (Bevir and Rhodes 2002). However, there are problems with Marsh *et al.*'s hypostatized notion of tradition.

We can best illustrate this point with Greenleaf's (1983: 15–20) account of the British political tradition as a dialectic between two opposing tendencies: libertarianism and collectivism. Libertarianism stresses four things: the basic importance of the individual; the limited role of government; the dangers of concentrating power; and the rule of law. Its antithesis, collectivism, stresses: the public good; social justice; and the idea of positive government. These strains exist in both the Conservative and Labour parties. They set the boundaries to political debate. Our view of tradition differs. Greenleaf's opposing tendencies are ahistorical. Although they come into being in the nineteenth century, they remain static, acting as fixed categories, ideal types, into which he forces individual thinkers and texts, even different parts of the one text or different utterances by the one thinker. Tradition is a starting point, not a destination, and instances cannot be constructed by comparison with the features of a tradition. Traditions do not constitute the beliefs that people come to hold or the actions they perform. Marsh *et al.* (2001) are essentialists who equate traditions with a fixed set or core of beliefs against which they assess variations.

So, when unpacking the idea of tradition, we must not reify traditions (Bevir 1999: 174–220; Bevir and Rhodes 2001). Tradition is a starting point, not something that fixes or limits later actions. Tradition is not an unavoidable influence on all we do, for to assume it was would leave too slight a role for agency. Rather, traditions are an initial influence on people that colour their later actions only if their agency has not led them to change it. Every strand of a tradition is in principle open to change. No doubt there are circumstances when we can identify core ideas that persist through time. But, alternatively, we might identify a tradition with a group of ideas widely shared by several individuals although all shared not one idea. Or we might identify a tradition with a group of ideas that passed from generation to generation, changing a little each time, so no single idea persisted across all generations. Finally, we should be careful not to hypostatize traditions. We must not claim an existence for them independent of the beliefs and actions of individuals. Traditions are not fixed entities. They are not given, sat in a philological zoo, waiting for people to discover them. They are contingent, produced by the actions of individuals. The carriers of a tradition bring it to life. They settle its content and variations by developing their beliefs and practices, adapting it to new circumstances, while passing it on to the next generation. We can only identify the beliefs that make up a tradition by looking at the shared understandings and historical connections that allow us to link its exponents with one another.

Traditions should be defined pragmatically depending on the events and actions we want to explain. We must recognize that traditions are contingent products of the ways in which people develop specific beliefs, preferences and actions. We must identify the tradition by looking at the background against which people come to hold their beliefs and by tracing the relevant historical connections. So, political scientists can locate an individual in various traditions depending on what questions they seek to answer. Because traditions do not exist as given and reified entities, the political scientist's task cannot be to place the individual in one of a finite set of fixed traditions. Rather, they should identify the tradition against which someone believed or did something by tracing the relevant connected beliefs and habits that intentionally or unintentionally passed from generation to generation at some time in the past. The value of the selected tradition depends on the explanatory power of the evidence for the conceptual and historical links between the beliefs and actions that make up the tradition. The more exact the account of these links, the more fully we will be able to grasp the nature of the tradition, so the more explanatory work it will be able to do. Historical or temporal links show how the relevant beliefs and practices passed from one generation to another and in so doing explain why the beliefs persisted through time. Conceptual links show us how the relevant beliefs and practices form a coherent set and in so doing explain why they persisted together as a loose-knit whole rather than as isolated beliefs brought together by mere chance.

The state and civil society

It is difficult to comment on Marsh *et al.*'s theory of structured inequality and asymmetrical power because they present only the beginnings of an argument. It would seem that the differentiated polity model is 'politicist and fails to acknowledge the socio-economic constraints on British governments'. This 'broader socio-economic structural context' constrains and facilitates 'the actions, and the likely success, of individuals and interest groups in the British polity'; 'British politics . . . isn't an even playing field'. We take the general point that changes in the differentiated polity must be placed in a broader context (see Rhodes 1988: 48–77, 372–87 and Figure 5.1).

The differentiated polity explores how the informal authority of networks supplements and supplants the formal authority of government. It explores the limits to the state and seeks to develop a more diverse view of state authority and its exercise. Broadly conceived, it explores the changing boundary between state and civil society. This broader notion of governance in Britain exercises historians of the twentieth century.

Harris (1990: 66–7) argues that one of the 'tacit understandings' about political community at the beginning of the twentieth century was 'a belief among politicians of all complexions that the relationship between government and society was essentially a limited one'. Civil society was 'the highest sphere of human existence', while the state was 'an institution of secondary importance'. The corporate life of society 'was expressed through voluntary associations and the local community'. She argues that these beliefs had 'enormous tenacity' (p.69). Between the wars, they were sustained not just by professional civil servants, who favoured a return to more limited government, but also by the British public who 'resumed their Victorian habits of voluntary action and self-help' (p.77). However, the Second World War led Britain to develop 'a far more powerful centralised wartime state than any of her more metaphysical-minded, state-exalting continental enemies' (p.91). It also fuelled a reformist mood, which led to a 'profound break with some of the major conventions of the previous hundred years' (p.96). 'Promises, programmes and planning' became the new norm (p.97). Harris concludes that, by the 1950s, 'the common constitutional culture based on tacit acceptance of common history and unspoken assumptions about the nature of political behaviour which had been so pervasive earlier in the century had virtually ceased to exist' (p.111). We should not write the history of the twentieth century as a battle between collectivism and the free market because they 'advanced in tandem at the expense of other more traditional social arrangements such as philanthropy, the family and the local community' (p.113). 'The ethos of voluntarism was . . . subtly transformed over the course of the twentieth century':

> They [voluntary associations] were the very sinews of autonomous 'civil society', supported by the state only through a general framework of law. This unpretentious and invisible private collectivism continued in some spheres throughout the period, largely falling through the meshes of the history of government. In many voluntary organisations, however, such autonomy progressively dwindled: they became increasingly the agents and clients of the state, holders of state licenses, beneficiaries of state tax concessions, recipients and competitors for state financial aid – or simply pressure groups urging government to change its policies on some deserving cause. The boundary between public and private spheres became more confused than in the late nineteenth century.
>
> (Harris 1990: 114)

Harris is describing the spread of organizational networks tied to the state. These networks are common to both the days of centralized planning and giant corporations and the days of governmental minimalism and neo-liberal economics.

Lowe and Rollings (2000: 101) similarly argue that the balance between state and civil society, 'between government and governance', was disrupted by two contradictions. First, British government had a limited or minimalist role in practice but unlimited power in theory. Although there were no constitutional checks on the powers of government, 'public compliance depended on their non-use'. Second, the state was supposed to be neutral between classes but it was partial whenever it intervened on controversial economic and social issues. Britain enjoyed 'an exceptional degree of continuity and order', but this was 'an achievement of governance broadly defined, rather than government' (p.105). The crisis of the 1950s saw the breakdown of this broader governance as the government responded to perceptions of relative decline by pursuing a policy of modernization through centralization. Thus, the history of differentiated polity in the twentieth century appears as a shifting balance between government and governance. It is through such an analysis of the shifting boundary between state and civil society that we would seek to explore the context of the differentiated polity (and for a more detailed discussion see Bevir and Rhodes 2002).

Conclusions

When trying to repair a gap in the map of British government there is always the danger of appearing one-sided. We seek to counter a view of British government that stresses Britain as a unitary state with a strong executive. We do not dispute the British executive can act decisively. Obviously, the centre coordinates and implements policies as intended at least some of the time. But the Westminster model attaches too little importance to the sour laws of unintended consequences. Governments fail because they are locked into power-dependent relationships and because they must work with and through complex networks of actors and organizations. To adopt a command operating code builds failure into the design of the policy. Such centralization will be confounded by fragmentation and interdependence that will, in turn, prompt further bouts of centralization. It is time to break free of the shackles of the Westminster model.

Devolution reinforces the existing pattern of functional differentiation with decentralized political authority and further constrains the capacity of the British centre to implement its policies effectively, creating the potential for a disUnited Kingdom. It is proving a hard pill to swallow. Devolved governments do their own thing. They elect first ministers the UK government does not want to deal with. They adopt policies the UK government does not approve of, which embroil the centre in disputes not of its making. Similarly, if at more mundane level, policy networks implement and vary policies in ways the centre dislikes. DfEE battles long and hard with the Treasury for extra money for the education service only to see local authorities spend that money on services other than education. Trusting devolved governments, local authorities, and indeed any decentralized agency, to deliver the services people want and to be accountable to those whom it serves is a big step for a British centre habituated to intervening at will. The administrative elite's concern for 'joined up' government shows that the centre recognizes that it has to manage not only packages of services and packages of organizations but also packages of governments. Managing intergovernmental relations is the new skill that the civil service must learn. Distinctions between types of organizations and levels of government become blurred as the centre seeks to manage a seamless web. But hands-off is a lesson no government has been willing to heed since 1945. Hands-on controls predominate although they are no way to manage a differentiated polity. Unless governments grasp this nettle and devise a central operating code that fits an institutional structure characterized by functional and political decentralization, the sour laws of unintended consequences will prevail and public cynicism will spread.

Our story is not just one that academics tell to one another. It is hard to draw a clear-cut distinction between academic commentators and elite actors. Tivey (1988: 3) uses 'the image . . . to denote the consequences of an interpretation . . . [of] a set of assumptions about "the system" . . . and how it works'. This image contains 'operative concepts' or 'operative ideals': 'the views of the authors are taken to be of some influence; what they have said has to some extent become operative . . . They have gained currency among those who study politics, and diluted and distorted they have reached the practitioners' (Tivey 1988: 1; see also Beer 1965: xiii, 404). So, today, elite actors talk of holistic governance, of joined up government even of networks (see Cm 4310 1999). The search is on for theories and vocabularies to understand fragmentation and its consequences.

The notion of the differentiated polity shows that words matter. The choice of words depends on prior theories; such theories are often implicit and, as in the Westminster model, best described as taken-for-granted assumptions which distort our understanding. When so formulated, these arguments apply to all west European systems whether we are talking about French exceptionalism, 'Modell Deutschland' or Danish associational democracy. As Wright (1997: 13) commented, the interactions of state, market and society throw up many contradictions and dilemmas that are common to west European democracies. Most important, a distinguishing feature of governing is its 'overarching and integrative function'. It provides 'ballast', 'a semblance of coherence', 'occasional steering ability', but above all it provides 'a degree of legitimacy to governance'. Public sector reform recurs throughout western Europe. The analysis of the differentiated polity seeks to identify the intended and unintended consequences of reforms and challenges the taken-for-granted assumptions built into the reforms. We want to correct faulty maps. Whether we succeed is a judgement that will be made by others.

The differentiated polity identifies important empirical gaps in the Westminster model and key changes in British government. It challenges the central notions of the Westminster model. In place of the classical model of a unitary state characterized by a strong executive and parliamentary sovereignty, we posit a shift to a differentiated polity with a power-dependent core executive hollowed out by internal differentiation and international interdependence. Second, it opens new avenues of exploration on key issues confronting policy-making and policy implementation in the 1980s and 1990s. Examples include the pluralization of policy-making; the mix of such governing structures as hierarchies, markets and networks; the uneven impact of joining up in England and within the constituent territories of the UK; and the relentless rise of intergovernmental diplomacy. Third, the analysis of traditions and the boundary between state and civil society necessarily locates the differentiated polity in a broader context, although one not limited either to an essentialist notion of tradition or to an 'economistic' notion of context.

The differentiated polity narrative is a valuable corrective to the traditional Westminster model. The causes of failure are not exogenous. They are built into the nature of core executive. To insist that the centre is dominant is to exclude the possibility that it is the author of its own misfortunes. The differentiated polity narrative offers the hope of finding 'new, better, more interesting, more fruitful ways' of speaking about British government (Rorty 1980: 360). We use the notion to develop a more differentiated view of state authority in its relationship to civil society.

Useful websites

www.scotland.gov.uk/who/senior.asp

www.wales.gov.uk

www.government-offices.gov.uk

www.number-10.gov.uk

www.cabinet-office.gov.uk/civilservice/scs/documents/htm/comp.htm

www.scotland.gov.uk/who/senior.asp

www.nics.gov.uk

Bibliography

Allsop, J. (1984) *Health Policy and the NHS*. Harlow: Longman.

Anderson, M. (1983) The political problems of frontier regions, in M. Anderson (ed.) *Frontier Regions in Western Europe*. London: Cass.

Arthur, P. (1989) *Government and Politics in Northern Ireland*. Harlow: Longman.

Audit Commission (1986) *Making a reality of community care*. London: HMSO.

Bach, S. (1999) Personnel managers: managing to change?, in S. Corby and G. White (eds) *Employee Relations in the Public Services: Themes and Issues*. London: Routledge.

Bains Report (1972) *The New Local Authorities: Management and Structure*. London: HMSO.

Banks, J.C. (1971) *Federal Britain?* London: Harrap.

Barberis, P. (ed.) (1996) *The Whitehall Reader*. Buckingham: Open University Press.

Barlow, M. (1940) *Distribution of Industrial Population: Report of the Royal Commission*, (Barlow Report) London: HMSO.

Barnes, M., Harrison, S., Mort, M., Shardlow, P. and Wistow, G. (1998) The new management of community care: user groups, citizenship and co-production, in G. Stoker (ed.) *The New Management of British Local Governance*. Basingstoke: Macmillan.

Beer, S. (1965) *Modern British Politics*. London: Faber & Faber.

Bell, E. (1985) What people should know about the role of the Civil Service in Northern Ireland since 1968, *Belfast Telegraph*, 29 January.

Bell, P.N. (1987) Direct Rule in Northern Ireland, in R. Rose (ed.) *Ministers and Ministries: A Functional Analysis*. Oxford: Clarendon Press.

Bevir, M. (1999) *The Logic of the History of Ideas*. Cambridge: Cambridge University Press.

Bevir, M. and Rhodes, R.A.W. (2001) *Interpreting British Governance*. Oxford: Oxford University Press.

Birrell, W.D. (1973) The Stormont–Westminster Relationship, *Parliamentary Affairs*, 26(4): 471–91.

Birrell, W.D. (1978) The Northern Ireland Civil Service – from devolution to Direct Rule, *Public Administration*, 56(2): 305–20.

Birrell, W.D. and Murie, A. (1980) *Policy and Government in Northern Ireland: Lessons of Devolution*. Dublin: Gill & Macmillan.

Birrell, D. and Wilson, C. (1993) 'Making Belfast work': an evaluation of an urban strategy, *Administration*, 41(1): 40–56.

Blair, T. (1996) *New Britain: My Vision of a Young Country*. London: Fourth Estate.

Bloomfield, D. and Lankford, M. (1996) From whitewash to mayhem: the secretary of state in Northern Ireland, in P. Catterall and S. McDougall (eds) *The Northern Ireland Question in British Politics*. Basingstoke: Macmillan.

Bloomfield, K. (1986) *Behind Stormont*. Belfast: Blackstaff.

Bloomfield, K. (1994) *Stormont in Crisis: A Memoir*. Belfast: Blackstaff.

Bloomfield, K. (1996) Devolution: lessons from Northern Ireland?, *Political Quarterly*, 67(2): 135–40.

Bloomfield, K. (1997) Central government and its operations, *Review of Northern Ireland Administrative Arrangements*. Belfast: Chief Executives' Forum.

Bogdanor, V. (1979) *Devolution*. Oxford: Oxford University Press.

Bogdanor, V. (1999) *Devolution in the United Kingdom*. Oxford: Oxford University Press.

Borooah, V. (1997) Economic dependency and development in Northern Ireland, *Review of Northern Ireland administrative arrangements*. Belfast: Chief Executives' Forum.

Borzal, T.A. (1998) Organizing Babylon – on the different conceptions of policy networks, *Public Administration*, 76(2): 253–73.

Bradbury, J. (1998) The devolution debate in Wales: the politics of a developing unitary state, *Regional and Federal Studies*, 8(1): 120–39.

Brand, S., Hill, S., Munday, M. and Roberts, A. (1997) Why isn't Wales richer?, *Local Economy*, 12(3): 219–33.

Brett, C.E.B. (1970) The lesson of devolution in Northern Ireland, *Political Quarterly*, 14: 273.

Bristow, G. and Munday, M. (1997) Economic development co-ordination in the periphery, *Regional Studies*, 31(7): 713–28.

Brown, A., McCrone, D. and Paterson, L. (1998) *Politics and Society in Scotland*. Basingstoke: Macmillan.

Buller, J. (1999) A Critical appraisal of the statecraft interpretation, *Public Administration*, 77(4): 691–712.

Bulmer, S. and Burch, M. (2000) The Europeanisation of British Central Government, in R.A.W. Rhodes (ed.) *Transforming British Government, Volume 1: Changing Institutions*. London: Macmillan.

Bulpitt, J.G. (1983) *Territory and Power in the United Kingdom*. Manchester: Manchester University Press.

Bulpitt, J. (1996) The European question, in D. Marquand and A. Seldon (eds) *The Ideas that Shaped Post-war Britain*. London: Fontana.

Burrows, B. and Denton, G. (1980) *Devolution or Federalism*. Basingstoke: Macmillan.

Butcher, T. (2000) The civil service: structure and management, in R. Pyper and L. Robins (eds) *United Kingdom Governance*. Basingstoke: Palgrave.

CAB (1964) *Pay Increase to Civil Servants – Long-term Settlement*, Memorandum by the Minister of Finance, CAB/4/1257/7, 17/2/1964. Belfast: Public Records Office.

CAB (1965a) *Civil Service Recruitment*, Memorandum by the Minister of Finance, CAB/4/1320/10, 4/11/1965. Belfast: Public Records Office.

CAB (1965b) *Civil Service Recruitment*, Conclusions of a Meeting of the Cabinet, CAB/4/1320/10, 1/12/1965. Belfast: Public Records Office.

CAB (1966) *Pay of the Higher Civil Service*, Conclusions of a Meeting of the Cabinet, CAB/4/1326/14, 3/3/1966. Belfast: Public Records Office.

CAB (1968a) *Operation of the Marriage Bar in the Civil Service of Northern Ireland*, Memorandum by the Minister of Finance, CAB/4/1393/5, 29/3/1968. Belfast: Public Records Office.

CAB (1968b) *Operation of the Marriage Bar in the Civil Service*, Conclusions of a Meeting of the Cabinet, CAB/4/1393, 4/4/1968. Belfast: Public Records Office.

Cabinet Office (1982) *Efficiency and Effectiveness in the Civil Service*, Cmnd 8616. London: HMSO.

Cabinet Office (1991) *Making the Most of Next Steps: The Management of Ministers' Departments and their Executive Agencies. A Report to the Prime Minister* (Fraser Report). London: HMSO.

Cabinet Office (1993) Civil Service Management Code. London: HMSO.

Cabinet Office (1994) *Next Steps: Moving On* (Trosa Report). London: Cabinet Office.

Cabinet Office (1995) *Department of National Heritage Annual Report 1995*, Cm 2811. London: HMSO.

Cabinet Office (1998a) *Public Bodies 1997*. London: HMSO.

Cabinet Office (1998b) *Devolution and the Civil Service*. London: HMSO.

Cabinet Office (1999a) *Civil Service Statistics*. London: HMSO.

Cabinet Office (1999b) *Modernising Government*, Cm 4310. London: HMSO.

Cabinet Office (1999c) *Circulation of Inter-ministerial and Inter-departmental Correspondence*, Devolution Guidance Note 6. London: Cabinet Office.

Cabinet Office (1999d) *Concordat between the Cabinet Office and the Cabinet of the National Assembly for Wales*. London: Cabinet Office. Also available at www.wales.gov.uk/cabinet/concordats/cabinet

Cabinet Office (1999e) *Memorandum of Understanding and Supplementary Agreements between the United Kingdom Government, Scottish Ministers and the Cabinet of the National Assembly for Wales*, Cm 4444. London: HMSO.

Cabinet Office (2000a) *Reaching Out: The Role of Central Government at Regional and Local Level*, A Report by the Policy and Innovation Unit. London: Cabinet Office.

Cabinet Office (2000b) *'Reaching Out': Action Plan*. London: Cabinet Office.

Campbell, C. and Wilson, G. (1995) *The End of Whitehall. Death of a Paradigm?* Oxford: Blackwell.

Cameron Report (1969) *Disturbances in Northern Ireland*, Cmd 532. Belfast: HMSO.

Carmichael, P. (1999) Territorial management in the 'New Britain': towards devolution plus in Northern Ireland?, *Regional and Federal Studies*, 9(3): 130–56.

Carmichael, P. and Knox, C. (1999) Towards a new era? Some developments in the governance of Northern Ireland, *International Review of Administrative Sciences*, 65(1): 103–16.

Carter, N., Klein, R. and Day, P. (1992) *How Organisations Measure Success: The Use of Performance Indicators in Government*. London: Routledge.

Chaney, P., Hall, T. and Pithouse, A. (eds) (2001) *Policy and Society in Wales: New governance – New Democracy?* Cardiff: University of Wales Press.

Charter 88 (1997) *Citizens Enquiry Factsheet – Wales*. Also available at www.gn.org/charter88/pubs

Civil Service Commissioners for Northern Ireland (1971–98) Annual Reports. Belfast: Office of the Civil Service Commissioners for Northern Ireland.

Civil Service Commissioners for Northern Ireland (1997) Recruitment Code. Belfast: Office of the Civil Service Commissioners for Northern Ireland.

Clulow, R. and Teague, P. (1993) Governance structure and economic development, in P. Teague (ed.) *The Economy of Northern Ireland*. London: Lawrence & Wishart.

Cole, G.D.H. (1921) *The Future of Local Government*. London: Cassell.

Collins, N. (1995) Agricultural policy networks of the Republic of Ireland and Northern Ireland, *Political Studies*, 43(4): 664–82.

Connolly, M. (1990) *Politics and Policy Making in Northern Ireland*. Hemel Hempstead: Philip Allan.

Connolly, M. and Erridge, A. (1990) Central government in Northern Ireland, in M. Connolly and S. Loughlin (eds) *Public Policy in Northern Ireland: Adoption or Adaptation*. Belfast: Queen's University of Belfast Policy Research Institute.

Connolly, M. and Loughlin, S. (1990) Policy making in Northern Ireland, in M. Connolly and S. Loughlin (eds) *Public Policy in Northern Ireland: Adoption or Adaptation*. Belfast: Queen's University of Belfast Policy Research Institute.

Constitution Unit (1996) *Regional Government in England*. London: University College London.

Cunningham, R. and McMillan, J. (2000) 'From here to diversity? The impact of equal opportunities training for middle managers in the civil service'. Paper presented to the Political Studies Association of the United Kingdom Annual Conference, London School of Economics and Political Science, April.

Davies, J. (1993) *A History of Wales*. London: Penguin.

Davies, J.S. (2000) The hollowing out of local democracy and the 'fatal conceit' of governing without government, *British Journal of Politics and International Relations*, 2(3): 414–28.

Davis, H. (1995) The fragmentation of community government, in S. Leach, H. Davis and Associates (eds) *Enabling or Disabling Local Government*. Buckingham: Open University Press.

Denham, J. (1999) Speech to the CIPFA/Public Management and Policy Association Conference on 'An epidemic of zones: Illness or cure?', Birmingham,

DETR (Department of the Environment, Transport and the Regions) (1997) *Building Partnerships for Prosperity*, Cm 3814. London: HMSO.

DETR (Department of the Environment, Transport and the Regions) (1998) *Quinquennial Financial Management and Policy Review of the Audit Commission: Prior Options Assessment*. London: HMSO. Also available at www.local-regions.detr.gov.uk//audit

DETR (Department of Environment, Transport and the Regions) (1999) *Regional Development Agencies: Regional Strategies*. London: HMSO.

Devlin, P. (1993) *Straight Left: An Autobiography*. Belfast: Blackstaff.

DFP (Department of Finance and Personnel) (1983) *Financial Management Initiative Within the Northern Ireland Departments.* Belfast: HMSO.

DFP (Department of Finance and Personnel) (1984) *Progress in Financial Management in Northern Ireland Departments.* Belfast: HMSO.

DHSS (Department of Health and Social Security) (1971) *Better Services for the Mentally Handicapped.* London: HMSO.

DHSS (Department of Health and Social Security) (1975) *Better Services for the Mentally Ill.* London: HMSO.

DHSS (Department of Health and Social Security) (1981a) *Care in Action: a handbook of policies and priorities for the Health and Personal Social Services in England.* London: HMSO.

DHSS (Department of Health and Social Security) (1981b) *Care in the Community.* London: HMSO.

DHSS (Department of Health and Social Security) (1988) *Working for Patients.* London: HMSO.

DHSS (Department of Health and Social Security) (1989) *Caring for People: Community Care in the Next Decade and Beyond,* Cm 849. London: HMSO.

DHSS(NI) (1975) *Strategy for the Development of Health and Personal Social Services in Northern Ireland.* Belfast: HMSO.

DHSS(NI) (1990) *People First: Community Care in Northern Ireland for the 1990s.* Belfast: HMSO.

Ditch, J. (1977) Direct Rule and Northern Ireland administration, *Administration,* 25(x): 328–37.

Ditch, J. and Morrissey, M. (1979) Recent developments in Northern Ireland's social policy, in M. Brown and S. Baldwin (eds) *The Year Book of Social Policy in Britain.* London: Routledge & Kegan Paul.

Donaldson, G. (1969) Scottish devolution: the historical background, in J.N. Wolfe (ed.) *Government and Nationalism in Scotland.* Edinburgh: Edinburgh University Press.

Donnison, D. (1973) The Northern Ireland civil service, *New Society,* 5 July.

Donnelly, M., McGilloway, S., Mays, N. and Perry, S. (1994) *Opening New Doors: An Evaluation of Community Care for People Discharged from Psychiatric and Mental Handicap Hospitals.* London: HMSO.

Dowding, K. (1995) *The Civil Service.* London: Routledge.

Dowding, K. (1995) Model or metaphor? A critical review of the policy network approach, *Political Studies,* 43(1): 136–58.

Drewry, G. (2000) The New Public Management, in J. Jowell and D. Oliver (eds) *The Changing Constitution.* Oxford: Oxford University Press.

Drewry, G. and Butcher, T. (1991) *The Civil Service Today.* Oxford: Blackwell.

Drewry, G. (2000) The new public management, in J. Jowell and D. Oliver (eds) *The Changing Constitution.* Oxford: Oxford University Press.

DSS (Department of Social Security) (2000) *Devolution.* London: DSS. Also available at www.dss.gov.uk/hq/pubs/fsheets/devolution

DTI (Department of Trade and Industry) (1983) *Regional Industrial Development.* London: HMSO.

DTI (Department of Trade and Industry) (1998) *Our Competitive Future: Building the Knowledge Driven Economy,* Cm 4176. London: HMSO.

Dyson, J., Wood, E. and Barclay, C. (1998) *Regional Development Agencies Bill: Bill 100 of 1997/98.* London: House of Commons Research Papers.

Efficiency Unit (1988) *Improving Management in Government: The Next Steps* (Ibbs Report). London: HMSO.

Elazar, D.J. (1997) Contrasting Unitary and Federal Systems, *International Political Science Review*, 18(3): 237–51.

Evason, E. and Robinson, G. (1996) Aspects of informal care in Northern Ireland, in R. Breen, P. Devine and L. Dowd (eds) *Social Attitudes in Northern Ireland*. Belfast: Appletree.

Evason, E., Darby, J. and Pearson, M. (1976) *Social Needs and Social Provision in Northern Ireland*. Coleraine: New University of Ulster.

Farnham, D. and Horton, S. (eds) (1996) *Managing the New Public Services*. Basingstoke: Macmillan.

Farnham, D. and Horton, S. (eds) (1999) *Public Management in Britain*. Basingstoke: Macmillan.

Farrell, M. (1976) *Northern Ireland: The Orange State*. London: Pluto Press.

Faulkner, B. (1978) *Memoirs of a Statesman*. London: Weidenfield & Nicolson.

FEA (Fair Employment Agency) (1983) *Report of an Investigation by the Fair Employment Agency for the Northern Ireland into the Non-industrial Northern Ireland Civil Service*. Belfast: FEA.

Finer, S.E. (1970) *Comparative Government*. London: Allen Lane.

Follis, B. (1995) *A State Under Siege*. Oxford: Clarendon Press.

Frances, J., Levačić, R., Mitchell, R. and Thompson, G. (1991) 'Introduction', in G. Thompson, J. Frances, R. Levačić and J. Mitchell (eds) *Markets Hierarchies and Networks: The Co-ordination of Social Life*. London: Sage.

Fredman, S. (1999) The legal context: Public or private?, in S. Corby and G. White (eds) *Employee Relations in the Public Services: Themes and Issues*. London: Routledge.

Fulton Committee (1968) *Report of the Committee on the Civil Service 1966–68* (Fulton Report), Cmnd 3638. London: HMSO.

Gaffikin, F. and Morrissey, M. (1990a) *Northern Ireland: The Thatcher Years*. London: Zed Books.

Gaffikin, F. and Morrissey, M. (1990b) Regional Economic Development Policies, in M. Connolly and S. Loughlin (eds) *Public Policy in Northern Ireland: Adoption or Adaptation?* Belfast: Queen's University of Belfast Policy Research Institute.

Gamble, A. (1988) *The Free Economy and the Strong State*. Basingstoke: Macmillan.

Gamble, A. (1990) Theories of British politics, *Political Studies*, 38(3): 404–20.

Gibson, J.S. (1985) *The Thistle and the Crown: A History of the Scottish Office*. Edinburgh: HMSO.

Gibson, N.J. (1997) Governance of Northern Ireland: Some Economic Considerations, in *Review of Northern Ireland Administrative Arrangements*. Belfast: Chief Executives' Forum.

Gladden, E.N. (1967) *Civil Services of the United Kingdom*. London: Frank Cass.

Government Office Central Unit (1998) Personnel policy and advice note: checklist of notes (and notes) issued. Unpublished documents, GOCU, London.

Government Office for Eastern Region, Annual Report 1996/97 (also 1997/98). Cambridge: GO.

Government Office for East Midlands, Annual Report 1997/98. Nottingham: GO.

Government Office for London, Annual Report 1996/97 (also 1997/98). London: GO.

Government Office for Merseyside, Annual Report 1996/97 (also 1997/98). Liverpool: GO.

Government Office for the North East, Annual Report 1996/97 (also 1997/98). Newcastle Upon Tyne: GO.

Government Office for the North West, Annual Report 1996/97 (also 1997/98). Manchester: GO.

Government Office for the South East, Annual Report 1996/97 (also 1997/98). Guildford: GO.

Government Office for the South West, Annual Report 1997/98. Bristol: GO.

Government Office for the West Midlands, Annual Report 1997/98. Birmingham: GO.

Gray, A.M. and Getty, D. (1999) Northern Ireland social policy review 1998, *Administration*, 47(2): 93–114.

Gray, C. (1994) *Government Beyond the Centre: Sub-national Politics in Britain.* Basingstoke: Macmillan.

Greenleaf, W.H. (1983) *The British Political Tradition. Volume 1. The Rise of Collectivism.* London: Methuen.

Greenwood, R. and Wilson, D. (1989) *Public Administration in Britain Today.* London: Unwin Hyman.

Greer, A. (1994) Policy networks and state–farmer relations in Northern Ireland, 1921–72, *Political Studies*, 42(3): 396–412.

Griffiths, D. (1996) *Thatcherism and Territorial Politics.* Aldershot: Gower.

Griffiths, D. (1999) The Welsh Office and Welsh autonomy, *Public Administration*, 77(4): 793–807.

Griffiths, R. (1983) *NHS Management Inquiry Report – together with proceedings of committee and minutes of evidence. First Report of the House of Commons Social Services Select Committee Session 1983–84*, HC 209. London: HMSO.

Griffiths, R. (1988) *Community Care: Agenda for Action. A Report to the Secretary of State for Social Services by Sir Roy Griffiths.* London: HMSO.

Hall, P. (1963) *London 2000.* London: Faber & Faber.

Ham, C. (1992) *Policy Making in the National Health Service.* Basingstoke: Macmillan.

Hanham, H.J. (1969) The development of the Scottish Office, in J.N. Wolfe (ed.) *Government and Nationalism in Scotland.* Edinburgh: Edinburgh University Press.

Harris, J. (1990) Society and state in twentieth century Britain, in F.M.L. Thompson (ed.) *The Cambridge Social History of Britain 1750–1950, Volume 3: Social Agencies and Institutions.* Cambridge: Cambridge University Press.

Harrison, R.T. (1986) Industrial development policy and the restructuring of the Northern Ireland economy, *Environment and Planning C: Government and Policy*, 4(1): 53–70.

Harrison, R.T. (1990a) Industrial development in Northern Ireland: the Industrial Development Board, in M. Connolly and S. Loughlin (eds) *Public Policy in Northern Ireland: Adoption or Adaptation?* Belfast: Queen's University of Belfast Policy Research Institute.

Harrison, R.T. (1990b) Industrial development policy, in R.I.D. Harris, C.W. Jefferson and J.E. Spencer (eds) *The Northern Ireland Economy: A Comparative Study in the Economic Development of a Peripheral Region.* London: Longman.

Harvey Cox, W. (1987) Managing Northern Ireland intergovernmentally: an appraisal of the Anglo-Irish Agreement, *Parliamentary Affairs*, 40(1): 80–97.

Harvie, C. (1994) *The Rise of Regional Europe*. London: Routledge.

Hayes, M. (1995) *Minority Verdict*. Belfast: Blackstaff.

Hayes, M. (1997) *A Report on Staff Deployment in the Northern Ireland Civil Service*. Belfast: HMSO.

Hazell, R. and Morris, B. (1999) Growing apart, *Public Service Magazine*, May.

Hennessy, P. (1992) *Never Again*. London: Jonathan Cape.

Hennessy, P. (1996) 'Shadow and substance': premiership for the twenty-first century, Gresham College, Rhetoric Lectures 1995–96, Lecture 6.

HM Treasury (1997) *Principles to Govern Determination of the Block Budgets for the Scottish Parliament and National Assembly for Wales*. London: HM Treasury.

Hogwood, B.W. (1992) *Trends in British Public Policy*. Buckingham: Open University Press.

Hogwood, B.W. (1996) *Mapping the Regions: Boundaries, Coordination and Government*. Bristol: Policy Press and Joseph Rowntree Foundation.

Hogwood, B.W. and Keating, M. (eds) (1982) *Regional Government in England*. Oxford: Clarendon Press.

Holliday, I. (2000) Is the British State hollowing out?, *Political Quarterly*, 71(2): 167–76.

Hood, C. (1991) A public management for all seasons, *Public Administration*, 69(1): 3–19.

Hood, C. (1995) Contemporary public management: a new global paradigm?, *Public Policy and Administration*, 10(2): 104–17.

Horton, S. and Farnham, D. (eds) (1999) *Public Management in Britain*. Basingstoke: Macmillan.

House of Commons Health Select Committee (1999) *The Relationship Between Health and Social Services, First Report Volume 1*, HC-I. London: HMSO.

Hunter, D.J. and Wistow, G. (1987) The paradox of policy diversity in a unitary state: community care in Britain, *Public Administration*, 65(1): 3–24.

Hutt, J. (1999) Partnerships for progress – community care in the 21st century. Speech at the Developing Partnerships Conference – Research and Development for Health and Social Care, Cardiff, June.

Johnson, N. (1975) The place of institutions in the study of politics, *Political Studies*, 23(2): 271–83.

Jones, B. and Keating, M. (eds) (1995) *The European Union and the Regions*. Oxford: Clarendon Press.

Kavanagh, D. and Seldon, A. (2000) The power behind the prime minister: the hidden influence of No. 10, in R.A.W. Rhodes (ed.) *Transforming British Government. Volume 2. Changing Roles and Relationships*. London: Macmillan.

Keating, M. and Midwinter, A. (1983) *The Government of Scotland*. Edinburgh: Mainstream.

Kellas, J.G. (1984) *The Scottish Political System*. Cambridge: Cambridge University Press.

Kellas, J. and Madgwick, P. (1982) Territorial ministries: the Scottish and Welsh Offices, in P. Madgwick and R. Rose (eds) *The Territorial Dimension in United Kingdom Politics*. Basingstoke: Macmillan.

Kickert, W.J.M. (ed.) (1997) *Public Management and Administrative Reform in Europe*. Aldershot: Edward Elgar.

Kickert, W., Klijn, E. and Koppenjam, J. (eds) (1998) *Network Management in the Public Sector*. London: Sage.

Kilbrandon, Lord (1973) *Report of the Royal Commission on the Constitution 1969–73*, Cmnd 5460. London: HMSO.

Knox, C. and Carmichael, P. (1998) Making progress in Northern Ireland. Evidence from recent elections, *Government and Opposition*, 33(3): 372–93.

Knox, C. and McHugh, M. (1990) Management in government – the 'Next Steps' in Northern Ireland, *Administration*, 38(3): 251–70.

Labour Party (1995) *A Choice for England*. London: Labour Party.

Lawrence, R.J. (1956) Devolution reconsidered, *Political Studies*, 4(1): 1–17.

Lawrence, R.J. (1965) *The Government of Northern Ireland*. Oxford: Clarendon Press.

Leftwich, A. (1984) On the politics of politics, in A. Leftwich (ed.) *What is Politics?* Oxford: Blackwell.

Levy, R. (1995) Governing Scotland, Wales and Northern Ireland, in R. Pyper and L. Robins (eds) *Governing the UK in the 1990s*. Basingstoke: Macmillan.

Lord Chancellor's Department (1999) *Memorandum of Understanding and Supplementary Agreements between the United Kingdom Government, Scottish Ministers and the Cabinet of the National Assembly for Wales*, Cm 4444. London: HMSO.

Lord Chancellor's Department (2000) *LCD and the Scottish Executive: Concordat between the Scottish Executive and the Lord Chancellor's Department*. London: LCD.

Loughlin, J. (1992) Administering policy in Northern Ireland, in B. Hadfield (ed.) *Northern Ireland: Politics and the Constitution*. Buckingham: Open University Press.

Lovering, J. (1996) New myths of the Welsh economy, *Planet*, 116: 6–16.

Lowe, R. and Rollings, N. (2000) Modernizing Britain, 1957–64: a classic case of centralization and fragmentation?, in R.A.W. Rhodes (ed.) *Transforming British Government, Volume 1: Changing Institutions*. London: Macmillan.

Lunt, N., Mannion, R. and Smith, P. (1996) Economic discourse and the market: the case of community care, *Public Administration*, 74(3): 369–91.

Maass, A. (ed.) (1959) *Area and Power*. Glencoe, Ill.: Free Press.

McAllister, L. (1999) The road to Cardiff Bay: the process of establishing the National Assembly for Wales, *Parliamentary Affairs*, 52(4): 632–48.

McConnell, A. (2000) Issues of governance in Scotland, Wales and Northern Ireland, in R. Pyper and L. Robins (eds) *Governing the UK in the 1990s*. Basingstoke: Macmillan.

MacDonnell Commission (1914) *Report on the Civil Service*, Cd 7338. London: HMSO.

Mackenzie, W.J.M. (1963) *Regionalism and Local Government Structures*. London: Institute of Municipal Treasures and Accountants (now CIPFA).

Mackintosh, J.P. (1968) *The Devolution of Power*. London: Chatto & Windus.

Macrory, P. (1970) *Review Body on Local Government in Northern Ireland* (Macrory Report), Cmnd 540. Belfast: HMSO.

Madgwick, P. and Rawkins, P. (1982) The Welsh language in the policy process, in P. Madgwick and R. Rose (eds) *The Territorial Dimension in United Kingdom Politics*. Basingstoke: Macmillan.

Madgwick, P. and Rose, R. (eds) (1982) *The Territorial Dimension in United Kingdom Politics*. Basingstoke: Macmillan.

Marsh, D. and Rhodes, R.A.W. (eds) (1992) *Policy Networks in British Government*. Oxford: Oxford University Press.

Marsh, D., Richards, D. and Smith, M. (2001) *Unequal Plurality: Towards an Asymmetric Power Model of the British Polity*. Canberra: Research School of the Social Sciences.

Massey, A. (1988) *Technocrats and Nuclear Politics*. Aldershot: Avebury.

Massey, A. (1993) *Managing the Public Sector*. Aldershot: Edward Elgar.

Massey, A. (1995) *After Next Steps: the Massey Report*. London: Cabinet Office.

Massey, A. (ed.) (1997) *Globalization and Marketization of Public Services*. Basingstoke: Macmillan.

Mawson, J. and Spencer, K. (1997) The government offices for the English regions: towards regional governance? *Policy and Politics*, 25(1): 71–84.

Means, R. and Smith, R. (1998) *Community Care – Policy and Practice*. Basingstoke: Macmillan.

Menon, A. and Wright, V. (1998) The paradoxes of 'failure': British EU policy making in comparative perspective, *Public Policy and Administration*, 13(4): 46–66.

Midwinter, A., Keating, M. and Mitchell, J. (1991) *Politics and Public Policy in Scotland*. London: Macmillan.

Morgan, K. and Mungham, G. (2000) *Redesigning Democracy: The Making of the Welsh Assembly*. Bridgend: Poetry Wales Press.

Morgan, K. and Rees, G. (2001) in P. Chaney, T. Hall and A. Pithouse (eds) *Policy and Society in Wales: New Governance New Democracy?* Cardiff: University of Wales Press.

Morrow, D. (1996) Filling the gap: policy and pressure under direct rule, in A. Aughey and D. Morrow (eds) *Northern Ireland Politics*. Harlow: Longman.

National Assembly for Wales (1999) *The Official Record, Tuesday 9 November 1999*, Questions to the First Secretary. Cardiff: National Assembly for Wales. Also available at www.wales.gov.uk/assemblydata

National Assembly for Wales (2000) *Statutory Instrument 2000 No. 253 (W.5), Constitutional Law, Devolution, Wales, The National Assembly for Wales (Transfer of Functions) Order 2000*. Cardiff, National Assembly for Wales/London: HMSO. Also www.wales-legislation.hmso.gov.uk

Neustadt, R. (1980) *Presidential Power*. New York: Wiley.

NICS (1997) Northern Ireland Civil Service Code of Ethics. Belfast: HMSO.

NICS (1998) Northern Ireland Civil Service Staff Handbook. Belfast: HMSO.

NICS (1998) Recruitment Service: First Annual Report. Belfast: HMSO.

NIG (Northern Ireland Government) (1960) *Government of Northern Ireland Digest of Statistics*. Belfast: Ministry of Finance/HMSO (and annually thereafter).

NIG (Northern Ireland Government) (1969) *Administration of the Health and Personal Social Services in Northern Ireland*. Belfast: HMSO.

NIG (Northern Ireland Government) (1972) *Summary of a Report on 'An Integrated Service: The Reorganisation of Health and Personal Social Services in Northern Ireland'*. Belfast: Ministry of Health and Social Services.

Northern Ireland Department of Finance and Personnel (1982) *Annual Abstract of Statistics*. Belfast: HMSO (and annually thereafter).

Northern Ireland Audit Office (1989) *Economy, Efficiency and Effectiveness – Examination of Certain Matters, Report by the Comptroller and Auditor General for Northern Ireland*. London: HMSO.

Northern Ireland Public Service Alliance (1972) First Annual Report. Belfast: Public Service Alliance.

Norton, P. (2000) Barons in a shrinking kingdom: senior ministers in British government, in R.A.W. Rhodes (ed.) *Transforming British Government. Volume 2. Changing Roles and Relationships.* London: Macmillan.

Office of Civil Service Commissioners (1996) *Guidance on Senior Recruitment.* London: OCSC.

Office of Civil Service Commissioners (1996) Civil Service Commissioners' Recruitment Code. London: OCSC.

O'Leary, B. (1998) The nature of the Agreement. Paper presented at the 9th John Whyte Memorial Lecture, Queen's University of Belfast.

O'Leary, C., Elliott, S. and Wilford, R. (1988) *The Northern Ireland Assembly, 1982–1986.* London: Charles Hurst.

Oliver, J. (1978) *Working at Stormont.* Dublin: Institute of Public Administration.

Osborne, R.D. (1990) Equal opportunities and the Northern Ireland Civil Service, *Public Money and Management,* 10(2): 41–6.

Osborne, R.D. (1992) Fair Employment and Employment Equity: Policy Learning in a Comparative Context, *Public Money and Management,* 12(4): 11–18.

Osborne, R.D. (1996) Policy dilemmas in Belfast, *Journal of Social Policy,* 25(2): 181–99.

Osmond, J. (ed.) (1994) *Parliament for Wales.* Llandysul: Gomer.

Osmond, J. (ed.) (1998) *The National Assembly Agenda.* Cardiff: Institute for Welsh Affairs.

Osmond, J. (1999) *Adrift but Afloat: The Civil Service and the National Assembly.* Cardiff: Institute for Welsh Affairs.

Osmond, J. (ed.) (2000) *Coalition Politics Come to Wales.* Cardiff: Institute of Welsh Affairs.

Parker, R.S. (1979) The public service inquiries and responsible government, in R.F.I. Smith and P. Weller (eds) *Public Service Inquiries in Australia.* Brisbane: University of Queensland Press.

Parry, R. (1982) The centralisation of the Scottish Office: an administrative history. Paper to the Political Studies Association Conference, April.

Parry, R. (2001) Devolution, integration and modernisation in the United Kingdom Civil Service, *Public Policy and Administration,* 16(3): 53–67.

Parsons, D.W. (1988) *The Political Economy of British Regional Policy.* London: Routledge.

Parsons, D.W. (1998) Being born lost? The cultural and institutional dimensions of Welsh identity, in A. Kershen (ed.) *A Question of Identity.* Aldershot: Ashgate.

Phillips, P. (1982) *The Anglo-Saxon Chronicles* (trans. Anne Sowage). London: Heinemann.

Pollitt, C. (1993) *Managerialism in the Public Services.* Oxford: Blackwell.

Pottinger, G. (1979) *The Secretaries of State for Scotland, 1926–76: Fifty Years of the Scottish Office.* Edinburgh: Scottish Academic Press.

Prior, J. (1985) *A Balance of Power.* London: Hamish Hamilton.

Prior, P. (1993) *Mental Health and Politics in Northern Ireland.* Aldershot: Avebury.

Privy Council (1995) *Civil Service Order in Council.* London: HMSO.

Pyper, R. (1995) Ministerial responsibility and the Next Steps agencies, in P. Giddings (ed.) *Parliamentary Accountability: A Study of Parliament and Executive Agencies.* Basingstoke: Macmillan.

Pyper, R. (1999) The civil service: a neglected dimension of devolution, *Public Money and Management,* 19(2): 45–9.

Randall, P. (1972) Wales in the structure of central government, *Public Administration*, 50(3): 352–72.

Raynor Scrutiny (1980) *Financial Administration in Northern Ireland*. Belfast: HMSO.

RCU (2000a) *Action Plan*. London: Cabinet Office.

RCU (2000b) *Summary of Progress*. London: Cabinet Office.

Redcliffe-Maude Commission (1969) *Royal Commission on Local Government in England 1966–1969*, Cmnd 4040. London: HMSO.

Rees, G. and Morgan, K. (1991) Industrial restructuring, innovation systems in the regional state, in G. Day and G. Rees (eds) *Regions, Nations and Europe: Remaking the Celtic Periphery*. Cardiff: University of Wales Press.

Rhodes, R.A.W. (1986) *The National World of Local Government*. London: Allen & Unwin.

Rhodes, R.A.W. (1988) *Beyond Westminster and Whitehall*. London: Routledge.

Rhodes, R.A.W. (1992) Intergovernmental relations in unitary political systems, in M. Hawkesworth and M. Kogan (eds) *The Routledge Encyclopaedia of Government and Politics*. London: Routledge & Kegan Paul.

Rhodes, R.A.W. (1994) The hollowing out of the state, *Political Quarterly*, 65(2): 138–51.

Rhodes, R.A.W. (1997a) *Understanding Governance*. Buckingham: Open University Press.

Rhodes, R.A.W. (1997b) From marketisation to diplomacy: it's the mix that matters, *Australian Journal of Public Administration*, 56(2): 40–53.

Rhodes, R.A.W. ([1981] 1999a) *Control and Power in Central–Local Government Relationships*. Aldershot: Ashgate.

Rhodes, R.A.W. (1999b) New Labour's civil service: summing-up joining-up. Paper presented to the British Council New Public Management Series, Palazzo Chigi, Rome, 5 October.

Rhodes, R.A.W. (2000a) Public administration and governance, in J. Pierre (ed.) *Debating Governance*. Oxford: Oxford University Press.

Rhodes, R.A.W. (ed.) (2000b) *Transforming British Government. Volume 1. Changing Institutions. Volume 2. Changing Roles and Relationships*. London: Macmillan.

Rhodes, R.A.W. (2000c) New Labour's civil service: summing-up joining-up, *Political Quarterly*, 71(2): 151–66.

Rhodes, R.A.W. (2001a) Unitary states, in Neil J. Smelser and Paul B. Baltes (eds) *International Encyclopaedia of the Social and Behavioural Sciences*. Oxford: Pergamon.

Rhodes, R.A.W. (2001b) What is governance and why does it matter?, in J.E.S. Hayward and A. Menon (eds) *Governing Europe*. Oxford: Oxford University Press.

Rhodes, R.A.W. (2001c) Putting the people back into networks. Keynote address to the European Group of Public Administration Annual Conference, Vaasa, Finland, 5–9 September.

Rhodes, R.A.W. and Dunleavy, P. (eds) (1995) *Prime Minister, Cabinet and Core Executive*. London: Macmillan.

Richards, D. (1997) *The Civil Service under the Conservatives, 1979–1997*, Brighton: Sussex Academic Press.

Riddell, P. (2000) 'Portrait of the Whitehall Programme'. Report to the ESRC, London, November.

Rokkan, S. and Urwin, D. (1982) *The Politics of Territorial Identity: Studies in European Regionalism*. London: Sage.

Rondinelli, P.A. and Cheema, G.S. (1983) Implementing decentralisation policies: an introduction, in P.A. Rondinelli and C.S. Cheema (eds) *Decentralisation and Development*. London: Sage.

Rorty, R. (1980) *Philosophy and the Mirror of Nature*. Oxford: Blackwell.

Rose, R. (1971) *Governing without Consensus – An Irish Perspective*. London: Faber.

Rose, R. (1982) *Understanding the United Kingdom*. London: Longman.

Rose, R. and McAllister, I. (1982) *United Kingdom Facts*. Basingstoke: Macmillan.

Rowlands, E. (1972) The politics of regional administration: the establishment of the Welsh Office, *Public Administration*, 50(3): 333–51.

Ryan, C. (1999) Growing apart, *Public Service Magazine*, May.

Salter, B. (1994) The politics of community care, *Policy and Politics*, 22(2): 119–31.

Scotland Office (2000a) *The Government's Expenditure Plans 2000–01 to 2001–02: Departmental Report by the Scotland Office*, Cm 4619. Edinburgh: HMSO.

Scotland Office (2000b) *Service Delivery Agreement*. Edinburgh: Scotland Office.

Scottish Executive (n.d.) Executive Terms and Conditions of Service Staff Handbook.

Scottish Executive (1999a) *Concordat between the Cabinet Office and the Scottish Administration*. Edinburgh: HMSO.

Scottish Executive (1999b) *21st Century Government for Scotland*. Edinburgh: Executive Secretariat.

Scottish Executive (1999c) *Aiming for Excellence: Modernising Social Work Services in Scotland*. Edinburgh: Executive Secretariat.

Scottish Executive (2000a) *Diversity in the Scottish Executive: Strategy for Change*. Edinburgh: Executive Secretariat.

Scottish Executive (2000b) *The Way Forward: Framework for Economic Development in Scotland*, SE/2000/58. Edinburgh: Executive Secretariat.

Scottish Executive (2000c) *The Way Forward for Care*. Edinburgh: Executive Secretariat.

Scottish Office (1998) *Modernising Community Care: An Action Plan*. Edinburgh: HMSO.

Seebohm, F. (1968) *Report of the Committee on Local Authority and Allied Personal Services*. London: HMSO.

Self, P. (1949) *Regionalism*. London: Fabian Society/Allen & Unwin.

Self, P. (1964) Regional planning in Britain, *Urban Studies*, 1(1).

Sharpe, L.J. (1970) Theories and values of local government, *Political Studies*, 18(1): 153–74.

Shea, P. (1981) *Voice and the Sound of Drums*. Belfast: Blackstaff.

Smith, B.C. (1964) *Regionalism in England. Volume 1. Regional Institutions*. London: Acton Society.

Smith, B.C. (1965a) *Regionalism in England. Volume 2. Its Nature and Purpose, 1905–1965*. London: Acton Society.

Smith, B.C. (1965b) *Regionalism in England. Volume 3. The New Regional Machinery*. London: Acton Society.

Smith, B.C. (1967) *Field Administration*. London: Routledge & Kegan Paul.

Smith, B.C. (1985) *Decentralisation*. London: Allen & Unwin.

Smith, M. (1999) *The Core Executive in Britain*. Basingstoke: Macmillan.

Smith, T.A. (1979) *The Politics of the Corporate Economy*. London: Martin Robertson.

Smyth, D. (1996) Speech for Priority Workshop. (Provided from the author's personal collection of papers and given to our research team.).

Spencer, K. and Mawson, J. (1998) Government offices and policy co-ordination in the English regions, *Local Governance*, 24(2): 3–11.

Tannam, E. (1998) *Cross-border Co-operation in the Republic of Ireland and Northern Ireland*. Basingstoke: Macmillan.

Taylor, A. (2000) Hollowing out or filling in? Task forces and the management of cross-cutting issues in British Government, *British Journal of Politics and International Relations*, 2(3): 46–71.

Theakston, K. (1995) *The Civil Service since 1945*. Oxford: Blackwell.

Tivey, L. (1988) *Interpretations of British Politics*. London: Harvester Wheatsheaf.

Tonks, A. (1993) Making progress – community care in Northern Ireland, *British Medical Journal*, 306: 262–5.

Verney, D. (1991) Westminster model, in V. Bogdanor (ed.) *The Blackwell Encyclopaedia of Political Science*. Oxford: Blackwell.

Walker, A. (ed.) (1982) *Community Care*. Oxford: Martin Robertson.

Walker, P. (1991) *Staying Power*. London: Bloomsbury.

Weller, P. (1985) *First Among Equals*. Sydney: Allen & Unwin.

Weller, P., Bakvis, H. and Rhodes, R.A.W. (eds) (1997) *The Hollow Crown: Countervailing Trends in Core Executives*. London: Macmillan.

Welsh Affairs Committee (1998) *The Impact of the Government's Devolution Proposals on Economic Development and Local Government in Wales*, Minutes of Evidence and Appendices. London: HMSO.

Welsh Office (1998) *Devolution and the Civil Service. Staff Guidance*. Cardiff: Welsh Office.

Welsh Office (1999) *Digest of Welsh Statistics*. Cardiff: HMSO.

Wilford, R. (2000) Designing the Northern Ireland Assembly, *Parliamentary Affairs*, 53(3): 577–90.

Williams, G. (2000) Research agenda and social care in Wales. Speech to ESRC Seminar Series Theorising Social Work Research, Seminar 5, What Works as Evidence for Practice? The Methodological Repertoire in an Allied Discipline, Cardiff, April.

Wilson, Sir Richard (1998) 'Modernizing Government: the role of the senior civil service'. Speech, Senior Civil Service Conference, October.

Wilson, T. (1989) *Ulster Conflict and Consent*. Oxford: Basil Blackwell.

Wilson, G. (1994) The Westminster model in comparative perspective, in I. Budge and D. McKay (eds) *Developing Democracy*. London: Sage.

Windlesham, Lord (1973) Ministers in Ulster: the machinery of Direct Rule, *Public Administration*, 51(3): 261–72.

Wolfenden, Sir John (1978) *The Future of Voluntary Organisations. Report of the Wolfenden Committee*. London: Croom Helm.

Wood, P. (1987) UK, in H.D. Clout (ed.) *Regional Development in Western Europe*. London: D. Fulton Publishers.

Wood, S. (1998) *Regional Government in England*, House of Commons Research Paper, 13 January 1998.

Wright, V. (1994) Reshaping the state: implications for public administration, *West European Politics*, 17(1): 102–34.

Wright, V. (1997) The paradoxes of administrative reform, in W. Kickert (ed.) *Public Management and Administrative Reform in Western Europe*. Aldershot: Edward Elgar.

Wright, V. and Hayward, J. (2000) Governing from the Centre: Policy coordination in six European core executives, in R.A.W. Rhodes (ed.) *Transforming British Government, Volume 2: Changing Roles and Relationships*. London: Macmillan.

Index

THE CHANGING WORLD OF TOP OFFICIALS
Mandarins Or Valets?

R.A.W. Rhodes and Patrick Weller (eds)

This book explores the roles and workings of the heads of government departments in six nations: departmental secretaries in Australia, departmentschefs in Denmark, directeurs d'administration in France, secretaris-generaal in the Netherlands, chief executives in New Zealand, and permanent secretaries in the UK. It also seeks to explore their 'infinite variety' by showing how inherited government traditions shape the response to reform.

It examines how such reforms as privatization and contracting out have affected who does these jobs and how they do them. It asks whether the demands of the new public management have made departmental heads more accountable, more public and more vulnerable. For each of the six countries the authors give details of departmental secretaries' backgrounds, their career paths, their conditions of employment, their impacts, and their changing positions. Central to each chapter are short biographies or portraits of top officials with extensive quotations from interviews in which they talk about how they see their worlds and how, for instance, they now focus more on managing their departments and less on policy-making. The experience of senior public servants is brought vividly to life.

This book is the first comprehensive, comparative portrait of top government officials, and is an important resource for students and scholars of politics, public policy and public management, and makes fascinating reading for all senior civil servants themselves.

Contents
Preface and acknowledgements – Introduction: 'enter centre stage' – France: 'dual structure, shared dilemma' – Netherlands: 'fragmenting pillars, fading colours' – Denmark: 'the Island culture' – United Kingdom: 'everybody but us' – Australia: 'mandarins or lemons?' – New Zealand: 'cautionary tale or shining example?' – Conclusions: 'Antipodean exceptionalism, European traditionalism' – References – Index.

288pp   0 335 20301 9 (Paperback)   0 335 20302 7 (Hardback)

EVALUATING PUBLIC MANAGEMENT REFORMS
Principles and Practice

George Boyne, Catherine Farrell, Jennifer Law, Martin Powell and Richard Walker

Governments across the world are pursuing reform in an effort to improve public services. But have these reforms actually led to improvements in services? *Evaluating Public Management Reforms* develops a framework for a theory-based evaluation of reforms, and then uses this framework to assess the impact of new arrangements for public service delivery in the UK. This book:

- identifies the conceptual and practical problems of finding clear criteria for evaluating reforms
- focuses on the shifts in public management towards markets and competition, towards the publication of performance indicators, and from larger to smaller organizations
- considers what impact these reforms have had on the efficiency, responsiveness and equity of services
- comprehensively reviews the evidence on the effects of reform on health care, housing and education
- discusses the implications for public sector management.

Contents
Introduction – Criteria of evaluation – Methods of evaluation – Health reforms – Housing reforms – Education reforms – Conclusion – References – Index.

192pp   0 335 20246 2 (Paperback)   0 335 20247 0 (Hardback)